Overseas American

Overseas American

Growing Up Gringo in the Tropics

Gene H. Bell-Villada

University Press of Mississippi   Jackson

Willie Morris Books in Memoir and Biography

www.upress.state.ms.us

The University Press of Mississippi is a member of the
Association of American University Presses.

13 12 11 10 09 08 07 06 05   4 3 2 1
∞
First Edition
Library of Congress Cataloging-in-Publication Data

Bell-Villada, Gene H., 1941–
   Overseas American : growing up gringo in the tropics / Gene H. Bell-Villada.
      p. cm. — (Willie Morris books in memoir and biography)
   ISBN 1-57806-720-0 (cloth : alk. paper)
   1. Bell-Villada, Gene H., 1941– 2. Puerto Rico—Biography. 3. Americans—
Cuba—Biography. 4. Americans—Venezuela—Biography. 5. Florida—
Biography. 6. Racially mixed children—United States. I. Title.

CT275.A1B45   2005
305.8′059942013′0092—dc22   2004019241

British Library Cataloging-in-Publication Data available

for Kanani, who also lived this and helped remember it
AND
for Audrey, who's heard more than her share of this,
put up with it, and helped me pull out from it

Contents

Acknowledgments

With special thanks for their help, encouragement, and advice, to Kanani Bell, Valerie Bell, Bonnie Tucker Bowen, Aviva Chomsky, Ronald Christ, Douglas Clayton, Leila (Villada) Condon, Miriam Dawson, Román de la Campa, la profesora y asesora Tamar Heller, Rachel Kranz (genius editor), Luce López-Baralt, Sarah Gertz Marion, Ronald Morin, Sara Muñoz, Nelson Quintero, Regina Rashkin, Estevan Romero, Shelley Salamensky, Carolyn C. Sloan, and Patricia Wilcox.

To Ron and Lisa, who introduced me to David Green, who in turn directed me to the Third Culture Kids (TCK) literature.

To the Hamilton College Academic Year in Spain, for infrastructural support during my 1995–96 tour of duty in Madrid.

To Seetha Srinivasan, director of the University Press of Mississippi, who early on saw value in my manuscript and gave support to its vision.

To Moira Crone, reader for the University Press of Mississippi, whose care and wisdom as a narrative artist helped make this a better, smoother, and more readable book.

To Carol Cox and Anne Stascavage, for a sensitive, thoroughly rigorous, and unusually erudite job of copyediting the final manuscript.

And to Audrey.

Foreword, with Hindsight: American, Overseas

"So where're you from?" someone asks me at a cocktail party, or a dinner.

"I grew up in the Caribbean," I say. My standard reply.

"Oh, where? That's kind of big." Or "That's a lot of places."

"Well, I was raised in three Latin American countries. Came to the States when I was seventeen and a half."

"Which countries?" they then ask.

"Puerto Rico, Cuba, and Venezuela," I say.

"Where were you born, though?" is the usual follow-up.

"Haiti," I answer. "But that was just an accident. My parents moved on a year or so after that."

"Oh, do you speak French, then?"

"I do, but not because of Haiti. I learned it in college, then later spent some time in France."

"Hmm. So why'd you travel around so much? Was your father in the Foreign Service?"

"No, he was in business, sort of a small-time adventurer, roving from deal to deal." And, in appropriate circumstances, I might add, "Someone out of a Joseph Conrad novel."

Here's the rest: My father was a lower-middle-class WASP from Kansas. My mother was part-Chinese, part-Polynesian from Honolulu, and she also had a Castilian grandfather in the Philippines—hence the

"Villada" part of my name, after a hamlet in the northern province of Palencia, Spain. (The Madrid telephone book lists just twelve "Villadas," so it seems to be a fairly rare surname.)

My parents divorced when I was thirteen, in Puerto Rico, when my father abandoned my mom for a blonde Cuban. During my early high-school years my kid brother and I fell under the custody of our dad (who more or less abducted us to Batista's Cuba) and his second wife.

Around this time, Mom moved with my baby sister to northern New Mexico. There she found a loving husband and, eventually, a supportive father for us three. Estevan was his name, a forest ranger of old, rural, Hispanic stock, from the type of community made famous in novels such as John Nichols's *The Milagro Beanfield War* and Rudolfo Anaya's *Bless Me, Ultima.*

My having been born of U.S. parents overseas automatically gives me American citizenship, by law. In some way, though, I'm pan-Hispanic as well: Iberian great-grandfather. Spanish-Caribbean upbringing. Chicano stepfather. And a Cuban stepmother on my bio-logical father's side.

I was not to set foot on continental U.S. soil until age thirteen and a half, during a five-day visit to Florida. My dad and his Cuban spouse had flown me there with my brother, on a brief vacation just before the new-lyweds went on to consign us to a military school in distant Havana. Back in Puerto Rico I had always described myself as "American." Once in Florida, though, my brother and I started experiencing the identity dilemmas we'd confront in later years. Now, when asked where we were from, I'd reply that we were Puerto Ricans.

The set phrase "Where are you from?" carries deeper implications on the order of "Where do you belong?" and "Where is your home?" and ultimately "*What* are you?" Where you first saw life and where you were then raised, after all, aren't necessarily the places you've since chosen to call home. Indeed you may find you don't much belong in either of them.

The question's possible responses become further complicated when you've been raised as an American abroad, and in more than one alien land. Under such conditions, the issue of where you are from, and what you are, will inevitably take on an elusive, slippery, and unresolved quality. You live with an identity that is in permanent dispersal, its bits and pieces scattered here, there, everywhere—and nowhere. And you're always both elucidating and withholding your strange tale every time someone comes up with the query.

How others see and hear you can significantly shape your own conduct or what you claim to be. For example, if a stranger remarks on how well I speak English, I don't know whether to quietly bask in this perceived aura of linguistic prowess, or to explain to them that, actually, English is and always has been my native tongue. Along with Spanish. On the other hand, sometimes they'll remark on my odd and unidentifiable accent, having already pegged me as an unclassifiable foreigner.

Another instance: on account of my Eurasian features, Americans I meet casually on my travels in Europe at times think of me as an expatriate from east Asia someplace. On occasion, I've gone along with their mistake in identity and told them I'm Cambodian. Or Vietnamese. Why not, really? If you've got several identities inside of you, then might as well try out a couple more of them, no?

The question "Where're you from?" is of course standard fare in the language of every nation, and its variants crop up early on in any Berlitz-style phrasebook. I'd speculate that it gets asked with special frequency within our U.S. borders. From seventeenth-century Dutch settlers and mid-nineteenth-century German exiles to the Bengali shopkeepers and the undocumented Guatemalan war refugees of our own time, most Americans trace their origins back to someplace else. About the only U.S. inhabitants who can rightfully reply, "Oh, we're from here" are the Hopi, the Lakota, and other indigenous folks whose presence on this continent spans millennia. The rest of us are Anglo-Americans, Irish-Americans,

African-Americans, Polish-Americans, Arab-Americans, Iranian-Americans, and the like. Our forebears, whether remote or immediate, deceased or still living, all hail from elsewhere, and we know it.

Our mobility on this landmass makes "Where're you from?" an additionally necessary gambit. U.S. education and media routinely celebrate an American frontier that remains present history. The now-mythic suburbanization that characterized the post–World War II years wouldn't have been possible without the widespread availability of good, cheap land (and, out west, massive federal water projects). And then there are our own individual itineraries, what we might call the frontier personal. A Connecticut-born professional might earn his degrees in Boston and Chicago, take an entry-level post in San Francisco, rise to something better in Dallas, peak in Manhattan, and finally retire to the golf links of south Florida.

At the other end of our social hierarchy is the roustabout-tinkerer, free yet rootless, aimless, drifting on the road from deal to deal or job to job—the kind of lonely individual portrayed in novels like Norman Mailer's *The Executioner's Song* or Russell Banks's *Continental Drift* (the latter title a complex pun with frontier connotations). This character is a very American type and in fact is an oddity elsewhere. In most other societies, custom and desire more or less dictate that you stick with a job and stay with what you know. By contrast, casual employment, student summer work, and migrant labor were for a long time essentially U.S. phenomena, at least in the degree to which we've assumed and depended on them. Granted, American working-class people incline toward traditional values—family, religion, personal ties, place. Yet when employment dries up in their communities, they'll often move on to where the jobs are. And the question "Where're you from?" inevitably resurfaces.

Foreigners sometimes find it puzzling to hear a Brooklyn housewife state matter-of-factly, "I'm Italian." What she means is that, around 1910, her great-grandparents arrived at Ellis Island from rural Sicily, perhaps with some intent of sailing back to Europe after a few years, though for any number of reasons they and their offspring ended up settling on these shores. Still, however residual, her Italianness forms part of the Brooklyn housewife's identity, given especially the slow demise, since the late 1960s, of the doctrine of the "melting pot" and its eventual replacement by what has been called the "unmeltable ethnics," by the mosaic of identity politics that characterizes our time. These new hyphenates—among them fair numbers of Jewish-Americans, Chinese-Americans, Cuban-Americans, Chicanos, and of course African-Americans—have their own heroes, community leaders, and politicians, and, in some cases, their own writers and filmmakers, all of whom compete within the multicultural market of U.S. life in the new millennium.

Within this mélange, one group—not exactly a hyphenate—that remains more or less invisible consists of those I call Overseas Americans. The phrase denotes the hundreds of thousands and maybe millions of corporate managers, military and diplomatic staff, expatriate adventurers, small-business people, schoolteachers, missionaries, clergy, and scattered individuals involved in the arts and film who settle abroad and whose offspring are brought up within American enclaves of varying size. (For complex reasons, few Overseas Americans are working class, unless you include the children of countless enlisted men who, starting with the Cold War, worked their way up the ladder at U.S. Army bases in Europe and Asia, but who also had little contact with the host country and its culture.) In addition there are the foreign-raised "red-diaper babies," children of American socialists who found it necessary to take jobs elsewhere following the postwar repression (the misnamed "McCarthy Era"), an obscure episode in political emigration virtually unknown today outside the tiny circle of the American left.

Despite more than two centuries of U.S. expansion, there's not much narrative on the subject of Overseas Americans. When novelists like James, Wharton, Fitzgerald, and Hemingway set their narratives in Europe, the tale is of individual expatriation, of an American abroad, rather than of a whole community and its array of businesses, bureaucracies, schools, clubs, churches, and gathering places, its politics, prejudices, and dreams. The literatures of England and France, by contrast, have had their venerable share of authors who deal in some measure with the experience of being a British or French person overseas. One thinks of novels by Kipling, Foster, Conrad (of course), and Graham Greene, by Orwell and Doris Lessing in their earlier incarnations, and by Camus, Duras, and Robbe-Grillet—all of whom deal on several occasions with the whole experience of being an overseas Briton or French person. Not to mention films like *Chocolat* (the one from the 1980s, set in Africa) and *Indochine*. And straight memoirs like Penelope Lively's *Oleander, Jacaranda*. All of these are works that speak of Brits in Africa, India, and Burma, of French in Algeria, West Africa, and Southeast Asia. They tell of characters who live, love, and muddle through during some era prior to the upheavals of decolonization in those lands, who've either never set eyes on a distant Mother Country, or have been on overseas duty for so long that they've lost touch with the motherland's everyday textures. Yet they still think of themselves as proudly English or French.

There's a simple matter of political geography underlying those French and English literary works: Britain and France were relatively small countries, limited by the countervailing military and demographic strength of their foreign neighbors. Their ventures in colonial annexation had, of necessity, to be overseas (starting with Ireland in the case of the British). A young, vigorous United States, by contrast, was blessed with weak neighbors (the Indian nations, Mexico, Canada), vast amounts of resource-rich lands to conquer and settle, and the natural protection provided by huge oceans—all features that to this day have determined the course of our historical development.

And so, as late as 1910, at the high noon of overseas European empire, such vast, contiguous expanses of land as Arizona and New Mexico still bore the official U.S. designation "territories"—our euphemism for "colonies," also applied at the time to Puerto Rico and the Philippines. Unlike with Europeans, up until 1898 or so the Overland American played a greater role in U.S. expansion than did the Overseas American. The process, familiar enough to us from the dime-novel mythologies of once-ubiquitous Westerns, was also illuminated in Mark Twain's nonfiction (*Roughing It*), while Willa Cather gave it poetry, beauty, and depth in novels like *O Pioneers!* and *My Ántonia*.

The changes in American thinking that came about in the wake of the Vietnam débâcle (what Tom Engelhardt calls "the end of victory culture" in a superb book by that name) have led to some fine imaginative work that captures certain kinds of Overseas-American experience. I think in particular of Robert Stone's wonderful novel *A Flag for Sunrise*, set in two fictional Central American republics, with its assorted gringo characters: small-time gunrunners, missionary nuns, a lumpen drifter, a CIA agent, and other such types familiar to anyone who has spent much time in the Caribbean. And I marvel at *The Poisonwood Bible*, Barbara Kingsolver's dazzling portrayal of an evangelical family from small-town Georgia, stationed for missionary work in a Belgian Congolese village in 1960, where the parents and four daughters bring their American ways; they start out more or less clueless as to the surrounding tribal culture and political intrigues—yet in the end will be variously transformed by sharing in the tragedies and struggles of the thoroughly non-Christian Africans they live with.

One unforeseen consequence of the enormous global U.S. presence following World War II has been the largely unacknowledged numbers of American youths whose schooling has taken place, in whole or in part, on foreign soil. In any given year since 1950, at least two hundred thousand U.S. children are enrolled at K-through-12

schools abroad. As a result, there's now an increasing body of nonfiction writing that deals with the assorted dilemmas of growing up as a
dependent overseas and then facing, as an adolescent or young adult,
the small surprises and long-term pangs of "repatriation."

Already in the 1950s the sociologists John Useem and Ruth Hill
Useem reflected on their time spent as an academic family working in
newly independent India. They coined the phrase "Third Culture
Kids," or TCKs. The term can be applied to any and all nationalities, but
in the Useems' research it refers to American children living abroad
"as dependents of parents who are employed overseas." The culture of
these kids is "third" because it freely and spontaneously mingles key
aspects of the host country's language, customs, and worldview with
elements from the passport country (in this case the United States),
though as an entity it doesn't belong fully to either. Later, most of these
TCKs will move to the U.S. for their studies and grow up as "*Adult*
TCKs." In the process, they'll tend to feel, in some degree, out of place
in the land of their parents and their citizenship. Having been perma-
nently marked by their upbringing overseas, they'll seldom reach a
sense of full integration in American life. As a useful piece of shorthand, "Third Culture Kids" and its acronym have taken on a life of its
own for those who write about the topic.

As the century waned, a few Adult TCKs who'd entered middle age
began seriously looking back on their formative years. They wrote a
number of social-science studies and personal memoirs focusing on
their still-nameless problem. Probably the pioneering work in this
regard is freelance writer Carolyn D. Smith's *The Absentee American:
Repatriates' Perspectives on America* (1990). For her preliminary research,
Smith sent out a two-page questionnaire to a sampling of Overseas-
American returnees. Responses came from three hundred individuals
whose ages ranged from twenty to seventy. Some of the questions asked
by Smith are highly suggestive: "If you returned to the United States

after an absence of many years, how did you respond emotionally to the reentry experience, and how did others respond to you?" Or, "Do you feel that you are well integrated into American society? Why or why not?" And her final question, the most telling and provocative of them all: "Do you readily identify yourself as 'an American'? If so, what does this signify to you? If not, how do you view yourself?" The responses are as searching and complex as the questions.

Smith followed up her strictly sociological opus with a collection entitled *Strangers at Home: Essays on the Effects of Living Overseas and Coming "Home" to a Strange Land* (1996). Most of the gathered pieces lay emphasis on the personal (though there's still some sociology), and they're therefore meditative, lyrical, often ambivalent. One of them (by Ruth Van Reken) concentrates on the particularly intense, self-contained universe of the "Missionary Kid" (MK) who grows up thoroughly immersed in a Third World nation; yet another (by Morten Ender) analyzes those brought up as "military brats" at U.S. bases across the globe. Though dealing with two very different subcultures, these two essays capture the series of overseas dislocations followed by inner trauma as their subjects reenter "normal" American life—secular in the case of the former, civilian in the latter. The titles of some of the book's essays are in themselves revealing: "Religious Culture Shock," "Where Will I Build My Nest?," and "You Can't Go 'Home' Again." Similarly, the very titles and subtitles of both of Smith's volumes—with words like "Absentee," "Repatriates," "Strangers," and "a Strange Land"—hint at the outset at something semialien, marginal, and unresolved.

As I first read through Carolyn Smith's two volumes (in just a couple of sittings each) and the briefer articles by the Useems, I felt repeated shivers of recognition, page after page. It was the very first time I'd seen in print the peculiar wishes and frustrations, the odd misunderstandings and misperceptions, the hard-won wisdom and inevitable wistfulness that come with being an Overseas American.

Moreover, to learn that there actually exist so many fellow Adult TCKs out there—who, in some measure or other, have shared in my complex, troubled emotions concerning my "absentee" past and my American "reentry"—has proved most heartening, even exhilarating.

Meanwhile, as a somewhat broader awareness of the psychological profile of the Overseas American has taken shape, there are now how-to books that confront the subject head-on. Their aim is to help outbound and returnee parents steer their families through the process of becoming TCKs. Their titles, naturally enough, zero in on the practical: *The Art of Coming Home* by Craig Storti, or *Homeward Bound: A Spouse's Guide to Repatriation*, edited by Robin Pascoe. In 2001, moreover, the term *Third Culture Kids* finally achieved full visibility as the title of a popular, snappy, and sensitive volume—part psychology, part sociology, and filled with revealing anecdotes—by David Pollock and Ruth Van Reken (both of whom had written previously on the topic); the book bears the subtitle *The Experience of Growing Up among Worlds*. Last but not least, there are even some small presses—Aletheia Publications and Intercultural Press, to name just two—that subspecialize in titles about matters of concern to TCKs, Adult TCKs, MKs, "military brats," "biz kids," and other sorts of Overseas Americans.

The matter of TCKs, then, exists as something to be studied, evoked, analyzed, and agonized over by select novelists, memoirists, social scientists, and pop psychologists. Meanwhile, what is it about the experience of growing up American someplace else that merits such intense exploration and soul searching? Well, TCKs represent a slice of American life and history, past and present. Yet they've also known a strange, otherworldly sort of existence with its strong elements of unreality—an unreality that is quite literally a part of the American Dream. To some extent, as a young Overseas American you're not completely in touch with, are even in denial of, the everyday world you live in, and are constantly waiting to enter the paradise known variously as the States, the U.S., the United States, America. En route to heaven, you might practice some indulgences and eventually go through some levels of purgatory, as Catholics do in their narrative of life and afterlife. And when finally you arrive "home" for school or for work, you find yourself always clarifying your past situation to strangers and acquaintances, and to yourself.

"Where're you from?" someone asks you at a party or on a bus.

And you reply, "I'm from Brazil/France/the Philippines"—or what have you—"but I'm American." And you've your own set answer at the ready.

I grew up as a Third Culture Kid. My schooling through the tenth grade was largely in Spanish, as was most of my socializing. At curbsides and street corners, at makeshift baseball lots, and at the YMCA and its summer camps in the mountains, my brother and I routinely had Spanish-speaking playmates. Our early home life and innermost thoughts, in turn, were in American English. The unstated assumption was that, even though we were residing in the Spanish Caribbean, our deeper ties were with the U.S.A., which was our ultimate destination. Together my brother and I formed a separate, self-contained, TCK entity. In our conversations we'd move effortlessly between the two languages, freely intermingling local with U.S. cultural references.

Of course, the two of us had never lived Up There. Had scarcely visited it. Yet we supposedly knew the place because of our regular immersion in TV shows such as *I Love Lucy*, or through teen flicks such as *Rock around the Clock* (the original one, with Bill Haley and the Comets).

Needless to say, our arrival and entry into the real, flesh-and-blood United States was something that bore but the slightest resemblance to those movies or TV entertainments. Like many a TCK, I "returned" to the U.S. for my college studies, where I'd experience shocks and ambivalences that I'd never outgrow, and that I hope to exorcise here.

And now, as I write this book, I make it my business to share what I know of Spanish language and culture with my students at Williams College and elsewhere. The Overseas American from our Caribbean colonies thus found himself a useful function here in the metropolis. My case is scarcely unique, though: not a few foreign-language teachers in the United States have backgrounds somewhat like mine. (I know at least a half-dozen of them personally.) In fact, education is among the most frequent career choices for Adult TCKs.

Of course, the role of cultural interpreter and casual, everyday relativist need not be the sole route taken by Overseas Americans once they're back in the States. Some may compensate for their rootlessness by becoming supernationalists, ardent defenders of U.S. ways and policies. They'll strive to become "mainstream"—even to *create* the mainstream, as did Henry Luce, who, having been born and raised in China of American missionary parents, later went on to found and rule tightfistedly over *Time* and *Life*, journals that, during the forty years he ran them, broadly reflected his right-wing, Liberty Lobby views. On the other hand, I've read that orchestra conductor Lorin Maazel grew up in Europe with U.S. parents; I like to imagine that he found in classical music a cosmopolitan, not specifically American world in which he would feel most comfortable (talents aside).

Although I started out as an Overseas American, I had no idea that's what I was as a child, adolescent, or young adult. I arrived at such a realization only after a decade or so of living in the U.S., and I didn't come up with the term itself until much later, in the 1980s. To some extent I *became* an Overseas American as a consequence of the '60s and everything that special era stood for. In this book, then, I hope to trace that long, complex, occasionally tortuous process of realization and self-discovery. Though the facts of my case are specific, the process certainly isn't. Most adult identities are not fixed essences but rather eventual outcomes, each one a resulting order that has evolved in response to varying degrees of conflict and struggle. We all become, not merely are.

In the following ten chapters I try to relate my one, small, personal instance of that becoming. In so doing, some retrospective thinking, construing, and commenting will be necessary. Childhood and adolescence are of course times of enormous illusion; and when you're growing up as an American overseas, the typical illusions of youth are further compounded by the grandest illusion of them all: namely, that you're an American too, just like those Stateside compatriots whom you see and hear in the movies and on TV, and whom you'll someday join for your studies or your work.

To arrive at last in the "homeland," by contrast, is to begin a long process of shaking off such notions, of looking back and realizing that you've been alien over *there*, and now are an alien *here* as well. Much of what I recount in these pages I finally understood only when I was crafting the words for it; and such informed retrospection, such sudden acts of insight and understanding, inevitably form part of this remembrance.

Yet I know there are readers—whether or not they're Overseas Americans—who'll sense some occasional frisson of recognition as they look into the narrative and the patterns brought together in these pages. After all, to enter U.S. life from abroad is a passage akin to immigration, a trajectory that has shaped our myths and history, from the salaried Italian navigator Columbus and the paying English passengers of the *Mayflower* venture on through the hardy Caribbean boat and raft people of recent date. Overseas Americans may have their own peculiar story, but in this regard they resemble native-born and immigrant Americans both, while differing considerably from either. This is an account of being an American while being outside the continental forty-eight States, and also a story of immigration (yet only after a fashion), a tale not so much of coming home as of going to where one was expected to go.

Part One: Overseas

The Absentee American belongs to no culture, or perhaps to all cultures ... To the Absentee American, all countries, including the United States, are "foreign." By the same token any country can be "home."

—CAROLYN D. SMITH, *The Absentee American*

Next Stop, San Juan

"Where're you from?" asked the freckled-faced guy sitting next to me in a Puerto Rican school bus. I must've been in third or fourth grade.

"From the States," I said.

"Where were you born?" he pressed on.

"Haiti."

"Well, then you're Haitian, not American." He mistakenly said *haitileno* instead of *haitiano*.

It was a foretaste of confusions to come.

My first home on this earth—according to my father—had been the Hotel Olafson in Port-au-Prince, a foreigners' enclave that serves as setting for much of Graham Greene's novel *The Comedians*. This odd fact has sometimes helped spice up accounts of my background. I wish I could say I vividly recall the broad, balustraded double stairways leading down to the hotel's outdoor swimming pool—a feature beautifully rendered by Greene. But, alas, I can't.

Two days after my birth, the U.S. naval base at Pearl Harbor was bombed by the Imperial Japanese Air Force. Following a few more months in Port-au-Prince, my parents and their infant son made landfall in Puerto Rico, presumably in order to be safe on overseas U.S. soil even as a belated American participation in an already vast global war was taking shape. With the birth, in 1944, of my brother Kanani—a Hawaiian name—we became a family of four residing in San Juan.

For my father, Puerto Rico was only the latest port of call in an ongoing odyssey. At age eighteen he had already packed his bags, bidding adieu to his stolid, German-Scottish parents in Missouri and going on to start college at the University of California, Los Angeles, where his brother and nephew lived. A couple of years later he transferred to the University of Hawaii.

Many cultures converged on that island campus. Among the eager enrollees was a petite sociology major by the name of Perlita Carmen Villada. Her Chinese mother, originally from the Middle Kingdom, worked in small-scale real estate. The father, Juan Mariano Villada, of Filipino extraction, had originally left Manila as a stowaway in search of a better life, jumping ship in Honolulu. The eldest of their five offspring, my mom was first known as "Perly." Neighborhood contemporaries would remember her as a cheerful, lively girl, filled with jokes and riddles.

At the university there, a twenty-year-old Perly, now called Carmen, meets the young man she eventually will marry. It seems to have been a classic, almost novelistic college romance: the blond, blue-eyed charmer who woos a native girl; the wide-eyed young maiden apparently quite taken with this movie-star-handsome guy from the States and his dreams of starting life anew, somewhere halfway around the world. Already he's making money by renting out halls for dances and running a private mailbox service near the university grounds. Also as in a novel, rumors circulate among friends about her parents' disapproval of the amour. Perhaps Mr. and Mrs. Villada sense something is amiss with the youthful and attractive Yankee adventurer. In time, I gather, he succeeds in winning them over with his winsome boyishness.

Late in life Mom would wryly recall the lengthy, Japanese-language sales pitch my dad had memorized for business use in the Far East. Around July 1940 he duly sets sail for Nippon, ostensibly to attend an international student conference there. Once the event is done, though, he journeys through Japan and China, speculating in currencies, selling magazine subscriptions (your typical avenue for college-age entrepreneurs), and renting his Hawaiian mailboxes to Japanese citizens sending out secret financial remittances to relatives abroad. In his many letters to Mom, filled with loving effusions, he characterizes his sales activities as "making money for us and our future." There are also verbal sketches of the cities he visits (Yokohama, Nagasaki, Kōbe; Pekin, Shanghai). And there are reports of encounters with colorful types along the way: rickshaw boys who moonlight as procurers, or the future *New York Times* writer Flora Lewis, whom they both know as their fellow student in Oahu.

In his early letters my father talks seriously of marriage, hoping for it soon. He also asks her to find him a Model A Ford. He wonders if Carmen's mum might loan him five thousand dollars (a considerable sum in those days) for initial capital or for a down payment on a house. Mrs. Villada, though, wants the young couple to finish college first, and Mr. Villada by then openly disapproves of their matrimonial plans. My dad must have later convinced or mollified them, though, for on October 21, shortly after returning from his Asian adventures, he and Carmen are legally married.

Then it's Uncle Sam's turn. Not long thereafter, the U.S. Army has drafted our youthful groom, who goes on to spend eight months in uniform at Hawaii's Schofield Barracks. In a loving letter dated February 6, 1941, he urges the newlywed bride to go see Lt. Col. Stevens, his battalion commander, and argue for discharge on grounds that federal regulations temporarily exempt from conscription those men who are their spouse's sole support.

Her efforts succeed! The couple are reunited. On the 11th of August 1941, with Carmen five months pregnant, the twosome set sail for the continental United States on board the SS *Mariposa*, which means "butterfly." (I still have among my parents' papers the ship's elegantly printed, imitation-calligraphy passenger list.) Their ultimate destination: Haiti. In his Asian letters, my dad has seriously entertained the idea of setting up shop on that remote Caribbean island and there making his fortune. Only a week before their departure from the Pacific, on August 5, he writes her from (of all places) Japan and notes, "Our first objective . . . is to make money. While we are making money we accomplish a lot in the way of building our character, strengthening our love for each other, finding out about each other. These are the things that count, but we must have money & we'll get it, darling."

After a short spell in Marshall, Missouri, with Dad's parents (Mom doesn't care for them much; later she'll recall her father-in-law yelling at her a lot), the couple arrives and settles in Haiti. Yours truly is born on schedule.

Meanwhile, with some help from my mother's savings, the twenty-two-year-old entrepreneur is launched in his ventures. In January 1942, just a month after my birth, Dad sends a letter from Havana, in which, after evoking the monumental beauties of its vintage, colonial-Spanish architecture, he dwells at length on a possible deal, shipping a load of mangrove bark for a lumber operator. He also describes himself as "a mag man" and, in his next few letters, becomes obsessed with getting the *Newsweek* concession for Puerto Rico. (The opportunity appears not to have panned out.) Only weeks have gone by since the attack on Pearl Harbor; he expresses relief at having slipped out of both the military and Hawaii, where he'd surely have been called up for combat in the widening Pacific war.

During their courtship my parents were far too naive to envisage U.S. entry into an armed conflict already engulfing much of East Asia and all of Europe. Now in the safety of the Caribbean, they quickly will become fluent in French, then Spanish. Meanwhile Dad learns about ships. Becomes a licensed pilot. Buddies around with small-time "pirates" (Mom's later term) and whilom gangsters. At one point he and a Belgian crony will actually establish the first civilian air link between Florida and the colonial French island of Guadeloupe. (The enterprise eventually peters out when, as part of postwar reconstruction and development, Air France moves in and, with its infinitely greater resources, puts an end to that pioneering endeavor.)

My earliest tropical, childhood memories are of a dark and spacious fifth-floor apartment in which browns and earth tones predominate. It's shaped like a double-armed T-square, with the living room, two bedrooms, and father's study in one arm, and the dining room, kitchen, and maid's quarters in the other. The living room and dining room both have entrances to the outer hall, with a long passageway connecting them, standing wide open to an outside patio—recognizably Iberian—with several identical apartments stacked above and below. Between the open ledges at either end there stretch multiple layers of clothesline, fully laden with bright wash during sunlit afternoons. Throughout the day, the mingled scents of cilantro, parsley, and deep-fried dough linger in the air, along with the sounds of small radios loudly sharing their situation comedies and sentimental soap operas.

There's a neighborhood atmosphere vaguely resembling that of a postwar Italian movie, people chatting with each other from their respective ledges or while standing about in the hall. Directly across from our front door lives Alfredo Matilla, at the time the island's leading classical-music critic, both in the press and on the radio. Later, I found out he'd been a lawyer in 1930s Spain, loyal to the civilian, republican government of the time, before fleeing Franco's fascists and ending up in Puerto Rico, where he'd somehow drifted into music journalism. My initial recollection of Beethoven's First and Brahms's Fourth symphonies is of their opening movements piping out into the corridor from Dr. Matilla's record player. His two children, Fredín and Mariloli, were slightly older than Kanani and I, so we scarcely played together. Fredín later went on to become a literature professor up in the States.

The building wasn't in any of the North American—preferred neighborhoods but in Río Piedras, an outlying district of greater San Juan, a bit as Queens is to Manhattan. The more significant American colony resided instead in El Condado (literally "The County"), an upper-middle-class district located next to San Juan proper, and right on a balmy, sea-lapped shore. That favored neighborhood was home to the corporate Americans who boasted their own beach club (called—what else?—El Condado) and sent their kids to St. John's, an élite school where English was spoken and which was also attended by the children of well-off, Americanized islanders.

Still, there were some Americans in the building and a few more close by. I vaguely remember, on the top floor, an extensive family called the Roses and their three flaxen-haired, loquacious girls. From one of them I first heard the word "Miami," to which I asked, "Your what?" Amused, she explained about the big, modern city across the sea.

At street level there was a well-lit bar and grill, owned by a tough, chain-smoking businesswoman called Lillian. Her jukebox listed several Strauss waltzes. Once, as the three-quarter time lilted in the background, she and Mom jested with my brother and me about the two of them exchanging their kids. Over the next day I kept expecting some follow-up, a total change of scenery with Kanani and me living for good at Lillian's place.

Just a stone's throw from Lillian's bar stood the lush, verdant grounds of the Universidad de Puerto Rico. It was our first playground, and its landmarks show up in outdoor photos of Kanani and me as toddlers. My sharpest and most vivid early-childhood memories are of the school's wide, grassy spaces, its ornate bell tower chiming classics at sundown, and its row of flamboyant tropical trees where the two of us occasionally clambered about and played.

Beginning at age five, I attended Colegio Espíritu Santo, a K-through-12 Catholic institution run by priests from the Fathers of the Holy Ghost and nuns of the order of the Holy Family of Nazareth; all were from the U.S. The school occupied a rectangular lot in a residential section of Hato Rey (pronounced AH-toe RAY), the next district over in the direction of San Juan. As many little kids do, I cried apprehensively when Dad drove me to school to start first grade. Next year, on the same drive, I remarked with amazement that leaving home for the second grade wasn't making me cry.

I spent nine years at CES, where we boys wore short, wine-colored pants and matching neckties up through fifth grade, after which we shifted to full-length khaki trousers. The girls' pleated skirts gave way to jumpers with light-cream blouses after eighth grade. On the left shoulder of our white shirts and blouses was displayed the school insignia. CES being an American school, every morning we'd line up on the concrete-paved front courtyard and recite a Spanish-accented Pledge of Allegiance, then file in to the sound of amplified 78-rpm recordings, marches by John Philip Sousa ("Stars and Stripes Forever," "Washington Post March") or military choruses singing the U.S. Marines and Air Force anthems ("Off we go, into the wild, blue yonder . . .").

Spanish was actually the primary language of instruction from grades one to six, although we employed the English honorifics: Miss, Mrs., Sister, Father. Resident nuns from the convent a few doors up the road evenly shared the academic subjects with a roster of secular teachers. There was an hour a day of English as a second language, during which the nuns led us into the exotic world of *Here We Come* and other Dick-and-Jane books. Arithmetic was imparted to us by the secular women. To this day I can see and hear them, yardstick or chalk stub in hand, patiently drilling us, like a choral director, in the addition and subtraction tables—in Spanish. For many years after my move to the continental U.S., I'd feel more comfortable using Spanish when doing math.

CES was one of the better schools in Puerto Rico, and a not unpleasant or unattractive place. Three or four middle-aged priests—kind and even friendly men—loomed over the operation like venerable patriarchs and taught a few courses. The secular teachers, dedicated professionals, took their pedagogical mission seriously. Among my most touching memories from that time is of our short, stout, first-grade instructor, Miss Franco, weeping profusely on her last June day with us. She always became very much attached to her yearly charges.

The sisters ran a full gamut from the caringly sweet and sensitive (my kindergarten teacher Sister Consolata, for instance, who as of this writing still remembers me and my classmates by name) to the high-handedly vicious, tyrannical, nasty types for whom verbal bullying was normal speech. The latter boxed the ears of miscreants and ridiculed the weaker students, calling them "dumbbells" and "slowpokes." And they constantly compared us unfavorably to "the kids up in the States," who allegedly "knew how to behave" and were shining models of what we were not. A former schoolmate, three years younger than I, recalls nuns fretting in class, "Puerto Rico is trash!" and "Puerto Rico is junk!" Legends existed of a special room, located in some dark corner underneath a hall stairway, where a repeat offender would be taken and subjected to a thorough thwacking with a wooden ruler. (The identity of the thwacker remained, to me at least, unspecified.)

Among the nun's functions was to inculcate in us young lambs the teachings, practices, and hierarchy of the Roman Apostolic Church. Every morning, before taking our seats in class, we recited the Spanish "Our Father." ("Padre nuestro que estás en los cielos/santo sea/el tu nombre . . .") In time the ritual hardened into routine and the prayer took on a Latin beat, something akin to the rhythms of the "Habanera" from *Carmen*. Doctrine constituted a mainstay of our curriculum. We memorized the catechism, learned the differences between venial and mortal sins. And we eventually arrived at the grim awareness that, with so much as one, single mortal sin on our soul when we died, we'd end up in an eternal Hell whose flames lacerate and burn human flesh for all time without ever consuming it.

The standard Creation story was taught. Early on a nun broke to us the news that, were it not for Adam and Eve's first disobedience, there would have been no death. We pupils sighed as one, sincere in our sadness. The sixth commandment in Spanish was *No fornicarás* ("Thou shalt not fornicate"), and I remember my eight-year-old's puzzlement at first seeing that mystery word. And then there were the rules concerning personal conduct. Marrying outside the Catholic fold was explicitly forbidden. Divorce led to immediate "excommunication." (The very word spelled fear.) A weekly Index, in Spanish, was tacked onto hall bulletin boards, with recent movies listed on a sliding scale from "highly recommended" to roundly "**CONDEMNED**" (yes, caps and boldface) as contrary to church morals. Some condemnations made little sense in that they might anathematize a perfectly innocuous, run-of-the-mill Hollywood musical—perhaps because of its barelegged chorus girls, or because, in one of them, the lead couple goes through a divorce.

Still, our occasional mockery notwithstanding, the indoctrination got deep under our skins. At recess, some kid would casually mention having prayed to God last week and then getting a grade of "100" on the next day's test. Or we'd argue earnestly over whether God could create a stone so heavy He could not lift it:

"Of course He can."

"Yeah, but then He's not strong enough."

"Well, He can't."

"Yeah, but then He can't do everything."

Rumor had it that an unnamed priest had been about to divulge the most hallowed church secrets, whereupon—ZAP!—a ray of lightning charred him into bacon. And I remember the terror I felt, in bed at nights, of dying in my sleep with a mortal sin on my soul.

Nevertheless, I was a Protestant boy. I'd been christened, around age two, at the Episcopalian church downtown. As a result I didn't share in the group rituals of confession and communion with my schoolmates on first Thursdays and Fridays of every month. During those occasions I'd sit out the hour in an empty classroom, chatting with the two or three non-Catholic Americans also in my grade.

Still, I wanted to belong. I'd speak earnestly of the attractions of Catholicism to my parents. They solidly opposed my joining the fold, each for different reasons. I've a recollection of my father in his study, his blond hair shining in the afternoon sun as he dismisses, with amused contempt, the very notion that the body of Jesus could be present in a piece of bread. There's scorn in his tenor voice. My mother, for her part, felt I should wait till my eighteenth birthday before making any religious choices. Late into my adult life I'd find out that her entire schooling in Hawaii had been at an institution run by the Maryknolls, an American order, and that her Chinese mother was a devout Catholic. Yet my mom never expressed any feeling about the church, for or against. To this day, the nature of her personal, subjective relationship to the Roman faith remains a total mystery to me.

Whatever Mom's motives, I think she made a mistake—if an honest one—in not letting me go all out and convert. Even if I'd eventually abandoned the fold and passionately spurned the whole thing (the most likely outcome), I could at least have claimed "lapsed Catholic" as a past phase. Instead, I can only say now that I once held Catholic views and fears, without ever belonging to the church ranks or engaging in its many practices. Strange as it sounds, I wish I'd been Catholic, wish I'd had that experience, that full tradition, to reject, rather than having been raised "neither/nor," neither Protestant nor Popish. It would have meant that at least I had once been *something*, rather than merely an in-between Puerto Rican or an incomplete American. And I now wonder if my mom, being a mélange of

Chinese, Filipina, Hawaiian, American (and Catholic?) herself, might actually have preferred those in-between identities to choosing a more specific and concrete status, both for her own life and her offspring's.

Outside of school, Kanani and I led isolated lives. The Americans Mom and Dad dealt with, being transients or otherwise uprooted, weren't given to forging bonds. I don't recall having friends among their children. There were Puerto Ricans in my parents' circle of acquaintances, particularly Mother's. The head of the government-run radio station WIPR lived next door to us; Mom often talked about him and his wife. Yet I never exactly understood what ties existed between our household and theirs, if any. Within the building I had no island friends, save for the occasional playmate. During a drought, I vaguely remember, our bathtub stood prudently brimful of water; a neighborhood kid and I played what seemed an amusing little prank as we surreptitiously peed into that makeshift reservoir.

Aside from the daily press, there were no Spanish publications in the apartment. We all knew the language, and fluently, but the continuity between the immediate outside world and our abstract Americanism was fractured and sadly incomplete. Our graying and affectionate Puerto Rican maid Paula cooked us some island dishes—*asopao* (a chicken-and-rice stew) or fried plantains. (And Kanani has fond memories of her running her fingers through his hair and giving him headrubbies.) For our desserts and breakfasts, though, rather than take advantage of the fresh, succulent, easily available tropical fruits—mangoes, pineapples, guavas—we mostly ate canned peaches and packaged cereals brought in from the States. The choice seemed perfectly normal; it would never have occurred to us to seek daily nourishment in the local fare.

The one time when Puerto Rican events impinged on our lives happened during the rise of the *nacionalista* movement. Its charismatic leader, Pedro Albizu Campos, was engaged in a fervent bid for island independence and the creation of a separate republic. The main-stream local press and radio were thick with mention of Albizu, always referred to in vaguely sinister terms. (Even the photos of him, I now realize, seem to have been chosen for their unflattering aspect.)

One morning a *nacionalista* demonstration at the university campus turned violent, with thousands of angry students fleeing cops at full speed and clouds of tear gas floating inexorably down the avenue. Kanani and I happened to be standing within the chaotic crowd's line of flight, waiting for our Espíritu Santo school bus. Scared, the two of us ran off together, ducking for cover in some building's front hallway. Otherwise, the movement was an issue that had little effect on us. I simply fell in with my parents' vague opinion that the *nacionalistas* were a bad thing.

We were Americans, Kanani and I learned, and we thought of ourselves as such. We understood this even though our parents were the only "gringos" with whom we had any ongoing contact. (My mom was a Hawaiian colonial, at that, and till sometime in her thirties was required by law to carry a government ID card and photo that classed her as being of "Mongolian" origin.) I wrote a few Christmas notes to Mom's parents and siblings in Hawaii, and to Dad's mother, now in California with her other son, Rex. (My grouchy, paternal grandpa had died in 1945.) But, except for short visits from Auntie Leila Villada and from Grandmother Bell in the late 1940s, there was no sense of our belonging to a larger American fold or even to some particular small fragment of it.

Kanani and I thus lived a vast absence, day after day, year upon year. Our parents aside, we knew virtually no blood ties, no caring, quirky grandmamas or grandpapas somewhere nearby to bring us into past history, no uncles, aunts, or cousins to link us to the continental Forty-eight or to insular Hawaii. There were hardly even family albums, pictures, to prompt reminiscence and reverie. The family tree's branches were minimal—just us two—and its roots were nonexistent. Continuity, connectedness—they were, in a word, nil.

Overseas Americans usually have their sights set on their "return" to El Norte. In our case, however, there was as yet no Norte known to us firsthand, whether in the form of places or people. What American life Kanani and I regularly led in our Río Piedras neighborhood was at a couple of movie palaces just three blocks down the avenue. There, on weekends and during summers, we'd go see any Hollywood picture we could. The bill changed weekly, so we must have seen a couple of hundred feature films, along with the cartoons and newsreels that were then standard fare. Vivid images stand out from a select few items: *Kim* (a scary final avalanche), *Beau Geste* (dead Foreign Legion soldiers lined up on the ramparts, rifles in hand), *Rocky Mountain* (white corpses littering some valley), plus glitzy, tuneful musicals, pistol-packed Westerns, and a horse-filled, Robin Hood saga with John Derek. *The Creature from the Black Lagoon,* both the story and the scaly beast itself, had a particularly profound impact on Kanani, who felt quite scared for some days thereafter. And there was the endless string of Abbott and Costello comedies, which Mom found unbearably stupid. (I chanced to see a snippet of one of them on TV in the '80s, and found myself belatedly agreeing with her.)

Usually we were the only English-speaking folks in the movie audiences, and we basked in the privilege of getting the jokes and other nuances left untranslated in the subtitles. (Later, when I moved to the U.S., films *without* subtitles struck me as odd, and also lacking in a useful supplement, especially for scenes featuring regional accents or low whispers.) Over the years we got many laughs out of what seemed willful misrenderings in titles and subtitles. *A Lion Is in the Streets* became *A Shark in the Streets* ("Un tiburón en la calle"), and a tough-skinned *Mildred Pierce* transmuted into the sappy *A Mother's Torment.* Behind the seeming mistranslations, of course, there were legitimate reasons—rhythm, semantics, context—which we didn't know about. "Un tiburón en la calle" actually sounds better to the ear than "Un león está en la calle," and "Mildred Pierce" as a proper name would've meant nothing to Caribbean Hispanics.

Subtitling was mostly of Mexican origin, so dollar figures cited in the dialogue were routinely multiplied twelvefold into peso amounts, though we didn't realize that and simply puzzled at the apparent discrepancy. Several neighborhood theatres regularly showed Mexican movies—back then a prime source of competition to Hollywood's Latin-American market share. But save for a starkly dramatic version of Steinbeck's *The Pearl* that Mom took us to, we scarcely set foot in those houses—a lost opportunity, I now realize.

Amidst my loneliness, much solace was provided by our living-room console and its 78-rpm record changer. My parents had their ten-inch disks of American pop tunes of the time—"Joltin' Joe DiMaggio," "Saturday Night (Is the Loneliest Night of the Week)," mere words to me then, or "Rum and Coca-Cola," of which I'd chance to hear a superb rendition by a Caribbean group on Boston radio around 1989. And some breakneck boogie-woogie piano solos.

Mom had also noticed my responsiveness to the classics; by my tenth birthday I owned bulky RCA albums of *The Nutcracker Suite, The Firebird Suite, Scheherazade,* and the Brahms First Symphony. WIPR also played several hours of classical music every day. I listened, ear glued to the radio at any opportunity, full of regret that I had to attend school and miss out on noontime concerts, sometimes crying disconsolately when "the pretty music" came to an end. So frequently did I steep myself in those classics that by age ten, with the aid of assorted guidebooks I'd memorized much of the orchestral repertoire and often sang along with recordings or broadcasts—a habit that continued through much of my adolescence, and that I even now resist with difficulty.

Meanwhile I desperately wanted piano lessons. When Dad was away on business, in my many letters to him I'd mention my fond hopes and ask to be taken to music school on his return. My wearisome requests led nowhere; the longed-for music lessons didn't materialize, year in and year out. And so at some point I tried my hand at "making" music on my own. I'd set up rows of chairs with signs saying, "violins" or "oboes" or "tympani." Pencil in hand, I'd "conduct" along with the orchestral piece emanating from the console. On one occasion, a nun at CES asked us, her fourth-grade charges, what we all wanted to be when we grew up. Sister enthusiastically called on me. Without skipping a beat I replied, "An orchestra conductor!" She echoed the phrase, "An orchestra conductor . . ."

Back home I'd "compose," too, after a fashion. Lying in the bathtub, I'd vocally improvise symphonies, some classical, others romantic in style. And I "wrote" pieces on makeshift staves peppered with random quarter and eighth notes. I remember something I worked on assiduously, called "Boom of the Cannon," my attempt at an *1812 Overture* bearing my own byline. Truly, I was a supreme oddity: a child musician who loved music, who knew a fair amount about music, who on some intuitive level understood music—and yet couldn't legitimately play, read, or transcribe so much as a note of music. Meanwhile, at home there was no talk of nurturing that bent either at the moment or in the future, in Puerto Rico or up north.

I also read. Books of all kinds. There was a branch library two blocks away and a good-sized Carnegie collection in downtown San Juan. I binged on many look-alike Hardy Boys and Bobbsey Twins volumes (all of them written by the same guy, I casually found out from a colleague in 1992!). There were also popularized histories of religion and of the world, biographies of composers and other famous men, opera synopses, illustrated astronomy books, and a house subscription to *Children's Digest*. Later, in junior high, I gobbled up scads of formula science fiction and two-bit Perry Mason pocket books, plus baseball novels, notably Bernard Malamud's *The Natural*. Had Mom and Dad owned literary classics, I might have attempted them too, but their bookcases were stacked with current best-sellers that I still wonder about—mysterious books with titles like *My Chinese Wife* and *Laughing Boy*, and other conspicuous items. I was too young for those adult volumes, whereas I did leaf frequently through their thick anthologies of American humor—the seeds of a future obsession with jokebooks that seized me in my teens.

Early on I also devoured books on geography—atlases, almanacs, descriptive volumes of some sort or other. In the process I became a walking (and talking) encyclopedia of geographical facts and figures: the capitals, populations, and chief products of different countries, the lengths of rivers, the areas of lakes, and the precise heights of mountains. And I'd stare at maps and pictures of faraway places—Tanganyika, the Sahara, Afghanistan, Argentina, France—and imagine myself residing there among the inhabitants.

Now I realize I was projecting globally the colonial, overseas romance that we as a family were caught up in. And of course in a basic sense I was responding with a small boy's wonderment and awe to the earth's multitudinous grandeur, as shown in those books. But I also was longing for a place—or perhaps many places—on that earth. Meanwhile I had put myself on the path of the proverbial bookworm and was perilously close to flowering into an insufferable little pedant with my monstrous knowledge of world facts—and my utter innocence of world living. My childhood fascination with maps has stayed with me, though. And any visit to a foreign town—Buenos Aires, Montreal, Avignon, Oaxaca, Cracow—sparks in some corner of my mind the vague fantasy of settling there to share a life with its regular folks, or at least with its literary and musical set.

The emotion originates, of course, in my having lacked any strong, organic ties with either Puerto Rican society or my Río Piedras neighborhood. Being rootless in a U.S. colony, yet having no connection to gringos either on the island or on the big mainland up north, I imagined, romanticized, and yearned for vital links—not only here but there, anywhere, and everywhere. My mental-cultural bonds were promiscuous, desire-stoked, unrealized. I was a restless cosmopolitan, if only by default.

The longings remain. Oh, sure, I've found a tiny niche of my own in New England, on academia's sidelines, in the world of books, ideas, and the arts. Not having the action-based temperament of an adventurer nor the amoral savvy of a wheeler-dealer, today I live that promiscuous cosmopolitanism through culture: still responding to, and learning, teaching, and sometimes writing about musics and literatures from the Americas and Europe. Because I could not fit into Puerto Rican life, could not belong to the States, a larger, more abstract world stopped, beckoned, and quietly put its claims on me. Then and now. Such has been my guiding impulse—from within, from without—ever since.

When I was about nine, my mom made what today I see as an unfortunate mistake: she brought us a few comic books (one of them being *The Fox and the Crow*, I remember clearly). And for the next few years I found myself hooked. At the magazine store by CES I'd browse through, choose, and sometimes shoplift from a wondrous array of animal fables, wholesome superhero hunks, gun-filled Westerns, teenage sitcoms, and small-town children's idylls. I especially liked Mighty Mouse flying about in yellow tights, in his ever-triumphant battles against fierce feline foes. During a brief spell I vividly imagined a planet where he and his brethren lived, where the small and weak could always hold off the big and strong. I even tried creating comics of my own, populating them with anthropomorphized rodents, filling notebooks with such creatures as the effete dandy, Percy Reginald Mouse. My artistic talents being negligible, the cast of characters never progressed beyond the stick-figure stage.

Still, for a couple of years I fed compulsively on those mass-produced comics. They temporarily replaced book reading, alas. The appeal wasn't just in their vividness and immediacy, or the ease and speed with which I could consume them. To enter their frames was to live vicariously a U.S. life I'd never seen from up close, let alone experienced directly. There I encountered in their most primordial form the standardized images of American utopia. Probably the most potent and seductive of these versions (say, *Little Lulu* or *Nancy*) evokes a happy small town where everybody is friendly and polite, dwells in middle-class comfort, and goes in for good, clean fun. The human characters and maybe even the animal ones too are all recognizably Anglo-Saxon, and they routinely speak sentences that end in three exclamation points!!! Their aw-shucks, golly-gee innocence is mostly untouched by social differences, conflicts, or wars. Into this idyllic neverland the forces of evil can scarcely intrude.

On the other hand there's the sheer wickedness relentlessly driving the action-oriented genres (Westerns, combat comix, tales of superheroes), where evil is routinely projected onto enemy aliens, inexplicable deviants, or purely fantastical monsters—always something ugly and "other." Later, during the 1960s, the art of R. Crumb and other "head" cartoonists, obsessed as they were by American culture's grotesque and sinister side, helped highlight, simply by contrast, the degree to which those '50s 'zines—be they about ducks, cowboys, or cute white kids—were idealizations of and even propaganda for the creeds, practices, and illusions of Americanism.

There was little actual family life in our household, I now grimly understand. Few memories stand out of the four of us doing the things families generally do. When Dad wasn't fully engaged in his home study or his office in San Juan, he was doing business elsewhere on the island or about the Caribbean. On an occasional weekend we might go swimming in the warm, bright-blue waters of nearby, picture-postcard beaches—Luquillo, El Dorado, Vega Baja. Or we'd sit in the chaises longues around the rectangular pool of the Condado Beach Hotel, where we'd actually see, hear, and maybe even chat with flesh-and-blood Americans. My only real memory of family warmth during those years is of the uncertain number of sunset strolls we took on the UPR campus amid the palm trees, with my parents holding Kanani's hand and mine as we gaze at the campanile and take in its early-evening bell concert.

During those years I got high 90s and some 100s in all my subjects, even for conduct, though praise was never forthcoming from Dad in that particular department. Mom felt pride in those grades and tenderly encouraged me, but few details stand out in relief. The entry for "Father's Occupation" in my quarterly report cards always read "Business," a word I found funny in the discrepancy between spelling (which to me suggested "BOOZ-ee-ness") and pronunciation. Kanani and I sometimes got a few laughs out of the word.

Actually, at the time I had no idea what my dad did for a living, other than that it had to do with buying, selling, and trading. I did know that he dealt in military accouterments. That at home there were often catalogs and samples—metal badges, leather holsters, military caps. That he corresponded with some Stateside firm called Gemco. And that he'd owned an orange-colored trimotor airplane, which I once saw parked inside a rundown, isolated hangar. During his many absences, Mom ran the home office, answered his business mail and phone calls—without receiving anything in the way of compensation.

Eventually Dad was operating his own three freighters, the *Etah*, the *Marlin*, and the *San Andrés*. Two of them were quite hefty and plied much of the Caribbean. Sometimes he'd take Kanani and me to spend the day on one or other of his ships. Their sharp, ammonia-streaked, metallic or wood fragrance, along with that of the salty, greasy docks and port waters, remains with me; any casual drive by a tropical harbor will reactivate the sensations. Dad's colorful business associates—Americans,

Americanized Puerto Ricans, a few expatriate Europeans—were free-wheeling adventurers. They'd hang around the apartment or the ships, and I got to know them about as well as a ten-year-old can. But my brother and I were clueless as to what went into the belly of those transports.

I finally got some idea when, following Mom's death in 1984, I came across my parents' voluminous correspondence. Hundreds upon hundreds of items sent by either of them. Dad's letters come from all over the Caribbean "lake," though most are posted in larger, wealthier centers of commerce like Florida and Cuba. Reading them, I'm struck by his persistent dwelling on two large topics: love and business.

The emotions he repeatedly expresses toward Mom are passionate and intense, surprisingly so. He certainly seems, in some way, to have loved her at the time. The main reason for his epistolary abundance, needless to say, is the fact of his frequent and prolonged absences from home, which on occasion he justifies as beneficial "for you, & for us, & our future." Yet throughout his letters there is scarce mention of his two growing boys, despite Mom's regular reports on our progresses, quirks, and misadventures.

In addition his letters brim with references to deals—prospective and actual—in, say, lumber, whisky, pipe, kerosene stoves, uniform caps and insignia, and molasses going to, for instance, Guadeloupe. A cattle shipment from Havana takes months to work out (he mentions tussles with customs authorities, problems with investors). On the other hand he writes jauntily that same year, "Sold 6,000 caps to the Cuban police" and "Got order from Cuban police for 14,000 shoulder patches." Another time he reports peddling a thousand dollars in fountain pens, even vends a batch of insignia to CES. He alludes constantly, relentlessly, to his ships, to demurrages, payments, letters of credit. And he instructs Mom about what to do with certain checks, money orders, and business contracts. He sends her directions aplenty about paying this, filling in that, or looking into the other as she minds the store.

Every deal he envisions is the "big" one that's going to provide full security. Among his favorite books back then is Napoleon Hill's *Think and Grow Rich*, a classic "self-help" volume of that era. Growing rich, I'll repeatedly realize over the years, is and has been my father's sole concern of any sort.

When We Were Almost Puerto Ricans

A neighborhood kid—let's call him Paco—has got me pinned up against a wall in somebody's front yard. Staring at me eyeball-to-eyeball, with a defiant smirk on his pretty face, he intones a perverse little litany.

"*Du-ru-á, du-ru-á, du-ru-á.*"

I stand there bewildered by it all.

"*Du-ru-á, du-ru-á.*" (Approximate English pronunciation: "Doo-roo-AH." They're nonsense syllables. His own creation.)

In the meantime a younger cohort, who lives in the house, is picking on Kanani, tossing him toward the grass and taunting him. Paco shouts, "Yeah, get his brother, too!" then keeps up his nonsense refrain. "*Du-ru-á, du-ru-á.*"

So new is it all to me that I never think to emulate my comic-book heroes and incapacitate the guy by kicking him in the balls and busting his teeth, then joining forces with Kanani to grind the duo into human sausage. Or maybe pluck their eyes out. I get an exhilarating high now just thinking of it. Wishing I could turn back the clock for that purpose only . . . and to this day I wonder: why didn't we? It would've been too easy. Yet it was so hard. I'd been almost totally unphysical till then, had fought only with Kanani, who was smaller than me.

By pure chance, though, I'd get back at Paco about a year later when we were choosing sides at a sandlot baseball game. I flip him the bat and somehow it lands bull's-eye right on his nose, bloodying it and then twisting it sideways forever. It'd be nice to claim the revenge as carefully planned, since a revenge it certainly was.

Our Overseas-American life has greatly shifted. I'm in my eleventh year. Dad has just been appointed Caribbean sales manager for a small but prosperous brassiere firm based in New York. It's his first stint as a salaried employee (and, as things would eventually turn out, his last). With our newfound stability, preparations begin for a change of residence, and my mind engages in constructing that "elsewhere." I spend long hours browsing eagerly through Sears, Roebuck catalogs, gazing at page after page of product photos and imagining the furnishings for our future home. And I picture a happy neighborhood idyll with lots of group activities, a place where I could share my musical and other interests with kids my own age, perhaps even finally get piano lessons.

In 1952, we move to Urbanización Umpierre, a quiet, suburban-style development in Hato Rey. Our one-story white-stucco house, located at the corner of Mallorca St. and a blind alley called Pachín Marín, has front and back porches enclosed in black-iron grillwork, and a carport right by the front door. A waist-level fence in matching stucco surrounds the house at its north and west sides. It'll often serve as seating for idle youths, my brother and me included. For the first time, we've got a lawn, where Kanani and I do the usual small-boy runnings-about and primitive acrobatics. Banana trees line the two rear fences. We'll often pick the yellow fruit right off the dangling bunches. In time I learn to mow grass, pull weeds, and—always a problem in the tropics—fend off mosquitoes and other bugs.

During my Río Piedras days I'd been shy, withdrawn, diffident at school, with scant occasion for extended contact with other pupils. In Umpierre, most neighborhood kids are schoolmates of mine. In the morning we often trudge the seven blocks to CES, then play together in the afternoons. As a result of the intense, daily coexistence, conflicts inevitably ensue, and for the first time I become aware of the power plays and threats of violence that are part of ordinary life.

And I learn what it is to get taunted, tormented, and beat up. The incident with Paco stands out only because it's the first. Actually, Paco was a fairly decent guy, and a good friend besides.

I also became aware of a nasty habit that's much more common in Latin America than in polite, middle-class El Norte: labeling individuals with malicious nicknames. (There is at all levels of Hispanic life a side that is overtly cruel to the weak, the handicapped, the unattractive—for instance, blithely dismissing somebody as "that blind old woman" or "the fatso.") A kid at CES by the name of Leo got it into his head to refer to me scornfully as "Marupepa," after a pathetic, homely, freckle-faced character in a local comic strip. He kept at it so relentlessly that one day I lashed out and grabbed him by the neck, nearly strangling him. The Marupepa routine stopped thereafter.

As for me, I can't claim having resisted the name-calling drift. There was at school a bright, serious, cultured boy who was also rather big, and I gave him the sobriquet *tonelada* ("ton"). Others picked up on the theme, teasing him with it daily.

Social life also produces the first challenges to my idea of myself. A boy from down the street approaches me on his bike and asks, "Hey, Gene, take off your glasses."

I do.

"Japonés," he says with a grin. (The tone suggests, roughly, "Jap.")

I get peeved that time. The next few times too. When playmates and peers address me as Japanese or Chinese or Filipino it strikes me as incomprehensible, since it goes counter to what Mom and Dad have taught me about myself. My initial, hurt response to such labels is, "No! I'm American!"

Today I realize that the kids who'd mouthed such terms hadn't ever set eyes on an Asian, save for the stereotypes they knew from the Hollywood mill. To them, I was simply an oddity.

There was to the experience another dimension that for some time I couldn't figure out: among Hispanics, referring to and addressing individuals by their physical traits isn't necessarily rude. Saying in Spanish, "Hi, redhead," "Hey, skinny," or "Black girl, how are you?" can be simply neutral or even amicable in appropriate settings. Part of it stems from Spanish grammar, in which adjectives readily become nouns, taking what linguists call the vocative case. "*Negro*" in fact remains a common term of endearment among both black and white couples. Many of those calling me "*chino*" or "*japonés*," then, weren't being all that offensive and in some cases might even have been heeding a friendly impulse. Time passed and I eventually interpreted it as a set formula whenever someone called out to me, "*¡Oye, chino!*" ("Hey, Chinese guy!"). In the U.S., by contrast, the underlying idea is that we're all individuals and thus it is unfair to place people in any sort of categories.

Literally a stone's throw away from our house, on the other side of a high metal wall sealing off Calle Pachín Marín, stands a slum known as El Modelo. It's the classic Latin shantytown, with makeshift dwellings built from stray wood slats and recycled tin cans, and topped with corrugated zinc. A shortcut to CES actually runs through El Modelo, and Kanani and I take it from time to time with neighborhood friends. I still remember my bewilderment at first seeing the rugged yellow-clay roads, the gullies that serve as open sewers, the sheer human deprivation. Barefoot kids running around in rags. Naked toddlers standing about, some with distended bellies. Seeing them, I feel more of a sense of threat from them than compassion for them. As is only to be expected, they're not actively friendly, the Modelo folks.

Before the move, on our family drives to San Juan I'd vaguely sensed the existence of such slums off Martín Peña bridge, alongside a muddy stream where a brackish stench always hovered. (Still does.) In the case of El Modelo, we can see the slum right from our backyard, walk by it from a variety of angles, even stroll right through it—anything but ignore it. Many of the slum dwellers are black or mulatto (a neutral, descriptive term indicating a mixture of African and European). A few kids from El Modelo will become occasional playmates of ours, yet we know that people on their side of the fence generally refer to us as *blanquitos* (whiteys). The diminutive carries a harsh, resentful scorn.

The poverty inevitably breeds some tough types, hardened young hoodlums with clear criminal potential. One, a colorful, clownish, fair-haired character by the name of Marcelo, sometimes swaggers down our street brandishing a knife.

A few years later I'll chance to play ball or socialize with a couple of somewhat older El Modelo guys. They're as educated and as mannerly (perhaps more so) as we middle-class Umpierre folk. The discrepancy baffles me at the time.

Many of the youthful slum dwellers, as in the rest of Latin America, have roots in the rural *jíbaro* (the Puerto Rican term for "peasant") class. They've left behind an impoverished countryside for greater opportunities in the city. By contrast, for Kanani and me, settling in Umpierre feels almost like a move to nature. In urban Río Piedras the one natural feature in our lives had been the well-tended university grounds. The only stray creatures we'd seen with much regularity were the many-sized roaches, which were common enough yet struck fear in our young hearts. (On one occasion, Kanani wouldn't enter the bathroom because of a cockroach he'd noticed on the basin.) For amusement, I'd sometimes find roach nests in a wall crevice and bombard them with Flit spray, watching with glee as the bugs scurried out to breathe their last. Still, though nobody's favorite fauna, in the tropics one simply gets used to their omnipresence. They're even immortalized in the comical song "La cucaracha," from Mexico.

Now we walk out from our back porch and face a row of banana trees—just one set among many in the vicinity. Lizards routinely dart about on outside walls and sidewalks. Iguanas sit squarely or lumber silently on the lawns, like tiny dinosaurs. Toads are an all-too-ordinary sight. Kids often throw stones at them, or cars squish them, and their flattened carcasses litter the asphalt. (A common insult is *sapo podrido*, "you rotten toad.") Perching birds are everywhere to be heard and seen, though to my present regret I never thought to learn to identify the local species.

Because many families on both sides of the metal fence raise chickens or fighting cocks, we often awake to the sound of crowing roosters. The folks next door keep rabbits and ducks ("Lala" is the name of one waddler) and treat Kanani and me on one occasion to a robust lapine stew. On Mallorca right across from our house are empty lots where livestock drink from crude troughs, cows and goats often graze, and we boys play, avoiding the fresh pies. (Only now do I wonder how those domesticated farm animals got there. Who owned them? Who tended them? And when?) Farther beyond stands the Hipódromo Las Monjas, a full-sized racetrack, where we watch bent-over jockeys spurring their horses out on practice runs and competing in regular weekend races to crowds cheering in the distant grandstand.

And the heat? The tropical sun? Well, you seldom gave it much thought. It was simply there, part of the world of *tropicalismo*, as that way of life is called. If anything, what seemed exotic and strange was the imagery of winter. I still remember, in one of my American children's books, an illustration of a stylized robin, shivering on a frost-covered tree branch amid swirling snowflakes, and accompanied by a rhyme called "The North Wind Doth Blow." To this day I'm affected by the combined beauty and sadness of that page, designed for readers ages seven to nine.

So powerful was winter's imaginative allure to us tropicals that, once a year, the San Juan city government flew in planeloads of snow direct from the States, distributed the white stuff ceremoniously at the grounds of the chief baseball park, and allowed some local youngsters to romp around within a faux New England landscape till it all dissolved into mush. Sears, Roebuck even showed up to sell sleds, which were bought in hefty quantities for one-day use. An annual media event, the snow day generated lots of excitement at the time, helping reinforce the idea, too widespread in hot climes, that winter is "good." That snow is "civilized." Brainwashing kids with snow.

Among my own winter fantasies at the time: to be strolling in the fresh New England snow with a group of merrily singing Christmas carolers. And then to accompany them on the piano in some parlor, with a fireplace crackling softly in the background (assuming that I would indeed learn to play that instrument someday).

One local, natural feature that does astonish us is the precipitation, which often pours down suddenly like an instant Angel Falls, causing flash floods that sweep cars and loose objects away—and then, almost as suddenly, will cease. The heavy, short-lived rains can be quite localized. Once Mom and I watch and listen to a storm move slowly across the nearby racetrack till it hits our front yard. On even rarer occasions, a downpour drenches the houses a block or two away while our section goes untouched by so much as a drop—it even remains sunny! Later, a few of us will go and stare in fascination at the line clearly dividing the wet asphalt from the dry.

A curious gender rule in Puerto Rico in those days is that, during rain, men and boys used raincoats only; and if you get your hair wet, Juanito, well, tough; gotta be macho! Umbrellas are for women. A guy foolish enough to take shelter under one of those contraptions could draw shrill whistles of scorn.

So far I've dwelled mostly on the jungle-like aspects of our new neighborhood. But that's only half the story. It's in Umpierre that I become aware of such things as camaraderie, friendship, sociability, the world of other people. Connection. For the first time in our lives, Kanani and I have regular playmates that we can simply hang around with, gabbing for hours as we sit on curbstones or somebody's front porch. (To this day, I prefer to let conversations linger on rather than heed the call of duty—another aspect of *tropicalismo* that hasn't left me.)

In our new neighborhood, even when alone you are aware of the humanity around—including nearby El Modelo, whence you'll overhear the *radionovelas* (soap operas), first announced by a painful melody from Tchaikovsky's *Pathétique* symphony, followed by tearful dialogues that you can hear blaring simultaneously from many shacks. And there are the vendors who walk the length of Mallorca Street with their distinctive food-hawking cries: *"¡huevos del país!"* (farm-fresh eggs), *"¡piraguas!"* (snow cones), and *"¡fiambreras!"* (stacked aluminum containers with freshly made meals in them).

We kids play, though our activities are not all of them gentle. Snails are everywhere to be seen. We pick them up, observe them, then squish them ruthlessly. Kanani and his friends climb to the tops of garages and pick mangoes and *quenepas* (small, grape-sized fruits with a shell around their gelatinous meat) from off trees and bushes. Out of hibiscus wood they fashion bows and arrows and shoot small reptiles with them. Or a boy might capture a lizard and carefully squeeze at its neck, making the creature open its mouth, then attach the animal to his own earlobe and leave the animal hanging there. We convert Popsicle sticks into toy boats by filing them at both ends and lacquering them with nail polish. After a heavy rain, we race the tiny barges in the water-filled gutters, sometimes for blocks on end. Kanani and I soon learn to ride bicycles, and with our neighborhood chums we pedal far afield, traveling what seems like miles at the time.

We discover baseball, playing it obsessively through the middle months of the school year, in empty lots or out on the street. I'll never be much good at it, partly on account of an astigmatism that makes me miss high fly balls. But I become an ardent fan, keeping a scrapbook filled with memorabilia about local heroes. And I devour many cheap, quickie U.S. books about the game, memorizing legends and statistics from the major leagues (this batter's home-run record, that pitcher's lifelong shutout and no-hitter figures). During baseball season I attend night games with various friends. Next day, I'll check out *El Mundo* for the attendance figures—"8,651" for instance—and muse, "Hey, Mom, if so-and-so and I hadn't gone, it would have only been 8,649!"

The island's season for baseball is during fall and winter. Players from the States take this opportunity to remain active and make extra cash by taking jobs with Caribbean leagues, not only in Puerto Rico but also in Panama, Cuba, and Venezuela. As a result I get to watch none other than Willie Mays from up close when he regulars for the San Juan Senators. And there's Roberto Clemente, a still-green nineteen-year-old rookie, barely competent the first year I see him. His subsequent flowering shows me how apparent mediocrities can grow into greatness.

I'll retain my passion for baseball through much of my teens. With our many moves and spiritual dislocations, though, it'll become one of the things I gradually shed and finally forget when coming north for college.

At just about this time I temporarily lose my receptivity to classical music. Side eight of my trusty old Brahms First leaves me cold. Shortly after our move into the neighborhood I've dropped in on a kid called Wally. In the living room he and his buddy Luis are dancing, quite ably and energetically, to the brass-rich rhythms of *Mambo número ocho*. I see a few classical albums stacked about—presumably belonging to Wally's parents—and ask if we might hear the Schubert symphony sometime later.

Wally replies breezily as he twirls about the easy chair, "This here is a symphony by Pérez Prado!" I recognize the piece, having heard it blaring out from countless barroom jukeboxes about town. At the time Dámaso Pérez Prado is widely known as "King of the Mambo" and enjoys an international reputation for his big band's unmistakably thick and sultry sounds, as well as for his famous grunts ("aa-AAGH, OO!") that actually serve as informal conductor's cues. One Pérez Prado tune, "Cherry Pink and Apple Blossom White," with its striking slide-trombone solo, will even score a hit on U.S. charts later that decade. Yet twenty-five years hence the Pérez Prado orchestra will be largely forgotten, a casualty of shifting musical fashions.

Meanwhile, peer pressure has its effects, and I'll come to share my playmates' tastes, at the expense of the classics. In time I'll also become a tolerably good Latin dancer. (To this day, I get pleasure out of the gliding steps and shared movements of a *guaracha* or a *merengue*.) And I especially learn to enjoy the Puerto Rican custom dictating that couples—even if total strangers—must always dance cheek-to-cheek to slow songs.

My insensitivity to the classics proves short-lived. Within a year I'll return to the Mozart-Beethoven-Brahms fold via WIPR radio. A Christmas gift from Mom of a Philco record player prompts me to purchase occasional LPs for myself, some of which still can be found in my library.

The Schwann record catalog becomes my preferred pickup reading for a while. I'll leaf eagerly through each monthly issue, circling those classical items I hope to own someday. Still, I have learned to love and respect the best of Afro-Latin pop (salsa, as it's now called) and no longer feel any conflict within me over the two musical traditions. So I develop early on as a musical relativist: I know that both Europe and the Caribbean have their respective musical "greats." Differences in prestige, I eventually realize, have more of a political than an artistic basis.

One curious, even astounding instance of shared experience in my neighborhood revolves around a dream. In Río Piedras I'd often been troubled by a vague yet horrific recurring nightmare: I find myself adrift on some gray surface that is devoid of other physical features. Suddenly, a little ball—a bubble, maybe—appears somewhere and starts to grow, grow, grow. Its steady increase becomes an unnamable menace that is about to suffocate and engulf me . . . at which point I'd wake up screaming, every time. Later on, in Umpierre, sitting on a doorstep, I'll hear a playmate recount the very same dream, with the very same sense of indefinable terror. The nightmare would never return once I departed the island a few years later. I now wonder: did my playmate's dream eventually disappear as well? Or did it continue to haunt him as long as he remained on the island? Is my weird delirium something specific to the tropics or even to Puerto Rico? Or is it as common as those famous childhood nightmares about arriving at school half-naked or forgetting about an exam? Meanwhile, the precise meaning of the dream has eluded me, though obviously a fear of being hemmed in by unknown forces (abstract shapes! that color gray!) has something to do with it.

In Umpierre I was ten or eleven, that age when boys first learn about sex and the many words that say it. As we sat on curbs or leaned against fences, I picked up from my more knowledgeable, worldly companions the local array of relevant nouns, adjectives, interjections. And—naturally—verbs.

Oh, how we marveled at the mystery of sex; how wondrous we all somehow knew It to be! Twelve-year-olds spoke of the delicious sensations you get down there when It's Happening. Others expressed puzzlement at how . . . well, how do you actually get a woman to Do It with you? To this day I feel a certain amazement at the fact that sex even exists; and on occasion, when strolling by a residential tower 'round midnight, I might vaguely ponder the possibility that right then, at that very moment, even as we speak and I smile, there are folks in there who are passionately enjoying their mutual pleasures. (To my relief, I've also found out I'm not the only adult on this earth who amuses himself with that stray thought.)

Suddenly I realized one day that girls were attractive. In the light of my grand discovery, I soon shared eagerly in the endless talk about pretty female schoolmates that was led by with-it young whelps at CES or around Umpierre. During one seventh-grade class that met afternoons in chapel, I joined in the daily mischief of those boys who spent much of the hour copping glances at the girls' side of the center aisle, seeing what we could see beyond their skirt hems, and occasionally wondering if so-and-so was purposely tantalizing us (though we didn't know the verb "to tantalize" yet) with her slightly bared knees.

Most of these experiences are taking place in Spanish. And though I'm not at all aware of it as yet, a cultural and linguistic split is taking place within me. Other than with our successive cleaning women, my home life is in English, as are my inner thoughts (except when recalling Puerto Rican conversations). Mom and Pop know fluent Spanish and also French. But English is their mother tongue and the medium in which they're most comfortable. If citing a Puerto Rican source or dialogue, we'll naturally quote the original words, as spoken. On occasion we might shift briefly to Spanish anyway, just for a change in register. But generally, English is what my brother and I speak within the family fold, and to each other. There's no linguistic snobbery involved, simply a practical habit, an everyday fact.

Thanks to the revolutionary new kinescope medium (and thanks to American power), probably half the programs on Puerto Rican TV are coming from the States. So we regularly see *I Love Lucy*, *The Ed Sullivan Show*, *The Milton Berle Show*, *The $64,000 Question*, and other U.S. cultural icons, all in undubbed, unsubtitled English, and with only a two-week delay. Kanani and I have a certain edge over our playmates in being able to follow the American dialogue with ease, and we can even understand most of the jokes.

As a U.S. school, CES conducts virtually all of its classes in English from sixth grade on, so there, too, I have an advantage, though I don't give the accidental privilege much thought. On the other hand the occasional Puerto Rican friend who's spent time up in New York sometimes taunts Kanani and me about never having set foot in the continental U.S.A. We're at a loss to counter such shows of one-upmanship.

At the same time I tune in to a lot of local radio, not only WIPR classics but also variety shows and situation comedies, even attending occasional live studio productions—in Spanish, of course. For a year or so, when listening to funnymen or comic broadcasts (featuring figures like Diplo and Yo-yo Boing, still legends on the island decades later), I jot down gags I like and accumulate several notebooks full. In seventh and eighth grades I'll write a number of half-hour skits in Spanish, in frank imitation of certain radio and TV farces, with some of those old jokes now recycled for my purposes. My miniseries depicts a schoolroom with a teacher and his four stereotypical pupils (the Brain, the Dunce, the Cut-up, the Goody-goody). I function as scriptwriter, director, producer, and straight man–teacher all in one. After a couple of rehearsals with four volunteers rounded up from among my friends, we perform the plays in our classroom for school-party dates—Halloween, Christmas, last day of school. (My fellow actors, serious in their commitment, memorize their individual parts cold. Being lazier, I read my lines throughout, script in hand.) To my surprise, our classmates like the show, greeting it with laughter, which spurs us on to further episodes the following year.

My childhood venture into theater proves short-lived, the result of family changes and disruptions, though I've sometimes since wondered if I would've continued writing light comedies had I remained in Puerto Rico and become fully Puerto Ricanized. Curiously, though, I did end up a teacher in real life, and my first fiction publications were humorous spoofs. In addition, Part 3 of my novel *The Carlos Chadwick Mystery* is actually a play in which the straight man has metamorphosed from teacher into talk-show host, while the four pupils have changed into three executives representing a think-tank called Perspectives Industries. Perhaps, when working on that play, I was unconsciously picking up on where I'd left off as a middle-school dramatist.

Because of the U.S. sway over Puerto Rican life, several of us youngsters can't envision a future on the island. Friends make comparisons between the two places, always in favor of the States—such as the measly prizes awarded on local quiz shows vs. the sixty-four-thousand-dollar jackpot on the famed program of that name.

The basic theme of comparison is, "Without the United States, we're nothing. If Puerto Rico became independent, mamá, papá, and I would leave for El Norte." And of course, being "American" myself, I passively and unthinkingly agree with them. Though such plans are never voiced at home, my vague assumption is that someday, five, six, ten years later, my parents and my brother and I are going to move north.

Incidentally, my friends allude to the U.S. not as "America," but as *los Estados Unidos*, since Puerto Rico is also America. "Los Estados Unidos" has indeed remained the standard usage throughout the Hispanic world. Like many folks from that region, I feel a surge of resentment today whenever U.S. reporters write about Mexicans or Guatemalans or Peruvians who come to "America." Spanish, I should note, has a useful and quite common alternative for the adjective "Americans"—*estadounidenses*, literally "United Statesians." Unfortunately the word does not travel well into English.

Given my two languages and multiple environments, I now realize, I was leading a double life without knowing it. On the one hand, CES was North American (if aimed at "the natives"). Our home life and virtually all of our spare-time reading was in English—*Mad* comics, *Time* and *Life* (which came to our p.o. box in old San Juan), *Look*, the *Saturday Evening Post*, *Saturday Review*, the Sunday *New York Times* (which arrived at the Condado Beach Club's magazine shop on Thursdays). At the Condado itself, besides relaxing in the warm pool or beach waters and watching the hairy-bellied, sunburnt men play shuffleboard, Kanani and I heard and spoke English with Mom's friends and their children.

On the other hand our entire day-to-day social life—at recess, after school, playing ball, at the YMCA and its summer camps, and even in my modest, truncated theater activities—unfolded exclusively in

Spanish. In the long run, I suppose, my linguistic split personality was a better proposition than the easy alternative of living in the strictly U.S. enclaves, safely sealed off from the surrounding language and culture. My brother's and my own world, however, qualifies in many ways as an oddity, an unreal situation in which we were cast adrift, developing neither as Puerto Ricans nor as *norteamericanos*. The utter strangeness of it all only began to dawn on me during my coming-of-age years amid the variegated ferment of 1960s Berkeley.

Sometimes my life in two languages led to curious misunderstandings. For instance: I'm sitting with a few neighborhood friends on a street curb. Casually I note, "Bad luck today. It's Friday the thirteenth."

My playmates laugh at me with puzzled looks. One of them says condescendingly, "Where'd you get that idea? No, Gene, you're thinking of Tuesday the thirteenth!"

He's right. As I'll find out repeatedly, in the Spanish world, a thirteenth on a Tuesday is the ill omen, the day of misfortunes, perhaps because of a Spanish proverb that demonizes all Tuesdays: "Los martes, ni te cases ni te embarques" ("On Tuesdays, don't get married, don't take trips").

Besides that, the Spanish phrase *martes trece* repeats the *t* and *r* sounds, making for fluid diction. In English, conversely, "Friday the thirteenth," with its threefold fricatives, comes more easily to our tongue and lip muscles than does "Tuesday the thirteenth," in which our mouth would do triple the amount of labor it exerts for "Friday."

Another instance: at CES one morning I refer in passing to cats and their nine lives.

Laughter all around. "It's *seven* lives!" several of my schoolmates inform me. And seven it is, if you're Latino, I'll hear enough times thereafter.

Again, sound and rhythms probably determine the number gap, though I still don't know where or when the notion of multilived felines first came up. But I do know now that the old saying "Cats have nine lives," with its double assonance and monosyllabic spondees, has a lyric texture that the hypothetical "A cat has seven lives" lacks. Along the same lines, "Un gato tiene siete vidas" has its own assonant rhyme pattern—*"tiene/siete"*—and a trio of *t* sounds to boot. By contrast, "Un gato tiene nueve vidas" limps as language, is itself lifeless, undistinctive. In a proverbial phrase, sound wins over sense.

None of this analysis is available to me back then. The differences strike me as simply arbitrary. In English, cats have nine lives, in Spanish, seven—and that's that.

Dad is often away in Cuba, Venezuela, Miami, and New York, keeping up with operations for the bra company. Usually we're alone with Mom. She fills her time by going to the U.S. crowd's socials, chatting on the phone with the women she feels closest to, and, more rarely, entertaining Puerto Rican women friends from Río Piedras days.

At some point Dad has a mail-order house ship us an 8-millimeter Bell & Howell home projector plus three silent shorts, including a couple of silly cartoons. Mom, Kanani, and I watch them repeatedly—maybe twenty, thirty times—in Dad's study-converted-to-theater. Sometimes there are a few playmates present, lying about the floor or roughhousing. I translate the titles for them, when needed.

My feeling as I now recall those silent-movie rituals, organized as they were around a high-tech toy of that era, is of a general pointlessness and desolation. We're supposed to be a family, yet what's bringing us together on those occasions is not any conjugal bond or my father's physical presence or both parents sharing in activities with their offspring—but this clunky gadget and a library made up of three soundless, ephemeral short flicks.

Later we'll adopt a cute, floppy-eared, brown puppy, a sleek-haired mutt we dub Ginger. My brother and I play with her, torment her, and love her intensely as only little boys can, projecting onto her the affection we crave from the family fold. These feelings are frustrated when, one afternoon, word reaches us that Ginger has been hit by a car on a nearby street crossing. Somehow the wounded creature is retrieved and delivered home to us.

After tending to her for the rest of the day, we say goodnight to Ginger as she lies whimpering on the back porch. Next morning Kanani first sets eyes on her body. Slowly he approaches it, touches it.

From the neighbors' front yard he hears a woman's voice. "No, m'ijito. Está muerta." ("No, sonny. She's dead.")

As my brother and I tearfully bury her near the banana trees, Dad (who happens to have been present for a brief spell) tries to assuage our grief with the words "And now she's in Dog Heaven."

Some positive memories stand out. In 1953 our little sister, Valerie, was born. I can still conjure up the joy felt by Mom, Kanani, and me as we listened to her typical baby cries, her infant laughter, and her first articulated word—"Hi-ya! Hi-ya!," which she'd utter enthusiastically whenever addressing and referring to Mom, and later anyone else. We cuddled and played with our small sibling (more than eleven years my junior), and the experience gave us a powerful sense of being a loving family as no Bell & Howell gadgets could. For years afterwards we reminisced over Valerie's first sound for requesting food ("Aahm"), her pronunciation of "yellow" as "lellow" and of "hairdo" as "hair doe-doe." We laughed together at her misimpression that the "God" in our exclamations was a family friend called Bob, or that dogs can smile.

Valerie grew up as a fully bilingual Overseas American for her first five years, speaking Spanish with the neighborhood kids, English at home and at the Lola Brown ("Yoda Brown," she pronounced it) day nursery. During the separations that evolved as a shaping force in Kanani's and my existence, she would become a symbol of basic family affection, the simple sanity, caring, and joy we knew was lacking in our daily lives and in Dad's subsequent households. Together my brother and I would fix our memories on her, beaming with delight as we saw, in any random child about the streets of Havana or in the churches of Caracas, a reminder of our kid sister in distant Puerto Rico.

At various times in my childhood, we'll visit other Caribbean havens: Curaçao, St. Thomas, St. Martin, the French islands, with a different, more run-down architectural look than in Puerto Rico, and with people—African as well as white—who speak with other accents or in the tongues of other countries. There, too, the soft, warm breezes are ever pungent with the smells of sea salt and fresh fish, both raw and cooked.

Kanani especially will recall, quite vividly, a ride we took in one of Dad's ships alongside the offshore, serpent-shaped, Puerto Rican isle of Vieques. The boy, who is nine years old at the time, has accidentally dropped a broom overboard into some jellyfish-infested waters. Dad peremptorily orders Kanani into the purple-dotted sea to retrieve the precious artifact, which he duly does. Fortunately the jellyfish aren't attacking nine-year-olds that day. (Nor are U.S. Army troops anywhere to be seen and signaled for help, even though they occupy one third of the island.)

The excursion that most stands out in my memory is a five-day break that Mom, Dad, Kanani, and I spent together in St. Barthélemy some-time in 1952. "St. Bart's" to English speakers, the place has since gained fame as an obscenely expensive watering hole for the international rich. At that time it slumbered as a quiet, hilly, French island village whose airport, a slightly inclined lawn flanked by equally green ridges, was accessible to small craft only. There being no electricity, Coleman lamps provided nocturnal indoor lighting. In daytime the seawaters were so absolutely clear that, from a glass-bottomed boat, you could gaze dozens of feet down to the ocean floor and observe a multihued spectacle of marine life swimming this way and that. The islanders, it goes without saying, enjoyed an excellent fish diet, and at one point we watched a local fellow spearfish a sea turtle that later became his family's evening soup.

When on terra firma, Kanani and I played and somehow talked with island boys, who wore the French garb of short pants and European-style sandals. I picked up some French vocabulary. The four of us (Valerie hadn't been born yet) even went for a few strolls along the village's unpaved paths. Just like our university-campus days. For years thereafter my brother and I would associate the smells and tastes of fresh seafood with St. Bart's. We entertained wistful images of that trip as a brief idyll, a time when we all of us were together as a family unit.

Ah, well. As I began work on this memoir in the mid-nineties, Kanani casually informed me that, sometime before our excursion, one of Dad's PT boats had been caught in a hurricane and run aground near St. Barthélemy. With logistical and legal matters to tend to, Dad had simply invited us along for the ride. And who knows? The outing may have been Mother's idea.

Actually our family situation had begun to deteriorate not long after our move to Hato Rey. Dad was away on business more often than not. Playmates made occasional wisecracks to me about his having mistresses overseas.

"Dear Daddy, When are you coming home?" Several loving notes scribbled by Kanani and me during his long absences start out that way, or with plaintive words to that effect. A letter Mom writes him cites me as having casually remarked, "Daddy means four months when he says 'soon.' "

Mom herself composes affectionate, longing missives to her husband, sometimes twice daily, in which she all but begs him to come back, saying that his love is infinitely more important to her than any of his material successes. She feels terribly lonely. Yet only once amidst her hundreds of letters from those years does she raise her voice to complain of the "lousy deal" he's been giving her. Tells him he treats his home as if it were "a hotel." Informs him he's "a good father but an indifferent one." Indeed, even when Dad is in Puerto Rico he will customarily be away at the office and factory until 8 or 9 p.m.

The strains will eventually become more manifest, dramatically so. One terrifying evening, Kanani and I accompany our folks to a casual get-together in San Juan with a group of Dad's business associates. The men talk business and nothing but business through well past midnight—maybe until 3 a.m. On the drive home Mom starts alternately laughing and crying hysterically. Later, from our bunk beds, Kanani and I listen in silent fear as she continues, her state worsening. Dad responds by shouting furiously throughout the night.

(I'm reminded of a *New Yorker* cartoon from the '60s. Two middle-class, middle-aged couples are sitting around over drinks in a middle-class home. One of the men has dozed off. His wife whispers to the other twosome, by way of explanation, "You stopped talking about business.")

Following Valerie's birth, Dad is scarcely around. In all, he'll spend maybe two weeks in the infant's presence. One late Christmas day, after the packages have been ritually unwrapped and enthusiastically oohed and aahed over, it becomes clear that Dad has no gift for Mom. In my personal bewilderment and sadness for her, I stare at him and wonder.

I don't know exactly when, or why, or for how long (one year? two?) it is that Dad's mother comes to live with us. Kanani and I will call her Gammie. Of German stock, she's a thin, frail, austere-looking woman with rugged features and braided gray hair. Usually dressed in dark grays and thick-heeled black shoes, she speaks with a midwestern accent and tends to sniff a lot when helping about the house. Over dinner she'll at times remark on the many "colored people" there are in Puerto Rico. On occasion, she reportedly complains right to our playmates' parents about the "broken English" she hears spoken by the islanders. (Of Spanish she will learn scarcely a word.) For a couple of months, there's an equally thin, and mustachioed, cousin of Gammie's living with us. Name of Fred.

I've since assumed that Dad sent for Gammie so that she might, in classic extended-family fashion, help bring up baby Valerie. If so, the experiment seems not to have worked. According to my mother, Valerie was a great deal crankier during the period when Gammie was around. Though Valerie had not sucked her thumb previously, Gammie now took to sticking it in the baby's mouth and taught her the habit because she found it "cute." In time, Grandma came to feel as if Valerie were her own daughter rather than Mom's. Following her eventual return to the States, in her letters she consistently misspelled the little girl's name as "Valeri," in imitation of some minor movie star's stage handle.

That at least was Mom's version of events. Whatever the case, no positive bonds or memories resulted from Gammie's stay, a void that was further aggravated by the bizarre fact that she stayed on with us for a long while after Mom and Dad had broken up as a couple.

In retrospect, the dark signs of a breakup were certainly there. But to a confused, early-teenage boy they're necessarily opaque, mysterious, fragmentary.

Mom, Kanani, and I are watching a Hollywood musical at a Río Piedras theater. In an exchange of dialogue between Marge and Gower Champion, the lead couple, a fearsome word, "divorce," comes up. So I ask Mother casually, "What does 'divorce' mean?" She goes "Shh" and quickly explains that it's when you're not married anymore. After the movie I try to have her elaborate on this strange, new concept; she remains tight-lipped about it.

Late one weekday, an airmail envelope arrives from Miami, addressed to Dad. Mom, thinking it a business letter, opens it and reads it. Distraught, she now rages at Gammie with a tearful anger. (I manage to catch a glimpse of the contents: a trysting note signed by one Marcie.) Many an afternoon after that I'll overhear Mom in Dad's study, spending long hours on the phone, complaining bitterly to her gringa friends in San Juan about Dad and the home front, especially about Gammie and Fred.

Meanwhile, the ominous word "divorce" can be heard bobbing up mysteriously in the background. Mother actually asks me point-blank if I'd like living with Dad elsewhere. (Only now do I understand what she was after. My answer at the time is flip: "Oh, sure, yeah, it'll be a chance to see other places!")

Secretly, I begin to wonder if it all means Kanani and I will have a mom and dad no more. When married couples cease being couples, do they also stop being parents? Where do their kids end up, and with whom? Do they become sort of like orphans? At school or on the street I occasionally speculate that my brother and I are going to be parentless, but friends explain to me that it doesn't work that way.

The culminating incident is one I will not witness but rather hear about from Mom's lips sometime after it happened. As she would recall it to me on numerous occasions, Dad returned from Cuba in early January, took her out for a drive, and sweet-talked her into putting her head on his lap.

Imagine Mom's surprise, then, when the two of them arrived at a nearby mental asylum and he proceeded to have her locked up under her maiden name. (According to Mom, it was to get her out of the way because of the impending arrival of his Cuban mistress. According to one of Dad's letters, it was because of Mom's "neuroses of long standing.") Within a week, Dr. Ravitch, a family friend, managed to get her released. For Mom, the terrible episode eventually became an experience of self-discovery, recorded in part in her diary. Well into her last two decades, she remembered how one of the staff doctors said to her, quite pointedly, "You don't need a psychiatrist. But that husband of yours does."

There's also the disturbing yet vague memory I have of Mom running around the house in her underclothes one sunlit day, and muttering incoherently as Gammie stands somewhere in the background.

Then she goes over the brink, attempts to slit her wrists. Or so Dad will subsequently tell us, with a certain contempt in his voice.

Kanani and I can remember little else about it. I'm not even sure how much of what I've just related is in chronological order.

Before the onset of these family complications, I'd been a model student. Now, partly to attract the attention of my fellow pupils, I take to joining in with the class cutups. I mimic their antics. Belch loudly. Sneeze at the top of my lungs. My academic abilities are becoming scattered, diffuse, unfocused. My grades go steadily downward.

One particularly nasty nun informs my mother, who'd gone to pay her a concerned parent's visit, that I'm "lazy." Later, with a nyah-nyah-nyah tone of voice, Sister Nasty will mock Mom's visit and throw it in my face in front of the class.

Today, even my modest past misfortunes help me sense dimly the sorts of nonsense that kids scrambling at the bottom of the U.S. pyramid put up with from year one. When family life is scarcely working; when your best talents aren't recognized or sustained; when too much out there seems stacked big and tall against you and hardly anything seems right—well, in such circumstances it's easy to lose heart and take your schoolwork, and any of the world's less-visible goals, less than seriously.

Raise hell, though, and you'll get immediate results—an easy public identity, an audience (even if an audience for the bitter buffoon), maybe even a few friends and cohorts, connection. Book knowledge, good grades: their rewards are quieter, less tangible, when so much is missing from your life. That nun dismissed me to my mom as "lazy," then taunted me publicly with it. I try to imagine the millions of less fortunate folks who hear such stuff casually, week after week, from a boss, a cop, a teacher—and from lofty right-wing sages and lucky authority figures largely untouched by ordinary human suffering, who will unceremoniously ridicule any attempt at finding out what it is about the life of the poor that discourages them and makes them seem, and perhaps even feel, "lazy."

Of course, even after Dad is no longer at home, our life goes on. Besides schoolwork to be done and a lawn to be mowed and watered, there are Valerie providing solace and fun, Mom being as affectionate and helpful as she can under the circumstances, and the usual round of distractions—baseball, radio, and TV, not to mention fence-sitting, dancing, reading, the beach. We haven't any idea of where our lives are heading, save for some vague notion about Dad's plans, which at the time include placing Kanani and me in a Cuban boarding school, a military academy that we've never heard about before.

Mom, for her part, has started doing journalistic work for a local English-language daily. She's attending more social events being thrown by the hard-core Overseas-American set in San Juan, and presumably is dating some of the men she talks about and introduces us to. (I remember one New Year's Eve, probably 1954, when Mom, wearing a bright, silver-lamé dress and golden high-heeled shoes, bids us good night out by the driveway as she leaves for some glamorous bash.) And just before summer 1955 she's making preparations to enroll in the well-known Publishing Procedures Course at Radcliffe College. The memories from that time, though less remote, feel more like a confusing daze, a crazy quilt of past fragments, than do those of my childhood years in Río Piedras.

My last remembrances of CES concern my eighth-grade graduation, held at a church near the school grounds. It's a sunny afternoon in 1955. The formal ceremony's over, and everybody's still decked out, looking sharp, their very best—girls in heels and bright pleated skirts. Boys in coats and ties. I see female classmates moved to tears, overwhelmed by the experience. I see entire families—parents, grandparents, siblings— lovingly flanking the well-dressed, well-loved, beaming, early-teenaged grads. I sense excitement in the air as my fellow thirteen-year-olds look forward to ninth grade at *"la high"* (the affectionate, casual nickname for CES's secondary-school ranks).

And I don't recall having talked to a soul, though surely I must have.

Father isn't there. I feel bad about it, and will convey the sad feeling to Mom that evening. (Her own absence hasn't affected me. Maybe she's too busy or otherwise engaged, and I understand that she has a good reason.) Family members—my American side—are not in attendance either.

I'm not continuing with my thirty-some classmates on to *la high*. So my Puerto Rican life is being phased out, seems finished for now. Thus ends my nine-year stint as a Catholic schoolboy who wasn't Catholic. I'm heading out, shipping out.

Back home, at least, Kanani and I share in our own exciting prospects. We're going to be spending summer in Caracas, Venezuela! Even if with our estranged, long-absent Dad . . . A new country, even a new life, is in store for us. So new, in fact, that only some three decades hence will we begin to figure out what had hit us.

Strange Interlude in Venezuela and Florida

We're among a planeload of recently arrived passengers, Kanani and I. Nervously seated with others in the plastic bucket seats along the picture windows. It's the foyer to the passport control office at the Aeropuerto Internacional de La Guaira, which services nearby Caracas. Eventually a uniformed official arrives, calling on Venezuelan citizens to proceed to the next room. For a split second I almost rise to join them, wishing briefly that I could. Wishing I were Venezuelan.

My next recollection from that day in June 1955 is of our smiling dad, chauffeuring his Nash Rambler on the spanking new superhighway that meanders through the mountains toward the capital city, about a forty-five-minute drive away.

He tells us about how, you know, Mother and he, well, they hadn't been getting along, unfortunately. And so they'd gotten divorced. And now he's got a surprise for us: he's recently remarried! Mary is her name, he says; we'd met her briefly during our visit to Cuba in 1953 . . . He describes her. I dimly remember the passing introduction in front of a Havana clothing shop.

Up through 1953, Dad's many letters to Mom had been consistently effusive, filled with longing. In a note from Caracas dated December of that year, though, he refers to a Cuban "fashion consultant" called

Mary, who's just come under subcontract with the bra firm to do some work for them. Her name comes up a number of times over the next few weeks' letters.

The next year Dad consigned Mom to the mental hospital. Later he stormed into the office of Dr. Ravitch—who'd helped Mom get released—and punched the guy in the face. (Dad will never once mention the entire incident—either the asylum or its aftermath—to Kanani or to me. Mom for her part will occasionally tell us that she'd considered the possibility of taking her husband to court on charges of illegal incarceration.)

Dad's mail to Mom thereafter turns curt and vicious. The letters are abusive, bullying, bellicose, nasty. While agreeing to send financial support, he truculently informs Mom that everything he's earned came "from the sweat of my brow," in contrast with her idle, parasitic existence.

In the year following the mental-hospital affair, Dad would go on to obtain legal residency in Cuba. From that island, on January 12, 1955, he sends Mom a blunt note informing her that they are now definitively and officially divorced.

So far as I know, he never sent much in the way of alimony. Within a couple of years, once he had gained thorough control over Kanani and me, his child-support payments for Valerie petered out as well.

Later that decade, Mother wrote Dad a polite letter expressing concern that his Cuban divorce might be invalid in the U.S. and that she might be liable for bigamy charges were she to remarry. He never replied, and his foreign, single-party divorce settlement amply protected him from any court actions on Mom's part, whether in Puerto Rico or El Norte.

Back then I was already acquainted with the plot of *Madame Butterfly*. Never would have I thought to liken my dad to Lt. Pinkerton, though! Mother, after all, was Hawaiian, not Japanese. Dad's new spouse was an upwardly mobile native girl from yet another exotic island, not your respectable, middle-class Anglo-American. And my father had long ago been mustered out from the military, as a lowly buck private, sparing himself any conflict with the Japanese. Still, from the perspective of today, some of the parallels are uncanny, especially the young couple's setting sail on the SS *Mariposa*.

Dad's new wife, Mary, is sexy, with big hips, shapely legs, and short, dyed-blond hair whose brown roots are easily perceptible. Often lively, with a big smile on her sensual red lips, she is also quite shrewd and acutely conscious of matters like clothes and status. Presumably to please Dad, she now lavishes her Latin warmth and womanly charms onto her new role of stepmom. Still, from the start Kanani and I employ the formal *usted* with her, never once venturing into the more familiar and intimate territory of *tú*. Nor do she or Dad encourage such a shift.

They're subletting a place on the top floor of a brown, four-story, stucco apartment building, with box-like balconies and a small front yard on the Avenida El Parque. The district, called El Bosque, is part of the newer, eastern portion of Caracas that, in the 1940s, started rapidly sprouting middle- and upper-middle-class *urbanizaciones*, an indirect result of the oil boom.

Puerto Rico was insular. Now the spectacle of a bigger, more cosmopolitan city fills Kanani and me with something like awe. The waiters, clerks, barbers, domestics, and other working folks we encounter are often immigrants from an impoverished southern Europe or from less prosperous Latin American nations. The women who wait on us at the Hotel Tamanaco's snack bar on our first day have Italian and Portuguese accents. Mary's live-in maid is from Galicia, Spain. Dad's roster of colleagues and employees at the bra factory includes Chileans, Cubans, and Germans.

Our encounter with all these nationalities will continue throughout the summer and further expand during our return two years later. So large and various is the immigrant population that ordinary

Venezuelans, we find out, occasionally lump them all into humorous categories such as *musiús* (from the French *monsieur*) or *portugueses*, regardless of ancestry. The migrants have come lured by the prospects of jobs and wealth. Streets paved with gold! Our maid's husband wryly recalls having taken those fabulous scenarios quite literally. (The immigration from Europe, I'm already vaguely aware, is being encouraged by the government, with a view to outnumbering Venezuelans of African and indigenous descent, thereby creating a "whiter" country.)

After San Juan, the visual panorama also seems greatly varied. City buses bear different colors—purple, green, or dark red, according to route. Paper money denominations are likewise color-coded. (The routine explanation for these broad spectra is Venezuela's widespread illiteracy problem.)

In keeping with the boomtown atmosphere, there are more shiny, tall buildings in the new parts of Caracas than I'd ever seen in all of Puerto Rico. It's the same with the automobiles: for the first time in my life I'm aware of Jaguars, Mercedes, and other expensive European cars buzzing about. Not to mention Thunderbirds, Cadillacs, and even the rare Mercedes taxicab.

At the same time I'm struck by a somewhat greater formality in people's manner and dress. On account of the altitude, Caracas temperatures seldom rise above 75 degrees F. The typical male denizen comfortably wears coat and tie when attending seemingly ordinary events—a movie, a Saturday-afternoon social. Greater "European" influence, Mary explains.

And then there are the oddities peculiar to Caracas alone. Owing to the oil bonanza, the inner city already boasts a couple of sleek high-speed freeways, while the regular arteries seem ever-congested with slow traffic. And yet blowing the horn is strictly forbidden; doing so can make one subject to a fine! Irate motorists pound on the outside of their doors and yell bloody murder instead.

Houses and buildings aren't numbered! They bear proper names, bestowed by the owner—"Palma" or "Penelope" or the like. If you're seeking an edifice on a lengthy avenue and lack information as to its whereabouts, you've no recourse but to walk or drive slowly along, reading façade inscriptions on either side of the road or asking people along the way. Moreover, in the older, downtown areas of Caracas, each *street corner* has a separate name. Dad's office is thus at Avenue So-and-So, Building Such-and-Such, between This Corner and That. Addresses on envelopes can get long and unwieldy. Also, though street crossings always have the now-familiar signs with crisp, one- or two-way arrows on black, virtually no street markers exist! Again, you study a map beforehand, then buttonhole bystanders—an oral tradition of sorts. I sometimes fantasize with Kanani about approaching the city authorities and offering to paint all those preexisting blank arrows with street names.

General Marcos Pérez Jiménez, a brutal military dictator with a potbelly and a big face, is in charge of the country. Stories run rife of ordinary folks being picked off the streets and thrown in jail for indefinite stretches of time. Given the situation, you always speak in hushed tones when alluding to anything remotely political, and avoid encounters even with traffic cops. The notorious plainclothes types from the Seguridad Nacional are supposed to be everywhere.

Like all dictators, Pérez Jiménez ordered the construction of ostentatiously huge public projects: sumptuous traffic rotaries with grandly elaborate fountain displays on them. The mammoth highways. Or the infamous Hotel Humboldt, a silvery, cylindrical skyscraper set atop Mt. Ávila north of the city and accessible only by funicular cable car. A sister structure on a neighboring peak, on the same *teleférico* line, offers shops, eateries, and (of all things) an ice-skating rink. (Yet another first for this island kid.) Owing to its remoteness, room occupancy at the Humboldt is reputed to be pretty low. On each of my casual visits I glimpse three or four lone businessmen lolling about in the lobby. The place—always beautifully lit up at night and, in fair weather, visible from any point in Caracas—is quietly referred to as "the white elephant" by English speakers.

There's one habit I retain from Puerto Rico: find the music! Soon after arrival, I seize possession of a small radio in our bedroom, jiggle the dial, and zero in on the government station. I take in its regular broadcasts of the Old Masters at every shot.

Musical life in Caracas, it turns out, is far more active and busy than in San Juan. Early on I hear a live performance of Mischa Elman performing Tchaikovsky's Violin Concerto with the Orquesta Sinfónica de Caracas. On another occasion the orchestra plays Stravinsky's *Symphony of Psalms*. (In my first encounter with the piece, its dark instrumental sonorities are a disquieting experience.) And one morning I tune in to an interview with the ubiquitous Czech pianist Paul Badura-Skoda, a follow-up to the recital he'd given locally the night before.

Just a block down the street from us, on a broad and busy Avenida Miranda, stands a tiny, hole-in-the-wall audio and record shop called Fidelitone. Right by the front door, on a metal rack, I discover the monthly magazine *High Fidelity*. I sneak-read a couple of issues till the store owner gets wise to me and tells me to quit. So I buy the mags, combing the music features and reviews from cover to cover (and learning a new word, "discography"). The *High Fidelity* habit will stick with me for much of my teens.

To my enduring surprise our nameless landlord has left a spinet piano in the living room, plus a tabletop record player, and a few classical and "semiclassical" LPs. I play the records often. Soon I'm picking out on the piano the melodies of some of the simpler pieces, reveling in my accomplishment as I play along with the vinyl. Mary actually marvels at my newly acquired skill. She says to Dad, "We've got to get this boy a piano teacher."

He nods in apparent agreement, maybe even answers, "Yes." He never acts on it, though. In fact, whenever I ask him about music lessons, he always says the same thing: "We'll see."

Once again, as in Puerto Rico, the fabled lessons do not materialize. Instead, early that summer, Dad drags my brother and me to the office and assigns us each to paying jobs. Kanani ends up in the silk-screen section, where he helps make posters. Through a quirk of fate, the knowledge he gleans from that experience will serve him well some ten years later, during his long stint as art student and practicing artist.

As for me, I'm placed in shop, at the far end of the factory. There, to the constant hum of several hundred sewing machines, this immature, out-of-it thirteen-year-old is "apprenticed," so to speak, to a German mechanic named Ernest and his Puerto Rican assistant, Juan. Sad to say, never will time and payroll money be more thoroughly wasted. Though I only dimly sense it then, the simple truth is that I've no eye, no talent, no instinct for the arcane craft of putting objects together or working on and maintaining them. Ernest seems to have known this from the start. At the end of the very first day I'll overhear him casually remark to Juan, in his German-accented Spanish, "Ese no aprende nada" ("That kid'll never learn a thing").

I mention it to Dad on the way back home.

He promptly reacts, almost without emotion, "I don't believe that."

We're inching our way through downtown rush-hour traffic. "What is it you don't believe?" I asked. "What Ernest said? Or whether I heard it?"

His gaze remains fixed on the congested road. "I just don't believe you heard that."

So I continue in my fruitless daily routine at shop. Still, the boss man must've finally caught on. Later that summer I'm transferred to the silk-screen operation with Kanani, where everything—the work teams, the atmosphere, the poster-making activity—is far more manageable, even enjoyable.

Our labors earn us a modest weekly wage. And every Saturday I spend a portion of my salary on a brand-new classical LP. After about a month, though, Dad orders a moratorium on my record purchases. Naturally, I complain. I cry and ask, "How come?"

" 'Cause you're too specialized," he observes, with benevolent, fatherly care and concern. "There's more to life than classical music."

Mary, for her part, often expresses to me her frank dislike of that simply dreadful, horrid *"música de muertos"* ("music of the dead") with which I'd been filling the apartment.

Around midsummer there emerges at the office an intrigue to oust one of Dad's managerial staff. The target of these machinations is a jovial, tweedy, bespectacled American, married to a jet-black-haired, creamy-complected Puerto Rican. Kanani and I like them both. So it's bewildering to us whenever, after work, we overhear Dad and his four or five managerial colleagues conniving to do the guy in. They draw and quarter him verbally. They savagely mimic his contemptible pleas for mercy.

"Joe Farley is a jark," I recall my dad summing things up, and changing "jerk" to "jark" (for rhyme's sake) in a nasal voice, when it's all over. (Joe comes by to shake my hand and say adiós the day he quits the office.)

Over the years I often hear our father mocking some of his salespeople and other staff employees. One of them is a kindly, probably lonely, middle-aged Hungarian lady who often brings Kanani and me little trifles. Or he'll say, with utter ease, "We've *got* to get rid of so-and-so." So-and-so might well be someone we'd dined with just recently.

Among Dad's closer associates is Manuel Marín, a Puerto Rican fellow he'd met and dealt with during island days. Mustachioed and handsome, suave, smooth, and flawlessly bilingual, Manuel is the very image of a Hollywood Latin charmer. In fact he's carried on a series of affairs with several women at and around the office while still supporting a wife and three teenaged daughters back in San Juan. Dad and Manuel have often gone on hunting trips and other outings in the Venezuelan back country.

So our "family" foursome and Mr. Handsome decide to hook up at the end of one of his excursions, in a coastal village called Higuerote (pronounced "Ee-gay-ROH-tay").

The drive itself, over narrow mountain dirt roads on which passing a slow truck is next to impossible, takes up the greater part of the day. To kill time, at some point in the morning I reach forward, flick on the radio, and tune in to the government station. They're playing some Beethoven concerto I can't identify. Dad and Mary repeatedly insist I turn the thing off (that "*música de muertos*" again), but I want to at least know what the piece is. The fourth, I finally find out.

"The fourth concerto by Beethoven," Mary repeats after the announcer. I'll always associate hearing the piece with that trip, and the sound of her enunciating the title.

Higuerote, being at sea level and less than a thousand miles from the equator, has daytime temperatures that sizzle unrelentingly. Modest, basic, and slightly run-down from the sea salt and humidity, it's the kind of forgotten coastal settlement that informed readers might readily associate with certain García Márquez short stories, written by him in the 1970s and set in comparable seaside hamlets in Colombia, west of us, next door. There are the few small fishing craft and rowboats. Abundant mosquitoes that seem intent on devouring us. Desperately poor black people.

And there's a local tavern where Manuel Marín and a hefty Italian-American, earth-mother type from the office do some slow, close, bod-to-bod dancing late one afternoon. They'll become a couple on that trip, sleeping together in a bunk bed in the boathouse where we all stay. I believe they eventually got married. Two years later, Marín will be one of those involved in a successful move to have my father dumped from the bra firm.

Though Kanani and I have no friends our age that summer, we do the sorts of things—some of them mildly naughty—that boys our age normally do. Play stickball on the lawn. Fill brown paper bags with water and drop them from the balcony, delighting in the final splash. And mischievously ring doorbells within the building while rushing down the stairs, till a señora on a lower floor catches us and gives us a sound scolding.

Sometimes I go on solitary strolls in El Rosal, a slightly more upscale neighborhood down the hill across Avenida Miranda. There, amid the tree-lined streets, with the attractive, red-shingle-roofed homes in the background, I'll occasionally see groups of lanky American youths sporting their loose-jointed American gait and that characteristic, 1950s American look: blond crew cuts, plaid or Madras shirts, blue jeans (then still rare overseas), horn-rimmed eyeglasses, and tennis shoes. I feel some odd, roiling sensations inside of me whenever I glimpse those types. They're Americans, and I'm supposed to be one of them, but I know that I'm not, really. At least, not for the time being. I'll wonder nonetheless if I should be in their midst rather than continuing to attend school with Latinos . . . Why, after all, am I not hanging around with "my fellow Americans"? Do I belong there, do I qualify, am I a gringo or what? On any casual sightings of this sort I'll fall prey to these anguished confusions. The life I see in those denim-clad Overseas Americans seems so near yet so far, so logical and natural to me, yet so foreclosed and unlikely.

Toward the end of the summer, Kanani and I have assumed, we'll head back to Puerto Rico and spend a week or two with Mom . . .

Not so. Citing lack of funds, Dad calls off our return visit sometime in August. (Years later, I'd find a slightly pained letter I wrote Mom at the time, informing her of the unexpected change in travel plans.) What Kanani and I do know is that, as of September, we'll be enrolled at Havana Military Academy, in the Cuba then ruled by Gen. Fulgencio Batista and renowned throughout the Caribbean as a haven of great beaches and nightclubs, fancy gambling and sex.

I still remember the front cover of the school's shiny prospectus, with a glossy photo of its annual, formal ball. Smiling cadets in white gala uniforms, gliding on a dance floor with attractive, well-coifed Cuban beauties, spectacularly decked out in their five-inch heels, their party dresses billowed out with multiple petticoats.

"Looks like the place might be fun," I remark to Kanani as we browse through the catalog in our bedroom.

"Oh, but ... It's just that ... I don't know," my brother replies haltingly.

As things turn out, eleven-year-old Kanani's inarticulate skepticism proves more reliable than my casual credulity.

And so we're going directly to La Habana. This next phase of our new life, however, will be preceded by a five-day interlude in Florida— our only visit thus far to the continental United States. The trip seems to be purely for pleasure, with no business purposes on Dad's part. (Perhaps he wants to show Mary the sights?) It never occurs to me to note the contradiction between this sudden, generous travel binge and his having claimed money woes when canceling our originally scheduled visit with Mom. In fact, I only catch the subtle discrepancy as I hurriedly revise this page.

Oh, but are we dazzled, awestruck, Kanani and I, by the look, the feel of Miami and Miami Beach! So clean! So orderly! So efficient! The geometric-grid layout, the numbered streets. The rapid-fire service at lunch counters. The businesslike impersonality of ruddy-faced waiters. Stacks of *Miami Heralds* sitting unattended on officially designated racks, with a special cup where customers drop their nickels and dimes. (Clearly, we say enthusiastically to Mary and Dad, the mark of an honest, trusting society!)

I even like the canned Muzak that I hear in the hotels (in 1955 a strangely novel phenomenon). And I find its processed sounds soothing, despite its not being either classical or Latin.

And of course the city is so sleek, so modern, so *rich*—traits easily noted in the endless array of glitzy hotels that line the long beachfront as far as the eye can see. Remarkably, the Latin American–type poverty I've grown up with is nowhere to be seen. Even though the climate and ecology scarcely differ from those of Puerto Rico or Venezuela, the human environment is a world apart. Fair-skinned, teenaged girls, to our amazement, wear shorts out on the street—something unimaginable in Latin America at the time (and still not fully accepted there today). Yet going bare-armed and barelegged makes perfect sense and seems to us far more comfy and more rational than the Latin practice of covering yourself in layers of clothing, regardless of how hot the weather.

Some of the fleeting encounters we experience at the hotels hint at the identity dilemmas my brother and I will confront in later years. For example, as I stand by the swimming pool one afternoon, a light-brown-haired American boy, about my height and age and also a nice guy, overhears us. He asks me if we're Cuban.

Without hesitation I reply, "No, we're Puerto Rican."

It's probably the first time I've identified myself with the island. And so *casually*, scarcely sensing the implications of my seemingly innocent statement. That conversation will last only a few minutes more. But the stray incident has obviously stayed with me as a small milestone of some sort.

On another occasion, some American women in their late teens or early twenties are lounging across from us at a small motel's diminutive pool. Apparently unaware that we're Anglophone gringos, they take to mimicking our Spanish among themselves. With a thick, American accent and intonation, they bandy about the words, "Oon mow-mayn-TEE-tow!" Then they giggle. Looking back, I wish I'd mimicked their mimicking, then mimicked their nasal American English, too.

I'm standing by the double doors of a hotel ballroom, observing the dancers through a porthole-shaped window. The big band is playing old standards. A uniformed doorman in his middle years emerges from the adjacent door. He says to me curtly, "Watch it."

I don't know what the guy means. So I simply stand there some more, watching.

Then he growls. "I said, 'Watch it!' Can't you hear me? Don't you understand English?"

Actually, I've never heard the phrase before. How long does it take me to realize the guy simply wants me to move aside? Anyway, I finally move.

Dad and Mary take me to my first U.S. bookstore on that trip. It's well lit, fully stocked, air-conditioned, efficiently run. Two teenaged boys are leafing through some cartoon drawings, explaining the punchlines to each other. I choose a pocket book of captioned drawings for myself, which I'll take to Cuba and chuckle at in my spare moments there.

In the New Titles section I hit upon *Masterpieces of the Orchestral Repertoire* by someone called Ferguson, a clothbound, music-appreciation volume of the sort I'd often consulted back in Puerto Rico. Browsing in it, I notice that the order of the pages has gotten jumbled up in binding. So page 240 might face page 113, say. And of course the alphabetization by composer is totally out of whack. I show the item to a pretty, bespectacled, dark-haired clerk who seems scarcely more than a few years older than I am. She and her equally young assistant leaf through the defective product with mild astonishment.

"Goes from Wagner to Mozart!" says one of them, pronouncing the names correctly. They let me have the thing for a buck.

I'm so proud of my purchase! In time I'll scissor out and paste the wrongly inserted pages into sequence. Over the next six or seven years, *Masterpieces of the Orchestral Repertoire* will accompany me almost everywhere I go. I'll turn to it for casual reading or for solace and wisdom. Even utilize it as source for a couple of college term papers.

Today I look back with bewildered amazement at the enormous personal significance that accidental volume took on for me. I've also wondered how Mr. Ferguson would have felt had he found out that his reelaborated concert notes—which is essentially what they were—had come to mean so much to a postpubescent Overseas American who desperately hungered for music in his otherwise directionless life. His book served as a surrogate instrument I could play on, play with.

All over Miami we're seeing posters and billboards that advertise weekend junkets to Cuba—by plane for thirty dollars, by ship for as little as nineteen. Clearly, any interested American can easily find cheap, abundant, easy access to the island. (Later on I'll realize that, for many potential visitors, Havana's lure is analogous to that of Nogales, or Tijuana, in Mexico. It's an offshore border town, a brothel-and-gambling stop.)

And now, in fact, Havana's our ultimate destination as, in a rented car, the four of us go due south on the famous seven-mile causeway that links two of the Florida Keys. As we reach the middle of the long bridge, we voice apprehension when not a speck of shore—neither sunny beach nor green fields—can be seen either ahead of or behind us. There's nothing but deep blue water on all four sides.

We're heading for Key West, where we'll spend just enough time for me to take in its oddly "West Indian" atmosphere (a sensation I'd recognize in 1974 when savoring Thomas McGuane's luscious novel *Ninety-two in the Shade*). In Key West we board a small passenger plane to Havana. Driving south instead of flying directly from Miami—I now assume—has been a way for Dad to save a penny here, a penny there.

During the next few weeks I'll often recall Miami and south Florida with nostalgia, and not just because of their paradisiacal unreality. For one thing, the five-day spell is our only visit as yet to the States and everything that that land represents to us.

And then, once we've enrolled at Havana Military Academy, our time as tourists in the mythic Miami Beach stands out as the most immediate memory of anything remotely resembling freedom.

Cuban Military Cadet No. 562

Dawn. First light falls on two long rows of metal bunk beds. The vivid sounds of the bugle's sixteenth notes have us all tumbling out as one. Cuban reveille: its staccato strains differ considerably from the arpeggiated tune familiar to me from American flicks and Puerto Rican media. So begins the day for us boarders at Havana Military Academy.

Following morning toilette in the large communal bathroom, we're under compulsion to ensure our lockers are neat, our shoes shiny, our beds properly made with a ten-inch fold on the top sheet. At inspection call each one of us—there are about a hundred in our second-floor dorm—is standing bolt upright at the foot of his bed. A student sergeant struts threateningly down the aisles, ruler in one hand, raised index finger on the other. Tight-lipped, he checks for dust in the closets, deficiencies in the sheetfolds, and other irregularities. Any reported infraction will produce demerits. A certain number of demerits will lead to assorted punishments. The most dreaded of these, known as *el rifle*, involves standing at attention in the afternoon sun with a rifle on one's shoulder.

Being in *bachillerato* (high school), I'm housed in the upstairs barracks. Kanani, still in sixth grade, sleeps in the primary-school section downstairs. My cadet number is 562; his, 565. The numbers don't seem to reflect any particular order.

Military routines will now punctuate our daily lives. There's early-morning formation where, amid the mists and chills of the hour after dawn, the respective flags of Cuba and the school are ritually raised, after which we march in step ("¡Un, dos, tres, cuatro!") to breakfast. A Spartan dining hall: gray, rectangular Formica tables, straight-backed dark wood chairs. We'll sit in groups of eight, a higher-ranking or older student at the head. We each of us get two rolls, a small box of cereal, and two ribbed plastic glasses, one for water, another for milk. We help ourselves to the beverages from brimfilled, gray metal pitchers. Throughout all meals, an impressive sight will be that of the workmen who tote huge, swaying, seven-foot-high stacks of those plastic glasses. Table barter: bread and cornflakes are commonly exchanged. At meal's end, emptied-out crusts and uneaten, doughy wads can be seen scattered across the tabletops.

There's military formation and step marching before morning classes and lunch. Before afternoon classes and sports. And, finally, before suppertime and evening study hall. And there's roll call at all major formations and meals, with each cadet answering some version of "¡Aquí!" ("Here!"). The distinctive, creative hollers developed by the cadets—for example, "Kep!" or "Hoe-ay!"—have evolved so much as to bear little resemblance to the original root word "aquí."

Our heads are now much changed: we all got brush cuts on day one. Military style is all-pervasive. During class hours we wear the school's gray uniform and black necktie, plus kepis when outdoors. At all other times, we sport HMA T-shirts with the regulation gray pants. When speaking about a fellow student to a superior, an administrator, or a teacher, you never refer to him as "this guy," but rather as "this cadet." Conflicts between individuals are resolved not by fistfights or scuffles but via formal boxing matches.

At daytime, student ranks are swelled threefold by the townies, whose civilian mobility and freedoms are resented by some of the boarding people. Lunchtime food for all seven to eight hundred of us is scarcely edible, save for the fried fish at week's end (the norm at the time in Catholic countries).

Most Fridays, following afternoon activities, there's a massive parade on the school grounds. Sounds of a drum-and-bugle corps fill the air. It's climaxed by the ceremonial lowering of the two flags as the bugles blare out Cuban "Taps" over a hushed, geometrically configured multitude.

The HMA grounds are approximately diamond-shaped. At the bottommost, southern tip stands the school lobby, where a cadet, one of a trio doing guard duty for the day, mans the front desk. Flanking the lobby are a few administrative and business offices. The bulk of the bottom diagonals is taken up by classrooms bearing plaques with the names of noted Cubans. My freshman classroom is designated "Carlos Finlay," after the Cuban scientist credited with developing the vaccine against yellow fever.

The dining hall, a small library, and an infirmary occupy the upper eastern diagonal, our barracks a portion of the western edge. Next come a swimming pool and a baseball diamond. A fairly large greensward, lined with benches, occupies the space between the building structures. The actual grounds stretch well beyond the sports area.

The school itself is surrounded on all sides by wire-mesh fencing. On the northernmost reaches of the greensward, though, a few bold students might occasionally find cover and even sneak out for a snow-cone purchase or a cigarette break. (Smoking is forbidden on campus.)

Dad and Mary have remained in Havana for the initial days of the school year. They visit us on the first weekend. After that, they're off to Caracas. Over the next couple of years, one or the other might drop by every few months or so, on business. Mom and Valerie are almost as far away, in Puerto Rico.

Academic and military routine now goes into full swing. I start my five classes: ancient history, physical geography, English language, Spanish grammar, and algebra. The second weekend arrives. No furlough as yet. And, in a disquieting contrast with our classmates and dormmates, no family visitors for my brother and me.

We're well into the HMA game of regimentation and survival. And only then do I start to grasp our situation, to wit:

—my brother and I find ourselves all alone at a military school in Batista's Cuba;

—our parents, recently divorced and in two different countries, are each of them more than a thousand miles overseas;

—at the overwhelmingly Cuban school, there are almost no foreigners, save for another American or two, a Venezuelan, and a Mexican (and they live in a fog of aloneness much like ours).

As I come to this realization my insides start churning in sheer panic. Spiritual terror, desolation. Disbelief. So we're confined here through Christmas! And after that, for the duration of the school year! And all by our little selves to boot . . .

This is not what we'd expected, though Dad in fact had told us little about the place. Still, what else *could* have we expected, given the larger picture of our lives?

Anyway, I want out. We both want out.

At some point that first month I call our mom. Or probably she phoned me, following some pained and anguished cry of help—a wire? a brief note?—that I'd sent her. Speaking excitedly, confusedly, over the front lobby phone I tell Mom we don't like the place and don't like the people and don't like Cuba or Cubans and simply want to get out and go back home to Puerto Rico. Even as I speak, the seated guard—a rugged type, somewhat older, with beard stubble—smiles a wry smile.

Mom says softly, earnestly, lovingly, "Well, son, we can't always do what we want."

In the long run she's right, of course, though I don't want to accept it at the time: we're stuck, Kanani and I, and can't do much about it. And she lacks the wherewithal to swoop down and fly us back to P.R. like a supermom. So she and I talk about this and that. And I get embarrassingly moist-eyed as I ask her to give little Valerie a big hug for us.

After I've hung up, the stubble-faced, wry-smiling student guard now ribs me, in Spanish, "Well, so you don't like the people here." As it turns out, he had lived a spell up in the States. Over the next couple of years he and I'll chat once in a while about Cuba and Cuban-U.S. differences.

I see little of Kanani during the school week, partly because of our separate living quarters, partly because of those age and grade differences that matter a lot in childhood and adolescence—but also because I sadly lack in any notion of being a protective, loving helper to my very vulnerable kid brother.

Today, it would be far too easy for me to attribute those emotional shortcomings of mine to Dad's gringo philosophy of "Take care of yourself, don't depend on others!" Granted, that was one of his stated justifications for dropping us off in a foreign military school, by ourselves, far from everything. Moreover, Mom, though always a loving parent, had found herself unwittingly caught up in (and later cast out by) Dad's individualistic schemes. Family continuities and traditions, no doubt, had been glaringly absent during our Puerto Rico years. Such absences inevitably played some role in shaping my unbrotherly conduct.

And yet . . . the above rings facile and false—sounds too much like rationalization, knee-jerk hindsight, passing the retrospective buck. Sibling ties, after all, have a dynamic of their own. Kids do decide among themselves how and what they'll be to each other in the course of growing up. Besides, the firstborn tends to enjoy intangible privileges that will hold sway over the next children. In my case, I had the privileges, but no sense of the responsibilities that go with brothering.

Occasionally, at HMA, during the half-hour evening recess, Kanani and I might sit a while on a secluded bench just to commiserate secretly. To cry a bit together, side by side, as we reminisce about home life in Hato Rey. That's about all, though, since we'd never really been that close before.

At HMA, Kanani and I comprise almost the entire English-speaking sector. Of course the mail to and from Mom, eagerly written and anxiously awaited, is in English. (Dad's is too, one would assume, though I've no memory of his letters then.) The magazines I read are also in the language of the Yankee north. *Time, Reader's Digest, High Fidelity*. I purchase them at newsstands when on furlough, then peruse them, cover to cover.

Though there's an illustrated Cuban weekly called *Bohemia*—well regarded, and a standard reading staple all over the Caribbean, much as *Life* is in the States—I'll probably look at its pages only once or twice during all my time there. The fact is, I don't feel Cuban. Don't feel connected to Cuban life or Cuban people. No reason, then, for me to make a habit of reading Cuban, either.

All of my personal stuff—my inner thoughts and fantasies, my private monologues and dreams, my occasional if intense prayers to a Catholic deity—happens in English, by habit more than by choice. (God is a gringo.) The rift between my home language and the surrounding, enveloping society now far exceeds what it had been in P.R., where at least there were the CES junior-high classes, the American radio and TV shows, the fractured family fold. At the military school, by contrast, Ameringlish lives almost exclusively inside the unhappily isolated little heads of Kanani and Gene. Yet it remains as the one functioning segment of my minimal American identity.

Objectively, I live, eat, and breathe Cuban. I study, chat, and play in a military microworld that is overwhelmingly Cuban and Cuban speaking. Subjectively, my inward language places me in some other, distant, powerful macroworld that I hardly know, and where I decidedly do *not* live, eat, breathe, etc. Ameringlish is my nowhere. It's the language of my utopia.

I look back at Miami with nostalgia, yet with no sense of my having a U.S. future.

Meanwhile, cadets and teachers are asking where I'm from. I answer, mechanically, "From Puerto Rico." So without realizing it, I've metamorphosed into an Overseas Puerto Rican. When asked what I *am*, though, I answer, "American." Then the rest of my background comes up: born in Haiti of a Hawaiian mother still residing in P.R. and of a gringo father currently stationed in Venezuela. Some humorist will invariably quip, "Shit, you're a regular United Nations!"

Oftentimes other cadets ask me why I'm enrolled at HMA. I haven't got a reply ready. The two I produce most frequently are, "Well, my father wants me to experience military life," or "My dad felt that my brother and I should learn to adapt to the world."

Now, decades later, I've arrived at the stark realization that we were there, quite simply, because our father wanted us there. HMA was his way of having control over Kanani and me, yet out of his hair, with no need to face us day by day. It also furnished a quasi-academic cover and faux-ethical pretext for spiriting us away from Mom, who at the time found herself more or less broke and lacking in resources. As generally happens after a divorce, the children had become pawns in a power play. And the power was his.

There exists an entire narrative literature focusing on boys' boarding schools and their institutionalized brutalities. Robert Musil's *Young Törless* and Mario Vargas Llosa's *La Ciudad y los perros* (translated as *The Time of the Hero*) come handily to mind. While allowing for poetic license and authorial exaggeration, I know from our experience that such fictional accounts are basically accurate. When I read those imaginative works I'll readily recognize the everyday sorts of cruelties and underlying sadomasochism that typify HMA life.

Most cadets pick on and prey on their fellow pupils. And the more vulnerable and exposed you are, the more abuse you must fend off. In my own case I'm ridiculed for my Puerto Rican accent, plus for my being 1) foreign, 2) American, 3) Asian-looking, 4) studious, 5) naive, 6) deracinated, 7) confused, and 8) bad at baseball, just for starters.

The alienation that grips me must be written on my face. Some guy looks at me during recess and says, "Coño, está jodido el chino éste" ("Shit, this chink here's all fucked up").

Another cadet, whose last name, Caos, is actually the Spanish word for "chaos," passes by me in the shower room, shakes his head, and remarks, "Oye, chiquito, qué extraño eres" ("Hey, kid, you're so weird").

Even my simple, Anglo handle elicits the occasional snide comment. At morning formation, after roll call, a stocky, round-faced student— himself often a target of abuse—remarks to nobody in particular, "Gene Bell. Strange name." Cubans find it even stranger that, unlike all normal folks in the Hispanic world, I don't sport a second, maternal surname. This lack had never come up as an issue back in P.R., where the widespread gringo presence probably made islanders more aware of Anglo-Hispanic cultural differences. Besides, as with many Hispanics, Cubans can't deal with a last name that's just one syllable long. And then, at HMA, given names are seldom used. So, throughout my two years there, peers will address me as "GeemBEL," uttered swiftly, like a single word that rhymes with "hotel."

And then, what about Puerto Rico? What's that? Some cadets, younger ones especially, confuse it with Panama or Venezuela. A handful are even surprised that Puerto Ricans speak in Spanish and have names like "Pérez" and "González." My first week there, one of the scarier-looking roughnecks informs me, "Hey, didja know that Puerto Ricans have dicks and hands just this size?" His thumb and forefinger frame a space a quarter-inch wide.

On my own, I make lists of my Puerto Rican friends. Write them the occasional letter, even a poem, and look back nostalgically at our times when we hung around street corners.

The sadistic attitudes and folkways at HMA can be encountered at every age and grade level. There's the practice known as *la pilita* ("the little pile"), in which a group of younger students, without warning, will zoom in on and swarm about a random cadet who happens to be alone out on the greensward, then "pile" onto him and rough him up.

The older guys, for their part, occasionally bully the grade-schoolers, whom they look down on and despise. Cuban Spanish, by the way, has two very unattractive and derogatory words for denoting little kids: *fiñe* (FEE-nyay) and *mojón* (moh-HONE). The latter noun can additionally signify "a dry, hardened turd."

There's also the sexual abuse, along with the homoerotic temptations. Early on in my first year, word gets around that a group of adolescents had been sodomizing a shy, scared, nearsighted ten-year-old, on a regular basis, each night. The whole crew gets swift, summary dismissals when they're caught. Though we all somehow know about the matter (I'm vaguely acquainted with one of the offenders), a public scandal seems to have been averted.

In another incident, it leaks out that two tall, hefty types in their late teens have carried on a furtive, mutually consenting affair within the school grounds. On the day of their expulsion, the pair are summoned up and publicly disgraced before a military formation of all boarders. As a parting gesture, the headmaster—a balding, graying, well-built and distinguished-looking sort known to everyone simply as *el coronel* (the colonel)—approaches the two transgressors and then punches each one of them in the chest.

For all we know, the expelled couple may well have been temperamentally gay; perhaps they went so far as to love one another. Still, girls being totally absent, the homosexual temptation is always there, even to us run-of-the-mill heteros. (Excepting weekend visitors, the only women we students ever set eyes on at HMA are its two youngish secretaries. We often talk about, speculate about, mythify the two-some, who are usually together.) So, as an instance, one pretty, delicate boy, a classmate, occasionally strokes my hand as we sit at study table. Though my homoerotic inclinations are close to nil, the sensation is certainly pleasurable.

It's at that Cuban school where I'll first hear a separate term for the guy on top in single-sex intercourse: *bugarrón*. I assume, today, that the word is etymologically related to the British verb "to bugger," though it exists in no other Spanish-speaking dialect I know of. I once overhear a hairsplitting discussion among some cadets as to whether *bugarrones* are or aren't *maricones* ("queers"). Later in my teens, I'll realize that, in Latino macho culture, the fellow who's on top bears less of a homosexual stigma than the guy on the bottom, who, as the phrase goes, "se deja" ("lets it be done to him").

Actually, among the popular, heterosexual, male segments of the entire Hispanic world, *maricón* is the standard insult, the barbed comment of choice. It's used indiscriminately for venting frustration or rage, contempt or fear, to convey that the targeted individual is nasty, stupid, obnoxious, dishonest, clumsy, incompetent, or just a general nuisance. And regardless of his actual sexual orientation.

At a place like HMA, where repressed sexuality is such a large part of life and where, outside the classrooms, there is no polite company, the "m" word surfaces constantly, obsessively, abundantly. You hear and employ the term dozens of times per day. A guy accidentally jostles you in a crowd, you call him *maricón*. A prankster helps himself to your bread or your books, you warn him not to be a *maricón*. There are no intended sex-ual overtones, any more than Anglo-Americans think of brown fecal mush or fleshy buttocks when labeling someone a "shithead" or an "ass-hole." Still, there is in those reflex insults a kind of cultural unconscious at work. In a society steeped in machismo, accusing someone—even casually—of *not* being a macho is the ultimate affront, a verbal assault surpassed in force only by alluding slyly to his female progenitor.

Of course, Cuba was (and is) a highly eroticized society. The trait manifested itself in countless ways. At the time, Havana had an enormous red-light district. Many of the older cadets would go brothel hopping during furlough. Back at school they'd boast of the experience. (One of them contracted gonorrhea and was mercifully cured by penicillin shots at the infirmary. For weeks thereafter, the guys around the dorm would express amusement at his mishap.)

In addition, Cuba's porno industry was a considerable force all over the Caribbean. Its crudely confected chapbooks (*novelitas de relajo*), extremely graphic in their swaggering prose and grainy photos of male-female couplings, circulated clandestinely about HMA. I recall being turned on by a few of the specimens that I once got hold of and read in some remote corner of the baseball field.

And then there were the *posadas*, hotel facilities that existed exclusively for heterosexual couples needing a quiet place for a bodily encounter, and with no sleaze or stigma attached to the (very Cuban) institution. They've continued to exist even throughout the revolution, as the opening scene in the movie *Strawberry and Chocolate* suggests.

Sexually explicit art movies from France and Italy were also widely shown at the cinema palaces on Havana's main boulevards, and without the censorious attitudes that, in the contemporary U.S., tended to raise righteous eyebrows and subject the films to isolation.

Sex was one economic sector that the Batista dictatorship more or less left alone.

It's not that the entire environment at HMA was brutal or Darwinian. On the contrary, positive and fruitful human contacts did exist: cordial conversation, youthful sharing of ideas and stories, expressions of warmth and camaraderie, even some friendship. I myself managed to forge friendly ties with classmates my own age; we buddied together during breaks or on weekends without leaves.

Among my more constant friends was an intense, gawky fellow from Santiago de Cuba. A thirteen-year-old, budding intellectual, he once loaned me Hesse's *Steppenwolf* (in Spanish). Coincidentally, he too was skinny, wore glasses, and happened to be called "Eugenio." At first he and I hung around a lot with one another. Even visited a brothel together once during a leave. Students and profs would sometimes confuse the two of us and even mix up our last names.

I don't know why but, one evening as I saw him dribbling casually with some cadets out on the basketball court, I took to ridiculing his surname, twisting it into a Cuban swear word. (Actually I do know why. It was the act of someone who was spiritually sick at the time. One who's since been lucky enough to find his way out of his soul-sickness.) I don't think Eugenio and I ever spoke again. Two decades later I'll find out through a mutual acquaintance from Santiago de Cuba that, at some point in the 1960s, Eugenio had committed suicide.

Certain wiser, saner, older pupils also took a special interest in me. Sensed my potential. Encouraged my better qualities. Urged me to mix not with just anybody but only with guys I was compatible with intellectually. A big and burly, yet refined and cosmopolitan fellow called Veranes attempted to give me just that sort of advice.

But, but, but . . . Owing to the mental morass, the tangle of confusion that I was caught up in and further sinking into, alas, I lacked the self-knowledge, the inner resources to enable me to handle any deep attentions of a positive kind. So, when hearing a silly sobriquet, based on some dumb Cuban soft-drink jingle, that other cadets had tagged onto Veranes, I joined the crowd and also started addressing him that way. Like a mental lumpen, I more or less spurned overtures of generosity such as his. Sometimes, in the worst cases, I turned against the very individuals who were offering them.

For want of much else to do, Kanani and I plunge into our studies. The school itself is first-rate academically. The faculty members—who're called *profesores* and wear white, knee-length robes over their civvies—are seriously dedicated to their scholarly traditions and their pedagogy. One of them, señor Íñiguez, even authored our Renaissance and early modern history textbook. A charismatic instructor, a delightful, orotund man, and also a freethinker, he has the gift of infecting us with his wry indignation at the Catholic clergy's sale of indulgences and the other church abuses that caused the Reformation.

The school curriculum, part of a national program and ultimately modeled—so I've since gathered—after the French system, was rigorous and demanding. Over my two years' stint there I had courses in world geography, European history, and basic algebra. In addition there was a year each of plane geometry and of "Anatomy, Physiology, and Hygiene," as the latter course was designated. In Spanish class we memorized definitions of twenty new words per week. What I learned during those years concerning grammar I still find useful in my own teaching today.

Had I stayed on, I also would've studied such compulsory subjects as physics, logic, and political economy. The levels of discourse in my ninth- and tenth-grade courses were comparable to what you'd find in a good U.S. college freshman class. We learned about earthly phenomena like river meanders, alluvial fans, old and new mountain ranges, and the low barometric pressure of a hurricane. And we talked about human events such as Rome's rise and fall, the French Revolution, European imperialism, and Argentine *Peronismo*. Socialism wasn't demonized but seen simply as a mode of organization, instances of which could be noted in nonsocialist systems. Accordingly, Soviet advances in industry, science, and education were duly mentioned in the textbooks, which were all serious, objective, high-quality volumes.

Sometimes, for my schoolwork in the years following Cuba, I found myself harking back to the knowledge I had assimilated in those military halls. (For example: year of the fall of the Western Roman Empire, AD 476. Fall of the Eastern Empire, AD 1453. Those dates, which I'd memorized in Havana, are conventionally accepted as the outer frames of Europe's Middle Ages. In my mind's eye I can visualize the thousand-year time frame.)

Kanani initially had it rougher. At first he was set back a year, partly because he seemed completely ignorant of long division. Luckily, the authorities soon caught on that, back in Puerto Rico, he'd simply learned the process via the U.S.-style configuration, with the mouth of the dividing sign facing down rather than up.

In addition, he happened to be at that age when kids are just starting to pick up bits and pieces of their national history. Unfortunately he'd been yanked out of CES precisely when those elements of the U.S. and Puerto Rican pasts were to be taught, leaving him temporarily unschooled in that area. Now he was dropped into classes on the history of Cuba, and he found himself totally mystified. Within months, though, he'd rally and learn to draw maps, memorize place-names and boundaries (Cuban and otherwise), and study rudiments of algebra and geometry.

He and I eventually shared most of the medals for top grades that were handed out, on a bimonthly basis, at the all-school Friday parades.

When first starting out at HMA, I sometimes complained to other cadets that I ought to be enrolled at a U.S. high school, not a Cuban *bachillerato*. Invariably I got from them a scornful or puzzled reply, along the lines of "An American high school? That's like our sixth grade!" Some years later I realized they weren't wrong. In fact the profound contrasts between the two systems still amaze me. (At many U.S. colleges, for instance, graduates of Latin American high schools get a full year's credit toward the B.A.) For a while I even entertained vague thoughts about finishing secondary school in Cuba and taking advantage of its superior training.

On the other hand, many Cubans I met, both youthful and adult, honestly believed their schooling enjoyed global renown and respect. It was a bit like those more naive Americans who automatically think that "our medical system is the world's best" and that every modern invention—including autos, movies, radio, and Rubik's Cube—is of American vintage.

Every other weekend we boarders have the right to a leave, unless somebody loses that privilege as a result of demerits. On weekends without furlough, the school gates are opened to visits from family members and friends. And on Sunday mornings, resident cadets have the option to board the school's buses and be shepherded to Mass at a church in nearby Miramar.

Most do go, if mainly as a chance to get away, and also to catch glimpses of teenage girls in their radiant Sunday best. I too attend, at the urging of some enthusiasts who wish to recruit me into the Catholic fold. For the first time I'm participating in the Roman ritual, watching the congregation, so as to know exactly when to stand, kneel, and pray.

Having no visiting kin to fill the other long hours of those nonleave weekends, I hide in books. Still lacking roots in Spanish or English literary traditions, I plow through mostly abstract, culturally nonspecific stuff in popular science—astronomy, physics, math, "sexology," even Freud. What novels I do read are by authors like Hermann Hesse (thanks to friend Eugenio), George Orwell, Jules Verne: alien imaginers with a strong philosophical bent. Anything too realistically grounded in a particular society would defy my comprehension.

Sometimes, at study hall, I'll browse in the textbooks of upper-level cadets sharing my table. And so I encounter Parson Malthus's seductive theory of population—to wit: food production increases arithmetically, whereas population grows geometrically, hence mass starvation is unavoidable!—summed up in a thick volume soberly entitled *Economía política*, required of all third-year students. The same book introduces me to the phenomenon of *latifundio*, the massive concentration of farmland in few hands that has long been the bane of Latin American society. When, during the late 1960s, ideas of Third World "overpopulation" as well as land reform would become heated topics of discussion in the U.S., I'd feel quietly grateful to that Cuban textbook for having first introduced me to those issues.

Most of my readings, I should note, are in Spanish, excepting Orwell and of course *Masterworks*, which I've toted along with me from Miami and now consult whenever my musical impulses move me to do so. It never occurs to me that I'm dwelling indistinctly in two languages yet am fully, solidly rooted in none.

Besides getting out of HMA and back to P.R., what I most want is to "do" music. During a weekend leave early that year, I take note of a private piano school on a street not far from where Kanani and I will be staying. My hopes are aroused! Getting up my gumption, I venture in that afternoon and inquire about piano lessons.

The middle-aged guy I talk to asks, right off, "Do you own an instrument?"

"No," I answer.

"Well, then, there's no point in taking lessons, really. You'd need an instrument, to practice."

And I leave, knowing there's not even the shadow of a chance. Not for now, at least.

The airwaves will prove once again to be my instrument. Like many resident cadets, I've got my portable radio. During the daily rest periods and on weekends I tune in to the classical station, with Ferguson in hand for guidance. In time I also come to appreciate and understand Cuban popular and folk music, their rich, complex textures, the culture that they belong to. Students at HMA intensely listen to and seriously discuss such esoteric genres as *guaguancó* (Afro-Cuban chants). They compare ballad singers' musical merits. They work at improving their own rumba and cha-cha-chá steps, an activity pursued by them in great earnest.

Through their example and some radio surfing I discover the special beauties of those distinctively Cuban ensembles, the *charangas*: three fiddles, used chiefly as rhythm background; a male-voice trio of singers; a piano-percussion-bass section; and—for instrumental melody and solos—a flute. Some of those *charangas*, notably the Orquesta Aragón, possess a velvety refinement, a virtuoso mastery and subtle artistry that can only be termed world-class. In their league they're comparable to the best of European classical and American jazz traditions.

Kanani, being three years younger than me, entertains himself with more physical fare. He swims a lot in the pool during the longer free periods. Or he runs about the quad with his set of friends, as ten- and eleven-year-olds anywhere will do.

One afternoon, though, he is hit by his very first mystical experience as he lies on his back alone, at the farthest reaches of the greensward. He's observing the edges of a nearby rainstorm as it skirts the school grounds without wetting them. And he marvels at such an amazing natural spectacle—at existence itself. It's the first of several such trances each of us will know in the course of our lives, and one of the few positive memories of our HMA days that he will eventually share with me.

Every other Friday, Kanani and I take the bus from the La Playera line. We're headed for Havana and our much-awaited furlough.

The mingled sounds of jukeboxes and slot machines greet us at the terminal some thirty minutes later. On occasion I play the notorious one-armed bandits, never achieving the combinations that might earn me more than a few dimes. The varied scent of deep-frying meats, fish, and dough snacks, sold by the ubiquitous street vendors, serves as a reminder that we're back in the urban fold. The sensation is further heightened by the outdoor lights, the late-Friday crowds and the traffic surrounding us as we ride a city bus to our final destination.

Dad has provided a whole apartment for the two of us in upscale Miramar, directly above some in-laws—Mary's elder sister, Pepa, and the latter's husband, Santos—who reside on the ground floor. The place, a modern construction with bright primary colors and sliding closet doors, is scarcely furnished save for the twin beds where we'll both sleep on those free Fridays and Saturdays.

Now and then we'll share in quick snacks and conversation with our step-aunt and step-uncle downstairs. Truth is, though, we're alone. So, once in mufti, we take long walks around the neighborhood. Or go for bus rides about town. Sometimes we stroll on the Malecón, the spectacular seaside promenade that's Havana's prime symbol. We'll stand there and watch the waves splashing up against the retaining wall. And gaze at the happy young couples walking by, holding hands.

Inevitably, back in the apartment I'll loll about on my twin bed, leafing through books and U.S. magazines. Or listening to the radio with *Masterworks* at the ready.

Evenings, we both take in an American movie at a nearby theater. We see World War II uplift pieces like *Mr. Roberts* and *To Hell and Back* (the Audie Murphy story). A political drama with José Ferrer called *Feet of Clay*. An idiotically saccharine account of a performing vaudeville dog entitled *Kelly and I*. And *The Killers*, costarring Ronald Reagan, based on Hemingway's famous story of the same name. Kanani and I will joke around for months afterwards with the future president's hard-boiled line, "Bright boy," with which he repeatedly taunts a hapless waiter.

Those weekend leaves . . . they're by far the most unreal aspect of our time spent in Cuba. They amount to little more than a negative freedom, a brief escape from the inhumanities and confinement of HMA. The furloughs themselves are totally disconnected from most anything in Cuban life. We're these two crazy foreign kids—Americans? Puerto Ricans?—with no authentic roots in, no genuine kinship ties on the island. Our only motive for hanging around La Habana, outdoors or in, is to get out of a suburban military school where we simply prefer not to be.

HMA was in great measure a microcosm of mid-1950s Cuba. The Army men on the faculty—one of whom taught me advanced algebra—were dissidents who'd been purged from Batista's officer corps. A top civilian administrator, Raúl Chibás, was the brother of Eddy Chibás, the impassioned, legendary leader of the island's nonsocialist left. Eddy's suicide in 1951, following one of his fiery radio broadcasts, held mythic proportions among concerned Cuban citizenry.

Among the cadets was Agostini, a gentle, good-natured boy whose father, a career soldier, had been murdered by Batista's henchmen. On the other hand there was a big, vicious, aggressive bully called Varela, whose pop was a high-ranking *Batistiano* officer. (Perhaps he would be among those publicly executed in 1959, shortly after the dictator was overthrown.) The father of yet another cadet, Cantillo, served briefly as interim military mayor of Havana between Batista's flight and Fidel Castro's final victory. And one kid, Dorticós, was related to the lawyer who became the ceremonial president of the Castro government in the 1960s.

Another of my classmates, Alvarado, had a brother, renowned at the time as a university student activist. His life was to be tragically cut short in 1958, when Batista's police tortured him to death.

During free periods, political discussion was frequent and intense. One time, in study hall, I overheard García, a tall, politically articulate junior, quietly complaining to the instructor-monitor about the 1955 coup staged by the CIA against Jacobo Arbenz, the legally elected president of Guatemala. He bitterly mocked official U.S. pretexts to the effect that Arbenz's administration had been "Communist."

A physical education prof and basketball coach, apparently connected to the Freemasons, discoursed with us at poolside once on the discrepancy between the church's professed doctrines of poverty and humility and the pomp and palatial splendor of the Vatican.

Among themselves, and with professors, some students talked now and again about the problem of *latifundio* agriculture, the skewed economic system that plagued Latin America then and still does today.

The United States, and its relative worth as a nation and culture, came up frequently in conversation. A short, effervescent classmate called González, who usually sat behind me, remarked while waiting for our next professor one morning that the best movies were American.

From the back of the room a smart, rebellious kid by the name of Gómez shot back contemptuously, "False! The best movies are from Italy." That same Gómez often shrugged off certain notions or facts as "American propaganda." (It may have been from his lips that I first heard that phrase.)

A tall, sweet boy, whom everyone knew simply as Víctor, sometimes leaped to the defense, observing, "Well, with all its vices, the United States is a great country. That's what I say."

Still and all, U.S. policy toward Latin America couldn't go unnoticed. During one particularly tense siesta period at the barracks, a senior who'd spent years at HMA started baiting me from his upper bunk on the matter of Washington's support for Nicaraguan tyrant Anastasio Somoza. I'd never heard the word "Somoza" in my life. And so said nothing.

Another voice chimed in, "Hey, leave the kid alone. He doesn't know anything about that stuff."

Whoever that voice belonged to, he wasn't mistaken: that "stuff" did indeed slide right by me. At best, I was mildly puzzled at the very idea that U.S. benevolence could be subject to challenge. At worst, I simply didn't care. It was only in the '60s that I began to grasp what those Cuban students had been talking about, and to finally realize that their political analyses were on the mark. And also that Gómez's judgments about Italian film were basically right.

At the time, though, my mind was elsewhere, shaped as it had been by the mythologies imbedded in *Time* and *Reader's Digest*, or by notions picked up from CES and my home life in Puerto Rico. Despite my not being part of any immediate American community that went beyond my minuscule family, I still somehow shared in the blind dogmas of many Overseas Americans, who'll spend most of their lives in, say, Egypt or Holland or Peru, yet whom the U.S. enclaves will insulate and protect from the life-and-death issues of their host nation.

In my case, in Batista's Cuba, the enclave happened to be the confines of my mind. Had there been some sort of action against U.S. interests on the island, I would have been a natural target for vigilante attack—verbal, physical, economic, whatever. Yet I wouldn't have had a clue as to why. No more than your stereotypical, whiskey-sipping, monolingual, yacht-club gringos would have.

Not that all political discussion at HMA was high-level, subtle, or smart. Plenty of vulgar, formulaic prejudice also found expression. For the first time in my life I heard the nouns *indígena* (indigenous) and *indio* (Indian) employed as terms of abuse for somebody who bungled or who just looked dark. Years later, I realized that, throughout Latin America's past and present, the indigenous peoples had gotten the worst deal of all, much like the Jews in the darkest epochs of European history.

Cubans also had a reflex phrase, mouthed if you felt attacked or otherwise set upon, that went, roughly, "Stop it! Am I Chinese or something?" The recurring statement puzzled me until I eventually read in historian Hugh Thomas's monumental *Cuba* that, in the nineteenth century, some 140,000 Chinese were press-ganged to the island as virtual slaves. So the racist-Cuban "Am I Chinese?" is analogous to the racist-American "Get your cotton-pickin' hands off of me!"

Still, as I look back, I'm struck by the heightened political consciousness, the ideological articulateness and sophistication of those Cuban high school boys when compared with that of most U.S. students at all levels—graduate and professional schools included—and in most U.S. eras, the '60s excepted. Some of my immediate classmates even talked half-humorously of organizing a student *sindicato* (a union), on the model of the highly active university groups that were and still are common in Latin America.

In retrospect, the greatest political oddity of all was the presence at HMA of a small boy by the name of Fidel Castro, Jr., enrolled in first and second grades. His father, meanwhile, was spearheading a distant guerrilla war in the hills of Oriente province. And yet scarcely anyone at the school made much of this strange fact. Besides, the boy's parents were divorced. And in 1956 there was as yet no strong expectation that the guerrillas could actually overthrow the régime.

Among the especially hot topics, of course, was the elder Fidel Castro himself, who, during my second year there, was successfully holding off Batista's troops in the Sierra Maestra bush and communicating clandestinely with the nation via Radio Rebelde. Not a few HMA enrollees were openly pro-Castro. Sometimes they'd casually exclaim, "¡Abajo Batista!" and "¡Viva Fidel!" Around then, Castro was not openly Communist or even socialist, although his general outlook was vaguely radical, as of course were his battle tactics. Meanwhile the United States, realizing that Batista's days were numbered, would gradually ease into a cautious acceptance of the Fidelista movement. By 1957, the only thing that mattered to official U.S. policy makers was that Batista's sordid and corrupt barracks régime had lost substantial support among the local military and élites. Washington in turn had little choice but to hold back its suspicions of Castro, in an effort to appear both pro-democratic and anti-Batista.

There was a certain amount of impassioned anti-Castro opinion at HMA, though somewhat defensive and less than vocal in its stance, and Fidel's detractors did not necessarily support the current government. In fact, almost no one publicly admitted to favoring the Batista régime, and Castro's guerrillas were about the only effectively organized opposition at that time. Still, I remember a middle-class Afro-Cuban student, with whom I buddied on leaveless weekends, dismissing Fidel Castro as "that son of a bitch." I've sometimes since wondered what he meant, what in particular it was about Fidel that had prompted such a response.

At one point a Fidelista food fight broke out in the dining hall. Some cadets got to dipping wads of bread in their water glasses, hurling them about while shouting Castroite slogans.

Meanwhile, outside the school walls, the political situation rapidly deteriorated and became tenser by the day, with power outages and occasional bombs in movie theaters or other public places. One climactic event was the mysterious assassination of the head of Batista's hated secret police, the SIM (Servicio de Inteligencia Militar). The incident sent shock waves through HMA; it elicited constant talk, whispers that ruffled the quiet of early-morning formation. By spring 1957, political discussion had grown so intense and heated that, at lunch one day, a top school official announced over the loudspeaker system an indefinite ban on "all conversations dealing with political subjects" anywhere on HMA premises.

Many years thereafter I'd encounter in print the names and faces of some of my schoolmates or their families, from both sides of the divide—as Fidelista officials in some capacity (e.g., Chafik Homero Saker, a diplomat at the Cuban UN Mission who was expelled by the U.S. in the late 1960s), or as counterrevolutionaries (such as the Babún brothers, onetime big landowners in Oriente province, who led a commando raid on the island in 1971). To this day I come across references to HMA alumni who've had books published (for instance, Sergio Díaz-Briquets, a professor in the U.S. and a scholar of Cuban medical advances under the revolution), or who have otherwise involved themselves in cultural activities outside Cuba (such as Vicente Dopico, an artist, or Carlos Alberto Montaner, a novelist and anti-Castro publicist living in Spain).

When I was at Havana Military Academy, of course, these guys were merely my classmates, barracks mates, fellow cadets and not much else. That they belonged to various segments of the Cuban élite was a concern that scarcely crossed my mind or mattered to me. Now I feel an odd sense of amazement at having shared study halls, platoon lines, and joke-telling sessions with some well-placed whilom teens from Cuba, the island's future notables or vocal émigrés-to-be.

Sometime during my first year at HMA I learn to play the series of rhythm riffs and melodies that the school drum-and-bugle corps performs at key formations and Friday parades. There are five each of such musical sequences, one of them being section B of John Philip Sousa's "Semper Fidelis." I don't remember how, but at some point I get a bugle of my own. By the end of second term I've joined the musical corps as a regular member.

Presumably because of that experience and because of a lack of anybody else with the academic record to fill the post, in my sophomore year I'm promoted—stripes and all—to band sergeant first-class. (Kanani in turn is raised to corporal within the school's nonmusical ranks.) So, for the first time in my life, I've found a musical role of sorts. Needless to say, I relish the sensation of marching at the head of the ensemble, my right hand marking time with a baton, my left periodically signaling changes in drum riff or calling for a specific brass tune.

Kanani and I still dislike being at HMA, especially after having spent Christmas and summer vacations in Puerto Rico, where we've been showered with our mother's loving warmth and the wondrous company of our baby sister. But the simple fact of familiarity with HMA's ways and rituals, combined with our military promotions, allow us to negotiate the everyday jungle more adequately during our second year, help us feel as if we're somebody at the school.

The start of each successive term, though, still puts us in a blue funk. We exchange morbid utterances—"Six months! How'll we survive them so far from home?"—long before boarding the DC-3 from San Juan to Cuba in January of 1956. When you're eleven and fourteen, half a year can seem like an eternity.

In a scene I'll never forget, we're picked up at Havana airport later that year, in September, by our step-aunt and step-uncle. Following a collective automobile ride in near-total silence, we're temporarily dropped off in the empty Havana apartment, alone, before our imminent return to HMA.

And then a twelve-year-old Kanani, seated at the edge of his sheetless bed, breaks into bitter and uncontrolled tears. Staring down at the floor, amid convulsive sobs he blurts out how much we as a family mean to him, how he'll never forget Mom and Valerie and me . . .

Because of my own lacks and faults, I simply don't know how to deal with my brother's sincere outpouring. I neither hug him nor comfort him nor say something loving in return. I just sit there across from him, listening and doing nothing.

Now, decades later, as I remember and write about myself remembering, I realize Kanani's tear-drenched outburst was a simple, intense, once-in-a-lifetime expression of family feelings and kinship solidarity that, at the time, I failed to understand. Burdened then with an emotional intelligence that was close to nil, I was wanting in the most basic notions of responding to human sentiment, was lacking in the most ordinary means of showing fellow affection. Oh, to be able to turn back the clock to that one moment, to hold Kanani in my arms and cry along with him and tell him how moved I am by his feeling about the three of us that way! But I could not. Something big had happened between my brother and me, and yet I didn't understand it.

Given our ongoing uprootedness and serial displacements, the only long-range objectives Kanani and I can look forward to are the vacations with our mom and sister back in Hato Rey. So, when our dad conveys to us sometime in November of 1956 that Kanani and I won't be visiting P.R. during the upcoming Christmas holidays, we greet the news with consternation. And in response we hatch a plan: from our arrival in September we've already got the return halves of our round-trip Delta Chicago & Southern tickets, with return dates open. On a free weekend we secretly go to a Delta office and confirm reservations for a flight in mid-December.

Our escape is set for the morning after school lets out. No one on earth knows except us two. The appointed date slowly comes. In the 5 a.m. darkness we quietly close the apartment door behind us, and, suitcases and all, sneak down the stairs in silence, to avoid waking up our step-aunt and step-uncle. Once out of the building we walk stealthily along the deserted streets until we reach Quinta Avenida, the central artery of Miramar.

Suddenly two plainclothes agents from the SIM pull up in front of us. Obviously they're suspicious of anyone carrying luggage in the wee hours. They emerge from their car. We are terrified, and wonder if they know what we're up to. But, after thoroughly searching every inch and corner of our bags, they taciturnly wave us on. Nervous and relieved, we hail the first available cab to Havana Airport.

The trip itself proves uneventful. Our flight touches down, as expected, in midafternoon. Throughout the entire adventure, though, we're worried about the aftermath. What will Dad do in retaliation?

No one's at our Mallorca Street place when we get there and park our bags. Mom is at work. Valerie's at nursery school. So Kanani and I go out to see neighborhood friends. Misgivings continue. Will Mom throw a fit? As I saunter home again I nervously rehearse a few conciliatory phrases to say to Mom. "I'll wash the dishes. Do the wash. Anything to make up for it."

But I know everything's fine when, as I trudge anxiously up the front steps, she throws open the front door and, enthusiastically crying out my nickname, gives me a spontaneous hug. Her greeting sets the tone for a three-week break we all now spend together.

Years later, I'll learn that Mom actually felt proud of our having taken matters into our own hands—a sentiment that, for the sake of safeguarding parental authority, she chose to keep to herself at the time.

Still, there remain worries about reprisals from Dad once he's received Mom's informational cablegram. (She'd begun her first draft with, "CHILDREN RAN AWAY. . . ," then decided to soften the opening.) I too send him a conciliatory cable, followed by contrite letters. I even go so far as to ask if he might discontinue our HMA schooling and have us stay in P.R. (Privately I fantasize about returning to Espíritu Santo.)

But there are no retaliatory measures against us from our father, no furious phone calls, not even a written reprimand—presumably because of a serious imbroglio that he's having in Caracas with the law, an episode that will land him in jail for a brief spell. (Kanani and I won't find out about this incident until the following year.) Instead Dad simply has Mom pay for our new one-way tickets back to La Habana.

This time, though, the two of us will board the plane in a livelier mood than usual. Then, back at HMA, Kanani and I, in punishment for our shocking misdeed, are demoted to private first-class and ordinary sergeant, respectively. The news is read amid the official lunchtime announcements. And yet I'm utterly indifferent to my downward shift in status. Couldn't care in the slightest.

Every afternoon during sports period, a mauve-colored bus belonging to Ruston Academy, the American school in Havana, drives by on the road skirting HMA's front grounds. Sometimes I'm standing in the area, alone or with fellow cadets. Through the chain-link fence we watch the bus approach, stop, and move on.

The American kids can be heard chirping in their singsong voices. Occasionally, not far from us, a few gringas might get off. We find them exotic in their plaid skirts and casual loafers. Of course we all envy the girls' civilian freedoms, but the fact of their being American inevitably adds to the lure. *Las chiquitas de Rooston,* as they're referred to by the cadets, help punctuate the afternoon and also provide a topic for conversation. By pure chance, I'll discover a few years later that, from an academic standpoint, Ruston was among the American high schools that were most highly regarded by U.S. college admissions officers.

About American girls and general U.S. sexual mores, the HMA students entertain notions that can only be described as fantastical. In Cuban life at that time a boy and girl alone together constitutes the exception, not the rule. As a result, the whole U.S. ritual of dating is pretty baffling to my fellow cadets, whose imaginations come up with an entire mythology concerning that alien world.

An earnest, heavyset fellow, perhaps a couple of years older than I, seriously and authoritatively confides to us at the dorm one afternoon the sinister fact that those so-called dates are really polite pretexts for couples getting in some sex on the sly. His Cuban listeners sit in hushed amazement. As for me, I've already read the comic book *A Date with Judy,* and in my heart I know he's wrong; American girls are nice girls. They don't do things like that.

There are also rumors about so-and-so, the Cuban guy who went up north, where he had the pick of any *Americanita* he wanted and led the grand life of a stud. "Those gringas, they love Cubans," someone says off the top of his head.

Inevitably, stereotypes float about to the effect that, actually, those American women, they're all *putas* ("whores"). Or sometimes, in a kind of Orwellian doublethink, I hear from some cadets the opposite idea: that, unlike their steamy, passionate *Cubanas,* American girls are actually frigid, unappealing, and cold.

These assorted myths were fanciful variations on a well-known truth: adolescent girls and boy-girl couples in the U.S. already enjoyed far more freedom of movement than did most respectable Hispanic-American youths, who still clung to ancestral Iberian mores of family propriety and residual Catholic ideals of female chastity. In the Latin America where I grew up, teenaged couples always had either an adult chaperone to watch over them or a friend somewhere within shouting distance.

Today, in urban areas at least, the differences between north and south in matters of permissiveness have been much reduced, even abolished. Back then, though, the sexual and courtship customs of young sprouts in the nearby colossus inevitably aroused fascination, not to mention awe, among their opposite numbers in La Habana. And so you got these flights of interpretive fancy, outright delusions construed as fact. (It somewhat resembled the odd bit of erotic folklore that took hold in U.S. college circles during the 1960s, when Sweden was regarded as a paradise of free love, a fabulous Nordic land where Swedish girls would go to bed with anybody at any time, just on a whim.)

On the other hand, the negative visions that HMA cadets sporadically expressed about U.S. life were by and large fairly accurate. The forced segregation and legalized racism in the South. The actual and threatened use of atomic bombs in warfare. The aggressive, imperial policy in Latin America. The low-quality education. Crime.

It was from an advanced student called Villaurreta that I first heard the impassioned observation, "There's no country more crime-ridden than the United States." The idea sounded simply bizarre to me. When I reported the comment to my father and Mary on their next visit to Havana, they explained the existence of higher crime rates in the U.S. as a consequence of there being more people. And yet, whatever its worth then, that eighteen-year-old Cuban's sweeping condemnation is a sober and indisputable statement of fact today, when American homicide rates stand at five figures per year, as opposed to a couple hundred in England and maybe a dozen or so in Japan.

As the end of our second year at HMA approached, the possibility of Kanani and me being transferred to some other school, somewhere else, had frequently been discussed. In May it's finally decided: for the fall of '57, Kanani and I will start living with Dad and Mary in Caracas. We'll also be attending the American school there. I peruse the school prospectus with genuine excitement. And I field questions from fellow cadets, who ask me the name of the institution.

"Colegio Americano," I reply. American High School.

"¡Yes, yes! But," they press on in frustration, "¿what's it called?"

So I explain to them on repeated occasions that the generic phrase "Colegio Americano" is indeed how the place is officially dubbed. I imagine myself riding in a Ruston-type bus. When replying to HMA schoolmates' queries, I mention that local U.S. school as a shorthand analogy.

At the time, it seems as if our father is finally responding to our wishes to bail out of the hated military academy and start attending American schools. More likely, though, his decision has been prompted by the growing political turmoil in Cuba and perhaps even by some basic concerns for his two sons' physical safety.

Whatever the case, Kanani and I are overjoyed at getting away from the forced regimentation, and also at the prospect of having a home life in Caracas, however imperfect. In June, wearing light civvies on a bright, sunny day, we shake hands with a number of teachers and students, and actually feel twinges of sadness at leaving Havana Military Academy behind as we offer final farewells to individuals we like.

"See?" Mary says as we walk on the greensward for the last time, heading for the front gate. "I told you guys that you'd come to enjoy this place."

Family Interludes in Puerto Rico

"Hope these next few days go by as fast as our weekends do!"

During our two long years at HMA, Kanani and I will often toss around such conceits, like little boys tallying the days till the arrival of Santa Claus. The countdown in this instance is for our long-awaited date of departure from Cuba, and on to P.R. either for Christmas break or summer vacation.

Life on the smaller island now signifies our legitimate escape and place of rest, far from the solitude and severity of La Habana. The house on Mallorca Street has become the symbol of our childhood idyll, with our mom and sister as the emblems of affection in a loveless world. Our old neighborhood is a community that we think ourselves part of.

So we play these numbers games in anticipation of the return trips.

Our journey, on a large, two-propeller plane from Delta Chicago & Southern (as it is then known), will grow familiar with repetition. The long, bumpy flights cover a swath above the Greater Antilles at a poky 200 mph. After cruising over Cuba's north coast, we come in for our first stop at my birthplace, Haiti's capital of Port-au-Prince. From the descending aircraft, the endless sight of vast, barracks-like slums presents a wrenching, dismal spectacle. It's the hemisphere's most impoverished nation, as I've learned in my HMA geography class.

Our next port of call is the capital city of the Dominican Republic, then modestly designated Ciudad Trujillo by the nation's reigning dictator, Rafael Leónidas Trujillo. Gigantic red block letters top the air terminal's roof, greeting one and all with the proclamation, "DIOS EN EL CIELO, TRUJILLO EN LA TIERRA" ("God in His Heaven, Trujillo on Earth").

Trujillo and Batista have an ongoing regional rivalry. From profs as well as students at HMA I've heard occasional talk about security threats from the neighboring *generalísimo*. The brutalities of the Dominican régime are known even to a prepolitical kid like me, though I'm more familiar with its comical excesses, notably the extravagant amours of the tyrant's two sons, Ramfis and Radamés, both named after Egyptian pharaohs. Ramfis gained special notoriety when he purchased a red Mercedes convertible and had it sent by airfreight as a gift to movie star Zsa-Zsa Gabor out in Hollywood.

(It took my adult scholarly researches into the real-life sources of García Márquez's *The Autumn of the Patriarch* for me to learn in detail about the absurd horrors of the Trujillo clan. Their autocratic rule, which started in 1930, would last through 1961, when the CIA finally saw the strongman as a liability and had him unceremoniously bumped off on a country road, as publicly documented by the Frank Church committee hearings in the U.S. Senate in 1976.)

When we finally arrive at San Juan airport, Mom will meet us, and Kanani and I both feel wondrously glad to see her. This daylong island hopping is a fixed itinerary we'll do some seven times in either direction, until June 1957. On our very first return trip from Havana in December of 1955, though, the much-awaited family reunion has its touches of uncertainty, unreality. We haven't set eyes on Mother and Valerie since shortly after my eighth-grade graduation earlier that year.

Mom looks different—thinner, somber. To our surprise, our baby sister now speaks grammatically, in full sentences. And with phonemes from Boston, where she'd recently spent the summer with Mom.

Still, I'm home. Not just with the family fold, but on what I've begun seeing as native ground. Being sent into a sort of exile, paradoxically, has made me feel more Puerto Rican. I'll often second some old playmates—now in the prime of adolescence—whenever they make earnest, emphatic assertions concerning the good, happy life on their little island. The place where they belong. Where they fully intend to stay.

Kanani's reactions to these return trips are more confused, for several reasons. First, there's our new, "other" family. Early on during our first Christmas break, he whispers to me as we sit alone on the front porch, "Don't tell Mommy about Mary."

Since June, by tacit agreement, neither of us has dared convey to Mom the news of Dad's second spouse. Now, though, Kanani explicitly seeks to deny the situation. We cling desperately to the denial till Mom casually approaches us on that same porch one afternoon and asks, "By the way, boys, I was wondering. Has your father remarried?"

Ironically, she's probably learned of it months earlier through the gringo grapevine. Yet the three of us had eased into this strange game of gaps and silences.

Outside home, my brother's life as a returnee is exciting yet tense, fraught each time with dangers and imponderables. The readjustments to friends, who are growing as fast as he is, stoke in him fears of rejection. Past rivalries with homeboys his own age are inevitably rekindled. But he also can impart to them and younger kids the knowledge of gymnastics he's picked up at HMA.

Among his most vivid memories of our Puerto Rican interludes is a moment akin to that mystical experience in Havana: his lolling alone on a tree branch across the house on Mallorca Street late one summer afternoon, and loudly belting out "Sixteen Tons." A mineworker's song, it has metamorphosed into a 1950s hit via a superb minimalist rendition by Tennessee Ernie Ford. (How many U.S. teenagers, when singing and dancing to Ford's spare, soulful version, will realize it's actually a protest song? Certainly I can't, won't, don't.)

Kanani's and my studies abroad, even if only in Cuba, do give us an odd standing back in P.R. Simply describing our strange other existence makes for lively conversation.

Meanwhile, each time we return, neighbors, friends, and former playmates present a changed aspect. Quondam little girls, with whom we'd once played tag or hide-and-seek, in just six months have blossomed into young women.

Paco, the guy who'd first taunted me and whose nose I'd altered with a baseball bat, casually shows up on my block during my first Christmas holiday, his face now sadly transformed by a terrible case of acne. Over the next couple of years, he and a couple of neighborhood guys will become proficient on clarinet and violin. I envy them their musical good luck. All I've managed is to pick up some drum and bugle riffs . . .

One of those summers I'll read a newspaper story about a forthcoming concert by violinist Jaime Laredo. It mentions, in passing, that his parents left their native Bolivia for New York, the better to encourage his musical training. As I reach the end of the article I ask inside myself, "And why couldn't *my* parents do something like that?" Or, "Why hasn't my father even lifted a finger to help me be a musician in Puerto Rico, let alone in New York?" I won't know the answer to such questions until decades later.

Summer not being baseball season in the Antilles, that distraction is not available to me on these trips home. So I turn to my usual other activities: listening to the classical-music station (at home, by myself, guidebook in hand). Sitting on neighborhood fences and front porches with friends. Sharing my whole new set of Cuban dance steps at friends' parties.

There's also religion. In Cuba, thanks to HMA, I've discovered Sunday Mass, figured out its ritual sequence. Now, in Puerto Rico, I start attending the church near my local alma mater, sometimes catching a glimpse of former schoolmates seated in distant rows. Without receiving any sacraments or having been rechristened into the fold, I find myself becoming inwardly devout, praying at length to God before falling asleep at night. I drop by the church during spare moments to commune with Him tearfully, entreating Him for improved life and family circumstances (though I don't use precisely those terms). The prayers take on a special intensity during the melancholy nights just before our departures to Cuba, when—within a large, attractive, well-lit place of worship—I'm the only worshiper present, kneeling at a church pew.

Meanwhile I continue my reading. I chuckle over American joke-sters like Robert Benchley (*My Ten Years in a Quandary*), Ambrose Bierce (*The Devil's Dictionary*), and H. Allen Smith (*Low Man on a Totem Pole*). I dip regularly into such collections as Bennett Cerf's *Shake Well before Using* and that thick mainstay of middle-class end tables at the time, *A Treasury of American Humor.* Joke books serve me as a refuge, much as music does. Occasionally I'll drive my mother to distraction with the many gags I recite to her from those volumes. ("Hey, Mom, listen to this joke!")

I also read with fascination Edward Bellamy's utopian novel *Looking Backward,* and get hooked on Perry Mason, reading so many of those gaudy, thin, two-bit pocket books from Earl Stanley Gardner's pen that his formulaic plots become comforting and his cartoon-like characters—Lt. Tragg, secretary Della Street, lawyer-cum-sleuth Mason himself—begin to feel like old friends.

There is, I further recall, a memoir of some years in a mental institution, *Asylum,* by one William Seabrook. I'm halfway through the 25-cent paperback when Mom casually tells me Seabrook isn't that good an author. (I finish reading it anyway. It never occurs to me that she might have the book because she'd recently put in time in such a place herself.)

And there are the pop-therapy titles of the era. *Be Glad You're Neurotic. Psychiatry for the Curious.* They exemplify a distinctly American synthesis—part self-help, part social reflection, part moralizing, and of course huge dollops of psychologizing—that is attaining middlebrow genre status with the U.S. importation and adoption of Freud.

I picked up and read those books mainly because they were in the house, either as Mom's property or as items left behind by Dad. And it's not that my mother was a middlebrow or vulgar sort of person. On the contrary, her intelligence, refinement, and cultural inclinations were among the reasons for my parents' divorce. (One of the particulars she'd cite in connection with their breakup was Dad's parting comment to her: "Well, now you can hang around with all your egghead friends.") Hers was, if anything, a tale of talents that were stunted as a result of personal uprooting, a terrible marriage, and, finally, abrupt abandonment by a first husband who had lacked even the slightest appreciation of her best traits.

Curiously, for the remainder of the decade she would keep mum to her parents in Hawaii about the divorce, indeed somehow prop up the fiction that she was still with my dad! Only when she visited Honolulu in the early 1960s—her first return "home" since she'd left there, married and pregnant, in 1941—did her Asian-Pacific next of kin get the full story straight from her, although their daughter Leila had heard vague rumors about it through a mutual acquaintance. It would be years, moreover, before we kids ever found out about the charade she'd managed to keep up over a five-year period. As to Mom's motive for so elaborate a shadow play—deep shame? fear of her folks saying "I told you so"? a sincere desire not to upset her elderly mother?—Kanani and I will never know.

During the summer of 1955, while Kanani and I were with Dad in Caracas, Mom went up with Valerie to Radcliffe College and enrolled herself in its well-known Publishing Procedures Course. It was her first return to the classroom since 1940, when, at my father's endless urgings and much against her parents' wishes, she'd dropped out from the University of Hawaii in senior year, to accompany him and then support him on his overseas ventures.

Her decision to take the Radcliffe course had both professional and financial motives. Dad had obtained his divorce papers in Cuba, and was beyond the reach of Puerto Rico's family laws. The guy was proving to be obdurately stingy and unreliable with child support and alimony. So she needed to acquire credentialed and marketable skills in order to pull out of a situation dangerously close to poverty.

As a result of that training (a positive experience, about which she enthusiastically reminisced for years afterwards), Mom soon landed a job as society-page editor of the *San Juan World Journal*. A new English-language daily, funded by the island's leading newspaper, *El Mundo*, it was a predecessor of sorts to today's respected *San Juan Star*. For a couple of years Mom interviewed all kinds of VIPs—socialites, politicians, visiting dignitaries—for its columns, and ran features under her own byline, Carmen Bell.

Some of her colleagues would eventually achieve national reputations. Bill Dorvillier, her boss, received a Pulitzer Prize in the early 1960s for his editorials calling for separation of church and state, in response to the prayer in the public schools controversy of the time. And among her fellow staff members was a young reporter by the name of William Kennedy; already working at becoming a novelist, he later carved out an evocative slice of U.S. literary geography from the hidden corners of his native Albany, New York.

During my mother's tenure at the *World Journal*, there were always issues of the paper lying about the house. I often sat around reading them out on the fence or the front porch, partly from genuine curiosity about their contents, partly as another way of being the gringo kid on the block, the one who read in English. I remember first encountering strange, exotic place-names—"Dien Bien Phu" and "Suez"—prominently displayed across its front headlines. The columns by, say, Earl Wilson and Robert Ruark provided the occasion for reflection or laughter, though I didn't realize that, in the States, they weren't just names but syndicated icons—as famous in their time as Russell Baker and Anthony Lewis would be in theirs—with daily faithful numbering in the millions. To this day I much prefer sampling and savoring a commentary on events that demonstrates some personal touch. Better that than sifting through the dry, unadorned facts, facts, facts of supposedly "objective" news.

Several of Mom's friends from her married days remained loyal to her, even though, in those days, getting divorced tended to make a woman a pariah. Indeed, Mom continued to gab with her pals over the phone and on mutual visits, and they'd correspond, off and on, for decades. There was also a small, bohemian, arty crowd she mingled with, she presumably having met them through her journalistic activities. Now, though, thanks to her various society contacts, she also began moving partly within a circle of truly rich, classically blond and ruddy-faced Americans in San Juan. In some measure she probably came to think she was one of them. Despite my youth and innocence, during the few times I saw her in such company, their faces and mannerisms—or so I thought—suggested condescension, a sense of their having this Oriental girl as a mascot in their midst.

As for Mom, she seemed to have temporarily accepted her new crowd's delusions about the role of the U.S. in this world. At one point she assured me that if ever Kanani and I faced an outbreak of civil strife while overseas, we should go around wearing a small American flag, as a symbol of peace and democracy, just to protect ourselves from attack.

Of course, these are only my early adolescent impressions, interpreted with hindsight. I'm sure the full picture was more complex, contradictory. Mom fully favored African independence, for instance, and was passionately against the segregationist tyranny in the Bible Belt states. But I do know that, in ways that were not right for her, my dear, loving mother was in the grip of certain then-prevailing U.S. myths about American benevolence and belovedness. That, like a good colonial, she accepted them pretty much uncritically at the time. Just as I did for quite a while.

It's in 1955, the first of our Christmas interludes, when Kanani and I meet Steve. That's a nickname for Estevan, from New Mexico. A ranger in the U.S. Forest Service, he is stocky and well built, about five feet, six inches in height, with mixed Hispanic and Indian features; he's been sent to Puerto Rico on an eighteen-month work stint.

With the island's shift in status during the 1950s from colonial possession to affiliated Commonwealth, the administration of public lands is being restructured. The lands themselves are undergoing either redistribution to local authorities or conversion to environmental research facilities. As a bilingual Mexican–American and forestry professional, Steve is the individual officially designated to assist in carrying out the operation.

He likes Puerto Rico yet is often baffled by the humidity, which, after the dry heat of the American Southwest, he finds uncomfortable. The tropical lack of seasons also has its disorienting effects and occasionally causes him to lose track of chronology, since he can't place events within time frames such as "sometime last spring."

Mother and he had first met when, on a casual visit she was paying to a female pal, the battery on her car went dead. Steve, then fresh from New Mexico and renting a room in the pal's large house, helped her out with the battery. She first mentions him in passing on the drive home from our arrival that December 1955. Later on she'll introduce him to us as "a friend." We characterize him thus to our neighborhood chums. They josh ironically, "Yeah, sure, 'friend.'"

Steve drops by the house often during our vacations. A warm, kind-hearted man, from the start he is considerably more attentive to the three of us (and to Mom) than our biological dad ever was. He plays games with Valerie, buys her toys, and shepherds Kanani and me on outings. He takes us swimming at the pool of his apartment building, the Darlington. (Then the tallest edifice in the area, it'll be dwarfed in subsequent decades by an urban tangle of office and bank towers.)

There's more. With his superb craftsman's skills, Steve zealously takes on every manner of repair and construction chores for our mother—for instance, he single-handedly rebuilds her house closets. We all like him; Mom sometimes hints vaguely at his expressed desire for marriage. But, given the many current imponderables, as well as her own caution in the wake of Dad's cruel divorce, we scarcely have reason to believe him part of our future. Still, even at so early a date, Steve has grown into a normal, informal member of our family life whenever Kanani and I are away from Dad and military school.

Inevitably, a major activity during these Puerto Rican interludes consists of my going—usually, though not always, alone—to crude, low-budget films from Hollywood. A decaying, rundown theater in a nearby neighborhood features some flickery, black-and-white sci-fi serials as regular matinées. I attend *los episodios* (as we call them) week after week, more for their imaginative astronomy and simple continuity than because of any artistic qualities in the space operas themselves.

I'll also come upon a certain other grade-B, "teen" subgenre that will exert an unfortunate sway over me. One particularly vivid specimen—its title escapes me—goes something like this: there's a new girl at the archetypal (white) high school of an idyllic small town in Anywhere, U.S.A. Pretty and cute, with straight blond hair, half-moon-shaped glasses, and well-shaped legs, she also spouts science, reads poetry, and listens to classical music. Yes, this girl's real smart. Indeed, a "brain." And therefore an arrogant, stuck-up little twit. With her superior airs, she snubs her cheerfully smiling schoolmates and constantly wounds them with her sarcastic barbs. Ah, but, in time, the insufferable brat is won over by the caring efforts of her happy and normal peers, who initiate her into the true joys of teen life and rock-and-roll music. At a house party, our heroine finally sees the light! Tossing off her shoes, setting aside her eyeglasses, and joining in with the ecstatically jitterbugging crowd, she realizes the error of her ways and puts all that contemptible "brain" stuff forever behind her.

I'll encounter several variants of this plot in movies and other media during my Puerto Rican vacations, and thereafter, too. In my quest for legitimate values and for a society to which I might belong, I'll slowly and unconsciously assimilate this vision of U.S. high-school existence as one long party, as endless fun and games. I'll also start wondering idly if other, more serious realms are indeed as pretentious and hoity–toity as those quickie celluloids suggest. Where this leaves me—an Asian-looking, Spanish-speaking lover of books and classical music who wears corrective glasses—is a question that as yet fails to cross my unsettled mind.

As summer of '57 rolls on, further changes lie in store for Kanani and me and for my family as a whole.

One morning we all go see Steve off at San Juan airport for his return flight to the U.S., his work mission now accomplished. My mom says good-bye, showing no special emotion as far as I can see.

Meanwhile, the *World Journal* has been recently discontinued, for business reasons. Mom is again without work or steady income. Presumably she's scraping by on Dad's sporadic payments, though we're too young and/or confused—all three of us—to really understand her situation. (When, in the mid-1990s, I sift through Mom's papers, I'll come across her lay-off notice: just two lines of typewritten text on a half-sheet of yellowed paper and signed by *El Mundo*'s venerable publisher, Angel Ramos. Deepest regrets. We're ceasing operations.

That sort of thing. I've no recollection of Mom's writing or talking about the job loss to Kanani and me.)

What my brother and I do know is that, come summer's end, we aren't going back to HMA. That alone is sufficient comfort to us at the time. In my mind I entertain the fantasy that life at the Colegio Americano de Caracas—my first time ever at a regular U.S. school—will be just like what I've seen in those teen flicks. Classes conducted in English. Recesses with Americans. And healthy doses of *Mad Magazine* humor. That's what's in store for Kanani and me. Plus lots of rock-and-roll dancing and parties galore.

On Being Gringo in Caracas

It's past midnight. Some slightly boozed-up gringo boys roam casually down the hill, five, maybe six abreast. Cracking the typical teen jokes, they're returning from a pre-Christmas dance party thrown at Academia La Castellana, a small-sized American school located in the upper-middle-class enclave of La Castellana. They've had more than a few cups previously and are about to imbibe from someone's flask, when the sudden sound of a speeding, honking vehicle startles them. The group moves aside.

A bevy of rich, slick Venezuelans, who'd also been at the school bash, go barreling by in their luxury machine, almost sideswiping one of the young Yanks in the process. A long, tall, rugged type among the Americans, known for his grungy gray windbreaker and himself an object of lust to many a local *gringuita* teen, yells out, "Come back here and try that!"

The auto stops. Screeches into reverse. Zooms back up the hill. Some notorious Venezuelan toughs emerge. An honest-to-goodness rumble rapidly ensues, complete with sticks and chains and body blows, along with bruises and some blood wounds, though without serious injuries.

The clash soon fizzles out, a standoff. No one claims victory as the Latino adversaries, taking their unceremonious leave, peel off toward their presumed destination, the lights of Avenida Miranda, a central artery several blocks down the road. For the three-week break to come, news of the skirmish will stoke collective passions, becoming the number-one topic of everyday talk among American teens in Caracas. Just one more episode in the ongoing rivalry between two contiguous tribes: well-heeled Venezuelans vs. well-off overseas gringos.

As for me, I'd been present at that very same party at Mrs. Hayes's School (as we usually call it) but chanced to depart alone, just about a half-hour before the others did. When I first find out about the incident at some gathering or other, and then hear my American classmates endlessly describe it, replay it, and constantly comment upon it with expressions of shock and moral outrage, I'll feel relieved at not having had to choose sides in so pointless a battle. I won't say so out loud, though.

Presemester assembly has just adjourned at Colegio Americano. We're all filing out from its green-trimmed, balconied exterior halls into its spacious, unpaved courtyard. As we amble under the high, radiant Caracas sun, I talk casually in Spanish with a short, wiry Venezuelan, a sophomore who's also new to the school. We're maybe a few phrases into our conversation when the guy asks me, "Are you Cuban?"

I duly explain.

Not surprisingly, after two years' living on that island, its accent and speech patterns have rubbed off on me. Complete strangers could now think of me as Cuban.

I'm fifteen and a half and ready to embark as a junior at my first secular, civilian, American school thus far. (No uniforms! What an odd sensation.) The human environment seems intriguing. Blood relatives aside, I've never previously spent much time around Americans on anything like a regular basis. Now, as the academic year unfolds, I find myself sharing classroom and corridor space with those Americans and their tall frames, big smiles, and short blond hair. Some of these guys, to my surprise, are bilingual and Caracas-born.

Others scarcely know Spanish even after spending years in this country.

In addition there are the Venezuelans, plus Latin expatriates from elsewhere. They're mostly fluent in both Spanish and English and, in their outlook, more North American than Hispanic. Their tastes in clothes and music tend toward U.S. styles; they play baseball, not soccer; they go to Hollywood films and only rarely to Mexican ones; and they have their sights firmly set on attending colleges up north instead of in Venezuela or elsewhere in Latin America. Any political ideas that they (we) entertain are of a vaguely centrist, secular, somewhat apathetic U.S. variety. Paradoxically, they are Third Culture Kids, though from the host country rather than overseas.

Further components of the high-school population, which totals approximately 175, include kids from the then-British colonies of Jamaica and Guiana, and a few overseas Europeans (French, Italians, Dutch) who are trilingual and at the time quite enigmatic to me. During my second year, the roster will be additionally swelled by some quadrilingual Egyptians whose families—I'm only vaguely aware— have gone into exile as a result of the Nasser regime.

By the first week of school I've pretty much chosen the friends and mates I'll spend time with for the next couple of years: a next-door neighbor of mixed Hungarian and Castilian descent. A swarthy Venezuelan from the distant oil town of Maracaibo. A Puerto Rican actually named Carlos Fuentes (no relation to the Mexican novelist who'll become famous within a few years). Later the circle will include the two movie-star-handsome sons of an English-French couple; like the other Anglos I hang around with, they've spent most of their lives in Caracas, identify themselves as Venezuelan, and alternate effortlessly between English and Spanish in their conversation.

Everyone in my male "crowd" is, within that particular, closed environment, your fairly typical high-school teenager: fond of parties and dancing, neither bookish nor arty, untroubled by personal eccentricities or by any darker, deeper concerns, and either ethnically Hispanic or born and raised in Latin countries.

The regular Americans—the towering, broad-shouldered, athletic-looking, cool guys—live in another world. They seem like a breed apart. One fellow, a dashingly handsome Hollywood type, drives on occasion to school and to teen socials in his Thunderbird convertible. My Latin group and I try to avoid these folks when seeing them on the street. It's not as if they behave nastily toward us—if anything, they're invariably pleasant, polite, even engaging. It's more that we're intuitively, inarticulately aware of a vast breach between Us and Them. As a matter of fact, the Thunderbird man is unusually outgoing and friendly, and is a talented stage actor besides; yet some of us resent his bevy of admiring girls and his casual air of privilege. In time we'll find out that he suffers from cancer of the neck—a condition that eventually will claim Jim's life before age thirty. The fancy sports car, then, was presumably Jim's parents' way of giving him the very best while he still lived . . . To us back then, though, to a bunch of Americanized Latinos in our midteens, he represents the *gringos* plus everything they've got that we don't.

Right from the beginning of my two-year period in Caracas, I start juggling these issues of identity. It's a question I'd never confronted before. And now, in a brief conversation on the balcony of our apartment with my dad that September, I describe to him these vague feelings, saying something along the lines of "I realize now I'm a Latino at heart."

He merely echoes my words, noncommittally. "So you're a Latino."

Our discussion ends there. But the exchange is nonetheless the first time I'm seriously broaching the subject of my own identity with anyone at all. From that day on, the questions of "What am I?" and also "How Latin, and how American, am I?" will preoccupy me, shaping and bedeviling my conscious existence. At school and school-related events, Anglo classmates think of me as Latin, whereas my Latin buddies sometimes tease and mock me as a gringo. It's a dilemma I'll continue to live with for the rest of my life, if in progressively subtler and more complex ways. That starting year at the Colegio Americano de Caracas, though, is the first time I'm fully aware of my inner debate.

Curiously, during that truncated chat my dad will make no attempt to argue on behalf of my "Americanness." Given his own frequent business dealings up north and his attachment to an idealized United States, his lack of effort in claiming his eldest for the gringo fold seems a bit bewildering.

Besides, I'm in my junior year in high school. That is the time when American middle-class parents start weighing college plans for their children, encouraging them to write to schools, leaf through college catalogs, shop around. Over the next couple of years Dad will do next to nothing in that regard. Nor does he initiate a heart-to-heart discussion about my hopes for a college major. I'm idly considering engineering, mostly because my technically inclined classmates are headed that way. Only once, toward the end of my senior year in Caracas, will my dad speculate that I might not exactly be engineering material, and will actually suggest that I study music instead. This after he has spent most of my life ignoring, blocking, or otherwise discouraging my musical bent.

Sometime during my Caracas phase I come to realize that I'll probably earn my keep in the U.S. as an academic. Of course I've no idea of what that entails, how one prepares for it, what one does besides teach classes. At one point my friend called Carlos Fuentes will ask me, "Well, do you have the contacts to get a job like that?" I say yes although the answer is no. Still, in my mind's eye I can see myself as a professor, walking briskly and alone, casually dressed, in sneakers, amid the verdant slopes and green-shuttered frame houses of some indistinct, unnamed New England campus. No plan, just a recurrent thought . . .

And now, once again, I throw myself zealously into a new social and academic environment. At Colegio Americano I do fairly well in everything from plane geometry (much of it a review of what I'd learned at HMA) to U.S. history and American literature, though the latter is a territory still alien to me.

Meanwhile there are daily rituals to be learned. For the first time in my life, students, not teachers, change classrooms. And on the opening day of class, I duly rise when fielding questions. A considerate Carlos turns around and quietly informs me that, in this non-Catholic institution, you don't stand up when you answer.

From the outset I'm bewildered by the oddities of American education. Electives, for instance, a concept unheard of in most other countries, where choice is minimal, and curricula tend to be fully fixed and common for all students. Similarly, the term "extracurricular activities" sounds well-nigh indecipherable when I first hear it. Then I start singing in weekly chorus and eventually play the role of Captain in a production of *H.M.S. Pinafore* at school chapel. Gilbert and Sullivan's quotable ditties will forever resonate in my mind ("Things are seldom what they seem," and "What, never?" "Well, *hardly* ever!"), all thanks to those extracurriculars plus Mrs. Mock, the English instructor cum passionate musician and intellect who directs the show.

In Cuba, biology was the last and crowning science taught in high school—after botany, zoology, physics, and chemistry. U.S. sophomores, by contrast, start out directly with biology. Because I enroll at Colegio Americano as a junior, I miss out on this fundamental course of study. Only in midlife will I become aware of this huge gap in my knowledge, the accidental result of a difference in national curricula. (To this day I'm all but clueless as to the various parts and functions of an ordinary green plant or flower.)

Strangest of all to me is the personal, caring approach taken by the teachers toward their charges. This particular aspect of U.S. educational style will have a major impact on both my life and Kanani's.

Along with my puzzled fascination at this new setting, I'm shocked at the low level of discourse in the halls and classes. Outside of a couple of math and science courses, little of substance is examined. In a history class, when replying to a question about the causes of World War I, a good-looking Venezuelan-American kid raises his hand and solemnly pronounces, "The causes of the war were political, economic, and social."

End of answer, which, to my amazement, the teacher accepts. Back at HMA, such key issues as imperialism, scrambles for overseas markets, and rivalries between Great Powers were underscored by both profs and textbooks in explaining that bloodbath. Here at Colegio Americano, though, questions of imperial rivalry seem to have vanished. By the same token, anytime the then-Soviet Union comes up as a subject, the automatic formula is to call attention to the country's lack of free speech and elections, and the threat posed to a peaceful West by Moscow's alleged plans for military invasion and atomic attack.

At the Cuban school, by contrast, we'd been furnished a sober, balanced assessment of Soviet advances in education, technology, science, and social welfare. As for the tyrannical regime, well, the Cubans were living under dictatorship, too.

A few instructors at Colegio Americano attempt to stimulate greater cultural and intellectual awareness, but their half-hearted efforts come mostly to naught.

The problem wasn't just these information gaps but also the general atmosphere of frivolity and lack of seriousness prevailing at the school and its affiliated events. Outside of honor roll, few incentives existed to promote serious study, and matters of knowledge and intellect were scarcely recognized, let alone respected, by the students, who openly scorned such enterprises. For the first time, I actually heard terms like "bookworms" and "squares"—known previously to me only from balloons in comic strips—pronounced out loud, and now utilized to refer to myself, or to a shy, studious, bespectacled French girl in my class. Much as in those grade-B movies I'd watched during summers in

Puerto Rico, the atmosphere was so fiercely dominated either by stock intellectual formulas or by extracurriculars that the kinds of learning you might expect from an educational institution got short shrift. (Perhaps Ruston Academy, whose buses I had seen going by every day in Cuba, was better.)

The situation was further aggravated by staffing shortages. There were some fine teachers in English and mathematics, and a few in social studies and history. They tended to be the spouses of locally based U.S. businessmen who took on the job for reasons of their own and did their best under the circumstances. The school had real trouble, though, in recruiting and retaining quality faculty in the sciences. The instructors who were there during my time had been hired on makeshift sorts of arrangements. One of them, her Oxford accent notwithstanding, was manifestly incompetent, if charming. In fact the only position with a regular contract was the physical education slot, filled on a yearly basis by arrangement with the Stateside offices of the YMCA.

These personnel difficulties, in retrospect, are perfectly understandable. How many serious science professionals end up staying for long in an underdeveloped Third World capital like 1950s Caracas? How many would be disposed to share their knowledge of physics or chemistry, at a so-so salary, with a bunch of American or Americanized brats who showed no interest in the subject, routinely misbehaved in class, and even sassed their teachers? Many of those science instructors, in fact, lasted but a few months. One trigonometry teacher—a musician, an international Swiss missionary, the school administrator, and a man of broad culture—railed at us one afternoon, accusing us all of being "uncouth" and "vulgar." He was not wrong.

Still, these problems mattered little. Or were beyond me. What counted was that, at long last, I was at an American school. Taking courses in English—my native tongue. Studying American subjects. I felt home at last, I thought.

Sometime later that year, the Colegio will move lock, stock, and barrel from its location in urban Bello Monte to an isolated hill amid the wilderness of Baruta, at the farthest, southern edge of town. The new site is attractive enough, with its panoramic view of the city valley. Yet it poses inconveniences. Previously, I could walk to and from the Bello Monte campus, which I sometimes did. Now the only way of getting to class is by private wheels or school bus, which picks us all up in the parking lot of the Automercado, a sleek, modern shopping center. Standing at the gateway to the residential Las Mercedes district and purportedly run by Rockefeller interests, the Automercado is the first such American-style temple of consumerism in Caracas. The place also serves typically as a hangout for adolescents. And even more so when it becomes the loading and unloading zone for the Colegio's teenaged hordes.

The move has pained me in some vague way. Here, for the first time, I'm proudly enrolled at a school where I'd wanted to be, and now the grounds are literally being pulled away from under my feet. Shortly after the move has been completed, I quietly pay a visit one Saturday morn to the abandoned Bello Monte campus. I wander through its long halls, brush my fingers against its iron railings, take in the faded dark green of its trim and shutters. And I yearn for it all almost as much as I'd once sat and reminisced longingly about life in Puerto Rico. The new Baruta complex, with its squarish, multileveled design and its more modernistic organization of outside space, seems disorientingly alien by comparison.

Once again, nostalgia has already set in. And after only three months.

Besides the U.S. high school curriculum, Colegio Americano offers the local secondary-education sequence, *liceo* (as in the French *lycée*). It's all given in Spanish and attended exclusively by young Venezuelans. Though we share the same classroom complex, library facilities, and central, open-air snack bar, there's little human or social contact between the two sections. We live and operate in separate worlds.

The elementary schooling of local gringo youngsters is handled by two private institutions. The first is Colegio Campo Alegre, founded with oil-corporation money for the purpose of teaching corporate children. With a solid reputation for academic excellence and good instructors through eighth grade, its impressive physical plant sits atop a hill in the American ghetto of Las Mercedes, just a few minutes' walk from the Automercado.

But Kanani doesn't attend the pricey Campo Alegre. Instead Dad enrolls him at the other U.S. alternative, the Academia La Castellana, or Mrs. Hayes's School, which occupies a large, rambling house in the distant residential district of La Castellana. It's a smaller, cozier, and (I assume) less expensive outfit than its weightier, more prestigious rival.

Despite the intimate setting, my brother isn't spared a few shocks of adaptation. At a snack hour during his first days there, a German woman serves him a little brown sweet the likes of which he's never seen before.

"What's this?" he asks.

With her robust, Teutonic voice and guttural *r* she responds, "Dat, my boy, iss a *braunie!*"

Twelve-year-old Kanani feels as awed and puzzled at being in American surroundings as I do. He too is impressed at how well informed the European students are, several of whom speak at least three languages effortlessly. He too is awed by the Americans' profound sense of security and power, the sheer wealth, that makes them seem a breed apart.

He also has his first direct experiences with racial prejudice when American girls at the school ignore him because of his darker skin, Asian look, or Puerto Rican background. He won't do a whole lot of studying that year and will dwell instead on the frenetic fun and games he's having with his new school friends.

The Venezuelan girls at Colegio Americano for the most part are either upper-class or culturally aloof, even snobbish. They're pretty much inaccessible to my more modestly appointed circle of friends. And so for the first time my social life revolves around events at American kids' homes. Yet another source of bewilderment. My knowledge of Caribbean rhythms, while a novelty for this new environment, is of use only in about a third of the musical numbers played at their weekend parties. I need to pick up the jitterbug steps still associated with rock and roll if I want to dance all night.

Even more bewildering to me are the romantic-erotic mores of my new American crowd.

I've donned coat and tie for my first American party at a schoolmate's house. And I arrive with expectations of sipping, dancing, and chatting. That was how it was done at the island socials. Halfway through the evening, though, the lights are lowered. Couples huddle close in hidden corners. Or they disappear outside into the bushes, behind the trees. Finally it dawns on me that the whole setup exists for the sole purpose of twosomes pairing off and necking (or "making out," to employ the up-to-date slang phrase I'll soon learn and never much like).

What will amaze me over the next few months is the sheer normality, the *ordinariness* of this whole sexual scene. At almost every American house party I go to thereafter, I'll notice some instant couple feverishly smooching (et cetera) on the dance floor here, a girl's legs sprawled out under some beefy guy on a sofa there, and a dark air of desire that hovers over the night's proceedings. And then there are the smooth, conventionally handsome make-out artists of legend. They'll scout the terrain and can usually count on securing the warm touch of a female embrace for a few long hours. So it seems, at least, to this wide-eyed novice.

The routinized physical intimacy comes as a shock to me. In the respectable, traditional Hispanic societies I'd known, the very idea that you could publicly kiss a girl whom you weren't married to or involved with was simply beyond consideration. It takes me two years at the American school to adapt to these new rituals, and I never cease to find the weekend fleshpot freedoms a phenomenon both alluring and disquieting. At the same time, the lofty scorn expressed by Venezuelan girls toward their gringa peers for "allowing themselves to be manhandled," and for being somehow used up and impure before marriage, strikes me as self-righteous and hypocritical.

Given my confusion, there are moments when I'll feel more at ease just chatting with the prostitutes my Latin friends and I meet at the dives where we occasionally drop in after those gringo parties.

The U.S. schools in Caracas and their overlapping social circles are a community apart. They allow you to exist in blissful ignorance of the host country's major issues and events. The sole exception during my first few months is the military dictatorship of Marcos Pérez Jiménez ("P. J.," as he's sometimes dubbed by local Americans), with its atmosphere of relentless, unalloyed fear. Everyone—Venezuelans and foreigners alike—lives in dread of the Seguridad Nacional, the secret police force whose agents are known for plucking individuals from off the street and letting them rot in jail indefinitely.

As a result, you behave cautiously in public. And you make every effort to avoid cops, who are universally loathed and feared. At various moments I'll hear my father and his colleagues, or my teachers and fellow students, all joking nervously about tapped phones or mikes hidden in walls. But everything else about local politics is a big mystery to most of us.

Then, in January 1958, sociopolitical tensions will impinge on our privileged separateness. Few among us know about the details, but, over the past couple of months, a broad coalition of disaffected military sectors and civilian groups—economic leaders, mass organizations, clerics—have jelled into an opposition movement. P. J.'s forces in turn fight back with harsh reprisals and rhetoric.

Suddenly, out of the blue—or so it seems—a 6 p.m. curfew is imposed. The Spanish term for curfew, *toque de queda*, mingles with the

English spoken in the Colegio's halls. Soon thereafter, all schools are shut down till further notice. Without explanation, radio stations air nothing but instrumental classics. (The *Eroica* Symphony is a favorite.) For days on end the sole images on silent TV sets are broadcasters' logos. Finally, the news is announced: General Pérez Jiménez has fled to the United States, his suitcases crammed with American dollars.

The collapse of the dictatorship sparks a collective jubilation out on the streets such as I've never yet witnessed. (It'll be repeated less than a year later when, with the fall of Batista to Fidel Castro's forces, the Cuban expatriate community stages its own public celebration.) Everywhere you see impromptu parades, trucks filled with men shouting and singing, total strangers talking to each other on the streets with relief and even joy.

At the same time, unsettling reports circulate about explosions of popular anger. Buses are burned. Seguridad Nacional thugs are summarily beaten to death by spontaneous vigilante bands.

Meanwhile, at the higher governmental levels a liberal military junta takes shape, headed by Admiral Wólfgang Larrazábal (his first name given him by parents who reputedly liked Mozart). General elections are scheduled for December. Back at our reopened school, I see and hear Venezuelan classmates arguing passionately about Jóvito Villalba and Rómulo Betancourt, legendary activists now reemerging from underground or exile. Local electoral politics, though, seems remote and abstract to us Americans. For us gringos the only change that now matters is the absence of repression and fear.

Though a separate subculture, the Americans in Caracas and at Colegio Americano have their own internal divisions. The differences are pronounced enough to produce strains, tensions, even some heated debates. Only a handful of the Americans at my school qualify as rich. Most do belong somewhere in the upper middle class, though. They inhabit comfortable, single-family homes in Palos Grandes and La

Castellana, California-type enclaves with central boulevards that slope up, steadily and dramatically, to the northern foothills. Or they had settled early on into quaint, red-shingled, Spanish-style dwellings in Las Mercedes and El Rosal. These last two, erstwhile idylls that had once constituted the very edge of Caracas, are now just another set of semiurban districts that spread south of an ever-congested Avenida Miranda, the dividing line between my neighborhood of El Bosque and their more affluent communities. The heads of these American households tend to be small entrepreneurs. They own and run, say, a local chain of laundries. A potato-chip factory. Or a clothing store in the congested, middle-class Sabana Grande shopping area. And there are also the kids whose fathers work at the U.S. Embassy's military mission, drawing a government salary and living in the Las Mercedes–El Rosal area.

These three groups comprise the young Americans who, to a large extent, will set the tone at the school, even for the Latino students enrolled there. They will influence the social life I lead.

Come Christmas and summer, the character of Overseas-American teendom changes drastically when "the kids from the States," as we call them, descend on Caracas for vacation. They're the ones who're attending prestigious prep schools up north. Who formerly spent up to eight years at Campo Alegre and thus have local histories, but who were then sent north for their secondary studies.

Many of us from the Colegio at first resent these returnees. "They're such snobs!" is what we local gringos regularly say about them. Few are vicious or nasty, though, and many in fact are friendly and even fun once you get to know them. The difference is in their style: cool. Smooth. Somehow above it all. Or at least above us. They dress better. Have slicker hair and better posture. Radiate the polish, poise, and self-confidence you pick up at élite schools. Flaunt slightly bigger words or concepts. Make the occasionally weighty pronouncement about the international scene.

But the fundamental difference between us and them is economic. They're children of the corporations. Their fathers are employed at high levels by the petroleum giants and related firms such as Schlumberger, the French manufacturer of oil-exploring equipment. Or their dads work at global powerhouses like General Tire and Sears, Roebuck. They reside within the mansions that line the gently sloping fields of the Caracas Country Club and the Valle Arriba (literally "Up the Valley") Club. And within our world, already separate from the Venezuela that surrounds us, their privileged milieu constitutes yet another world apart from, if sometimes overlapping, ours.

The kids from the States are strictly Christmas and summer fare. Yet throughout the year we frequent their parents' watering holes, if illegally. The hottest spot is the Caracas Theater Club, at the outer edge of Las Mercedes, on a hill just beyond the massive, V-shaped Hotel Tamanaco. My friends and I will often sneak in by climbing the steep, grassy incline and then jumping over the wall. Or we might befriend one of the front gatekeepers, for instance, the kindly, gentle West Indian fellow by the name of Mr. Roberts. If he trusts us enough, he looks the other way as we discreetly file in.

Once inside, we encounter a glistening, open-air, kidney-shaped pool. And Americans everywhere! Swimming and splashing about. Sunbathing on lounge chairs. Playing cards at tables underneath an extensive, varnished wooden shelter, or sipping cocktails at the out-door bar. And all these Americans are precisely what we're not: namely rich, powerful, expensively clad, and absolutely sure of their future. Downstairs in the basement is the club's special pride: a modern, multilane bowling alley, with its own bar as well. Many of the "kids from the States" spend long hours aiming at those tenpins and swilling drinks of their own.

Meanwhile the Theater Club lives up to its name with its periodic theater offerings. I'll attend a creditable production of *Auntie Mame* there. And I'll also turn pages for a team of pianists accompanying the big event of 1959, a two-night run of *Oklahoma!*

By definition the Theater Club is a North American enclave, though a few Venezuelan hangers-on are always, well, hanging around. The Caracas Country Club, on the other hand, is an extensive, forbidding, shadowy sort of place, designed for the upper-upper class. Though it's the next neighborhood over from mine, I scarcely ever set foot within those grounds, save for the rare bike ride on the mysterious district's outer roads.

Then there's the Valle Arriba, the other country club in affluent east Caracas. Many of the urban really rich—Venezuelans, Americans, Europeans—live there. Equipped with a golf course, it boasts wide-open, gently rolling fields that anyone—including wannabes like my mates and myself—can hike across. Arriving at the Old World–style clubhouse and lounge, you see Americans as well as other nationals of all ages, idly playing dominoes and schmoozing.

In my mind's eye I will always associate sunlight and bright colors with the Valle Arriba, darker hues and an enclosed, gated landscape with the fortress-like Caracas Country Club. These dream worlds, though, exist outside a Colegio Americano that is bounded by the more banal limits of daily life.

A sizable minority of Americans at the school—students and faculty alike—are of southern U.S. stock. Their accents and views color much of our ambiance and conversation. A few of the Venezuelan students actually speak English with a slightly southern twang. One of the songs we'll practice during weekly school chorus has as its opening line, "Some folks say that a nigger won't steal/Way out yonder in the corn-field." Neither the choirmaster nor any of us students takes note of the pejorative, even though we may be nominally against racism.

One matronly teacher—who will do a great deal to help me personally—defends segregation with sweet reason in class, on grounds that "the Nigrahs" prefer being with their own kind. The gringos still in their teens naturally express their racial opinions in cruder form. A tall, pretty, sharp-tongued southern belle raves righteously from her bench one lunch hour. "Those people are just lazy! All they care about is sitting and singing under the trees, getting drunk!"

A Puerto Rican pupil, himself no nice guy, gets up from the same bench and lambastes her, ending his peroration with, "You simply do not know what you are talking about!" as he storms off.

The southern belle and her coregionalists routinely employ the term "niggahs." Sometimes with a humorous smile.

Other divisions at the school have to do with conscious identity choices. A fair number of children of Anglo parents, despite their U.S.-style upbringing and education, will end up opting for local ways. There's Alice, short and cute, who, though born in Texas, has lived since her infancy in Caracas, where her father owns a small communications firm. She has roughly equal numbers of Venezuelan and American friends. At a party late into my senior year I'll also meet for the first time her more sober and reserved sister Elena. As we dance, I ask Elena why we haven't seen her before at such events.

She replies tersely, "Because I prefer *lo Venezolano.*"

Things Venezuelan. She indeed has had minimal contact with the American set, attending national schools instead.

In another incident, on a corner of Avenida Miranda not far from my place, I run into a classmate, a strikingly attractive, slender woman, Venezuelan-born though with a classically English-sounding name. We chat. Amid the sounds of busy afternoon traffic I ask about her conspicuous absence from American socials. Her blunt if friendly answer is, "Oh, I just don't like wasting my time with *children.*"

In fact most of the American kids at the Colegio *are* quite immature socially. The students of Venezuelan and other nationalities have it way over us gringos in matters of conduct and decorum. We aren't about to recognize the fact, however.

At times the split between Americans and Venezuelans takes an ugly turn. One Venezuelan girl, of German origin, complains frequently and at length about gringo condescension toward her compatriots. Tells me about having overheard herself referred to more than once as "a spic" by her American cohorts in the ladies' room.

During a dispute that erupts in homeroom over equal representation in student government, the daughter of a U.S. diplomat acidly notes that half our class officers are Venezuelans. She is more or less right, though some of the "Venezuelans" are from other Latin countries.

World events affect our social climate. The Soviets launch their Sputnik in 1957. The U.S. attempt to counter the loss of prestige ends in a pratfall, with a satellite that aborts just yards off the ground. The more independent Venezuelans in our midst react with glee. "All those gringos are good for is launching spaceships that blow up at takeoff!" a fellow exults at recess. The Latins who are present roar with laughter, while I and a gringo kid maintain a resentful silence.

Sometimes the divisions take on an aggressive, physical turn. One big, stocky, handsome brute-of-a-gringo speaks in hushed tones on his front lawn about having mugged an occasional lone Venezuelan in dark alleys around payday. Other guys drive around Caracas on weekends in teams of three or four, and, from the safety of their automobiles, taunt pedestrians at random.

A more ideological brouhaha erupts as the result of a much-awaited 1959 state visit by Richard Nixon to Caracas. That afternoon the vice president's limousine is attacked, and the man is repeatedly spat upon by an unruly crowd of left-wing university students. (The sordid incident will be recounted—in Nixon's typically pompous, self-serving style—in his midlife memoir, *Six Crises*.) The occurrence inevitably sends shock waves throughout town, serving as sole subject of conversation next morning at the Automercado parking lot and on the bus ride. We all understand that something big will happen at school in the course of the day.

And happen it does. Mrs. Williams, probably the most beloved of all our teachers, delivers an angry and impassioned speech in her social studies class. She vents her sense of outrage, affront, and insult at the episode, angrily reminding us of the Venezuelan orphan boy she and her husband long ago adopted and lovingly raised. The class, Americans and Venezuelans alike, sits in stunned, shamed silence.

But it's not over. Throughout recess, angry political debates break out between Venezuelan and American student factions on matters going well beyond that of Nixon-as-victim. Gringos argue that if it weren't for U.S. know-how, Venezuela's oil would still be lying, useless, underneath the ground. The more articulate Venezuelans throw back at them the undeniable fact of generous U.S. aid and support once given to the dictator Pérez Jiménez, including a congressional medal. They cite the automatic granting of asylum to the tyrant after his recent ouster.

Nelson, one of my Venezuelan friends and a former resident of Colombia, notes pointedly that the nation of Panama had previously been Colombian territory. The U.S., he observes, had fomented its separation with a view to constructing its canal there.

Once again, as was the case in La Habana, I'm bewildered by the discussion, having no idea whom to side with or what to say. All I can do is mindlessly repeat the U.S. formulas from time to time. Though the Venezuelan students are fundamentally right and have data aplenty at their disposal, they've few means of driving their point across. The Americans, after all, hold the power and, in the wake of the Nixon affair, can claim righteous indignation, both out in the world and here in the schoolyard. The *venezolanos* might argue, reason, and cite facts; they can rave, bluster, and spit all they want. Yet their gringo adversaries—for all the standard Yankee rhetoric of civilized rationality and "open-mindedness"—aren't about to listen. Can't listen.

Throughout all the ongoing geographical, cultural, and familial changes, my love of classical music has stayed with me, along with my desire to be a musician.

Shortly after Kanani and I have arrived in Caracas for our Venezuelan phase, I ask my dad, "Could I have piano lessons now?" I have high hopes, given the new situation.

But he dismisses my inquiry with a curt "Well, I haven't got the money for music lessons these days." Mary, typically, still dispatches the sounds of Beethoven and his ilk as "dead people's music."

Meanwhile, during my free time I'll continue to tune in regularly to the government radio station. I'll sing along as before with whatever classical pieces are being broadcast.

This casual habit of mine will soon have fateful consequences. During my first few months in Caracas, we live in one of a pair of identical, graystone apartment buildings on Avenida Arboleda, an arc-shaped, diminutive little street in the upper part of El Bosque. (In the neighboring lot is the local American church.) Soon after the start of school, I begin recognizing the sixtyish, Montana-tinged voice of my English III teacher wafting from somewhere outside through Kanani's and my window. By the purest coincidence, Mrs. Williams and her husband, Dick, live in the other twin building, their unit just a single floor above ours.

One day between classes at the Colegio, a tall, gray-haired Mrs. Williams stops me in the corridor. She asks, "Gene, is that you who lives across the way from me?"

"Yes."

"Are you the guy who sings along with the classics?"

"Yes."

She looks at me intently. "You know, I've been telling Dick these last couple of months, 'Someone next door sure knows his symphonies.'"

Mrs. Williams somehow will figure out the tangled web of my musical desires and the chronic hostility I'm confronted with at home. By late spring of 1958, she's arranged to pay for my first piano lessons with Janet Langmead, a warmhearted, earnest music teacher in her late twenties, then married to an engineer with the international construction firm where Mr. Williams is an executive.

I'll study with Mrs. Langmead for about half a year—gratis, after the first couple of lessons that were paid for by Mrs. Williams. Then she passes me on to Mr. Petsch, a lanky, unforgettably hip and colorful twenty-fiveish Missourian in tortoise-shell glasses, a bravura pianist then earning his bread by giving private lessons from his Las Mercedes flat.

So there I am, finally able to make music! Mrs. Langmead and Mrs. Williams will give me free access to their own pianos during the afternoons and evenings.

From the start I throw myself wholeheartedly into learning piano. I put in two or three hours' practice a day and make rapid (if not always the most disciplined) progress. Within months I'm playing Bach minuets, Chopin preludes, and a Mozart fantasy, in addition to picking out American pop tunes on the sly, complete with correct harmonies. Sometimes I slip into a trance and merely repeat a left- or right-hand phrase, savoring the notes miraculously being produced by my very own thumb and fingers.

My speedy advances come as the result not only of sheer practice (though the long hours certainly help) but also because I know what I'm doing. In San Juan, during eighth grade, I'd briefly attended free classes in solfège—the European system for teaching beginners to read music—at the Escuela Libre de Música, a neoclassical building near the downtown Carnegie Library. From those few months' experience I picked up some of the rudiments of music theory. Later, in Cuba and within the confines of my mind, I'd gone on to reconstruct, through a personal system of visualized "slots," the entire arrangement of Western music's intervals and scales, plus a good portion of its harmonic organization, though seldom knowing the formal terms for them. Thus equipped, at HMA I started running every musical piece I could—whether classical or pop—through my mental-aural-visual scheme, playing the melodies in my head.

Years after that, I'd discover a kindred spirit of sorts in the seventeenth-century French philosopher Blaise Pascal, who, as a boy, reconstructed the history of mathematics from the ancient Greeks to his time.

Eventually my secret musical exercises took on a life of their own, indeed became an obsession: I simply couldn't stop some form of music from running through my brain—with the notes in the right slots, of course—even at this very moment, as I craft this page.

I now see that my inner musical world was a kind of psychological haven, a means of coping with my loneliness and isolation, and, more importantly, my own way of having the music I so much longed for but was being deprived of. Many years later, as a kind of therapy, I wrote and published a short story entitled "The Prize," focusing on this bizarre experience. In 1994 I sent the piece to Dr. Oliver Sacks, the neurologist renowned for his essays on the amazingly varied shapes that human imbalances can assume, along with a letter in which I described to him my odd, long-standing condition. In his kind and lengthy reply, Dr. Sacks informed me that he knew of several hundred instances of individuals obsessed by "musical hallucinations." And he noted that, in most cases, alas, the condition was "neither pleasant nor productive."

Luckily, as I finally took up the piano in Caracas at age fifteen, my musical hallucinations helped me assimilate its basic principles with ease. I could learn short piano pieces remarkably quickly, especially if

I'd already heard them over the radio or on a recording. From the musical visualization within my head to my hands moving along the keyboard was not that great a distance. Within a year I'd be playing occasional background music for school events—and feeling a strange combination of gratitude and vertigo at the yearned-for opportunity.

The dizzying sensation I felt then has stayed with me. Whenever I sit down at the piano, I'm astounded that I can play it at all. And thanks to the private system I'd devised in Cuba and Venezuela, to this day I can pick out on the piano any melody and its accompanying chords, so long as the scales and harmonies are relatively diatonic and pre–twentieth century.

All this initial musical growth I owe ultimately to my caring English teacher, Mrs. Williams. She was the prime mover; no Mrs. Williams, no music for little Gene, simple as that. But there's more, much more: she also determined my future course of study. As college-applications season approached I was actually considering—passively, with little conviction, and for want of a concrete alternative—the idea of doing a major in business. Well, at the start of my senior year, Mrs. Williams confronted me one afternoon in her apartment, and broached the subject of my academic plans. I argued the need for a practical degree, in business, because, you know, it'll guarantee me a job. Besides, what if there's another Great Depression? She challenged me forthwith, and passionately. In the heated debate that followed, she chipped away at my flaccid arguments ("In a depression," she remarked, *everybody* loses their job!") and started persuading me to set my sights on majoring in music.

Twelve months earlier, of course, it would've been unthinkable for me to embark on such a path. Prior to Mrs. Williams's selfless efforts on my behalf, I had received zero training as a musician; and as a raw, unschooled novice I never could've entered so arcane a guild, so hands-on and physical a craft. Now, having at least achieved some proficiency on the piano, I had within my grasp the beginnings of access to that formerly elusive world. To seek a degree in business, by contrast, would've been (needless to say) a monumental mistake that I probably would not have emerged from unscarred.

In some profound way, then, Mrs. Williams saved my life, or at least my sanity. I eventually got around to conveying my gratitude to her in a letter I wrote in 1969, telling her that, without her help and guidance a decade earlier, I might well have gone crazy. Lucky thing I wrote when I did. Mrs. Williams, I found out much later, died in 1970.

Cars and car-consciousness seem to dominate Venezuelan society. Its capital city is congested with Cadillacs and Mercedes-Benzes dashing about or just idling in stopped traffic. Among my male cohorts, when the talk isn't girls or gossip, it's cars. Sedans vs. convertibles vs. sports cars. American vs. European cars. Standard-shift vs. automatic-transmission cars.

"Seen the latest Buick? Radical change!"

"Hey, did you guys get a ride in so-and-so's Corvette?"

"Thunderbirds are pigs!"

"The Edsel—yuk!"

And so on ad infinitum. Many's the afternoon I'll sit with my friend Carlos at his bedroom window, watching metal hulks zoom down El Rosal toward the Automercado as we identify makes and models. Wishing for this Pontiac, that A. C. Bristol.

We can only wish and dream, since, owing to high tariffs, automobiles in Venezuela are prohibitively expensive. Besides, by law, you need to be at least eighteen years old in order to qualify for a driver's permit, though a sizable bribe can usually fend off the licensing and enforcing authorities. The only Venezuelan teens who drive—let alone own—cars, have money, lots of Papa's money, at their disposal.

To those of us without such resources, the solution is a motorcycle, an ordinary enough sight in Caracas. Motorists, mounted on two-wheeled machines of every imaginable size, brand, and look, ably snake their way between long lines of slower-moving, four-wheeled vehicles. Some of them sacrifice mobility and add luxurious, even ostentatious sidecars to show off their girlfriends. Deliverymen regularly stock their more sober-looking side attachments with the day's items— baguettes, for instance. At Colegio Americano, some members of the older, cooler set have hefty BMW and AJS cycles on which they arrive clamorously at the school grounds and weekend parties.

Desiring the motorized transport along with a piece of that street glamour and glory, and finding my 24-inch, single-speed bicycle much too small for me, I set out to secure a modest motorcycle of my own. First, though, I need the money, and my father isn't about to provide it. So I ask some teachers at the Colegio about any leads on summer jobs.

The school principal refers me to a small firm in the mammoth, tripartite, Galipán complex looming over Avenida Miranda. The operation, owned and run hands-on by a hardened, grizzled American woman—a heavy smoker who always wears thick, black heels—functions as a white-collar employment agency without really being one. Such agencies being against national law, Miss D., rather than charging the employees she has placed, bills the employers for providing them with qualified personnel. (In modern parlance, she's a kind of headhunter.)

I sit for an interview with Miss D., mention my teacher, and am hired on the spot for the equivalent of about twenty dollars a week. Over the next three months I'll function as receptionist, file clerk, typist, messenger-delivery boy, and translator-interpreter. The work itself proves to be a rewarding experience. I get to know a Venezuela that is more real than the closed, privileged circle of Overseas Americans. Delivering documents about town, I make contact with a wide range of Miss D.'s customers, from a shiny new tobacco factory in Caracas's eastern fringes to the cramped, Dickensian offices in the ever-busy city center. In the process I get to know in some detail the urban layout, and a grid-map of its street names and building shapes takes shape in my mind.

Every day I also receive and deal with the dozens of applicants who stream through the office, filling out standard forms. These are subsequently studied by Miss D. and me; she then files them by occupational category. General office workers—secretaries, clerk-typists—predominate, with a smattering of salespeople, accountants, engineers, and a lone chemist from Spain. Quite a few of them seem to have shown up in Caracas on whim, because they'd heard there was lots of work and money to be had there. It's the classic boomtown, frontier-capitalism pattern.

The job furnishes an unexpected glimpse at a more unsavory side of life in Venezuela—and in Latin America generally. If a candidate is dark-skinned or non-Caucasian, Miss D. routinely places his or her dossier in a separate file, unmarked yet clearly set aside for racial unacceptables. Mulatto/a candidates' photos are captioned in light pencil by Miss D. as "C & L" for "café con leche," the descriptive term often employed in Latin America to designate fairer-complected nonwhites, equivalent perhaps to the adjective "high-yellow" used by African-Americans. And one thirtyish fellow, a South Asian immigrant, has above his photo in prominent capital letters the stark, unforgiving word "BLACK."

These undesirables never get a callback, regardless of their credentials. One particularly attractive, experienced, multilingual West Indian woman—alas, a "C & L"—fills out her application form, and then remains in the office, forcefully arguing her qualifications to my boss, and politely reiterating her earnest desire "to take a position." Miss D. irritably replies that there isn't much available for her at that particular time.

The discriminatory policy originates not with Miss D. but with her clients and their hiring practices. Certain distasteful incidents will prove as much. One time we send a handsome, slightly swarthy youth in his early twenties for an interview with a respected small company. Soon afterwards I'll field a concerned telephone call from an officer of the firm, who states, more or less, "Thank you for sending us candidate X, who is quite good. But, please, next time, could you send us a *white* man?"

I relay the message to Miss D. She is dumfounded and amazed. The fellow, after all, didn't even have "keeky hair," in her words. (Next day we recall the young man and refer him to a vacancy elsewhere. They hire him.)

One often hears it said that Latin Americans are less racist than their U.S. counterparts. To some extent I agree. That summer's exposure to Venezuelan employment practices, though, taught me something about the informal, extralegal, voluntary barriers to nonwhites prevailing in the supposedly more liberal economy of late 1950s Caracas.

By August I've hoarded enough money to start looking around for a secondhand motorcycle. Needing advice, I enlist the help of Johnny F., a British cyclist familiar to me from Colegio-related social events, who's legendary in his knowledge of anything connected with recreational, gasoline-operated land vehicles. (His father, whom I'll also meet, has actually done professional car racing.) On the backseat of Johnny's souped-up Triumph, and with his expert guidance, I make the rounds of mechanics' and sales shops, and in time get fixated on a small, used, two-stroke DKW.

The monies are paid. The appropriate papers received. I thank Johnny F. He and I go our separate ways on our respective bikes.

The air streams by my face as I effortlessly, miraculously negotiate the steep hills of Caracas and ride into Avenida Arboleda. In front of my building, some neighbors standing idly about see me approach. They wave at me in surprise. I stop. We chat. As a demonstration I proceed to drive the machine around the building's street-level parking lot— and unceremoniously lose my balance halfway through the second lap, falling on my side as the horizontal wheels spin furiously. Still, my schoolmates, friends, and casual acquaintances are fascinated and awed by my metal steed, however modest in its dimensions. And I relish the feeling of having finally "made it."

I'll ride my bike all over Caracas. To school. To parties. To my last few weeks of work. On casual errands. And just for the sheer hell of it.

I also act dangerously and imprudently, at times barreling downhill at breakneck speed with some friend or other seated behind me. (And no helmets.) Once I turn a brusque left at an intersection where there are substantial amounts of sand loosely scattered on the roadbed. The bike's tires skid. I and my passenger—a Venezuelan cohort named Freddy—both go hurtling into the air and onto the ground. Luckily we suffer only minor flesh wounds that someone tends to at a friend's house nearby. In the seven months of recklessly driving that supposed glamour gadget, I greatly endanger the lives of myself and of others. All just to "belong."

In the long run my DKW, an aging clunker, can't be saved even by its original, high-quality German workmanship. By February, the mechanical problems are multiplying out of control. As I'm cruising home from school one sunlit afternoon, the bike transmission goes kaput. For the remaining half of the trip I'm forced either to coast in neutral or poke along in low gear. The constant visits to the repair shop begin feeling like a ritual, and I frankly regret having the machine among my few possessions.

My motorcycle days . . . A monumental if youthful mistake. An instance of the foolish extremes a kid might go to when there's little to sustain him spiritually. I'll have no concrete recollection of the DKW's final fate. Later on, Kanani will inform me that, somewhere, some-when, I finally junked the old heap for good.

To Kanani and me, the attractions of leaving HMA and transferring to Caracas had included the supposed prospect of a normal, civilian home life. In the meantime, Dad and Mary's domain has grown by a son, Hal, born in 1956. The boy's maternal grandmom has also since been flown in from Cuba to help raise our half-brother while Mary runs her wholesale apparel business.

There now looms over their living room a large, romanticized oil portrait, in predominantly red hues, of Mary—a gift to her from Dad. Two years have elapsed since the distant "honeymoon" summer of 1955. Kanani and I have never lived under the same roof with Dad's enlarged domestic realm. Rather than returning to a family fold, we're moving into our father's new household. And in with his expanded second family.

So from the outset there's something unnatural or unfamiliar about the situation, and, as the weeks unfold, home life for Kanani and me will scarcely exist. Dad invariably gets back from work around 9 p.m. and sits alone at the wrought-iron, glass-surfaced table, downing his dinner with a couple of beers as he silently peruses his evening paper. During the two years Kanani and I live with our father, he won't take us even once to anything not directly work-related, whether it be the beach, a movie, or a casual drive or stroll. (Sometimes he does drag us to the office to help with cleaning, though.) Neither does he go meet and talk with our teachers, save for a single visit that he'll pay to Mrs. Williams, at my urging.

Tensions between the two differing sets of members in the domestic environment inevitably flare up. Certain house rules applying to Kanani and me will grow harsher over the next two years and further heighten the feelings of ill will. For example, because there is a shower and lavatory next to our room in the rear, my brother and I are strictly forbidden from venturing into the main bathroom up front, the one easily accessible from the living-room area. Early on in our stay, Kanani casually brings home a playmate at noontime. Mary takes me aside to complain about their now having to treat the boy to lunch. In time the living-room furniture is declared off-limits to the two of us.

Any visitors of Kanani's or mine are to be confined to our own quarters. At some point Kanani and I start being required to take our meals in the kitchen.

As for me, I'll strain things further by contesting some of these limits. Or by defying Mary, even cruelly mocking and insulting her. At one point I confront Dad about Kanani and me feeling cramped "right here in our house."

"It's not your house," he observes calmly. "It's Mary's house."

Things get further complicated when, sometime in 1957, Dad is suddenly fired from the bra company. The details of his dismissal elude me, though his Machiavellian and conniving ways, which I'd seen in action two summers ago, may have created bad feelings among his staff and now come back to haunt him. What I do see is Pop describing himself as the victim of an unsavory conspiracy by "the Jews" at his office and in New York. Previously there had been the obscure financial scandal that had blown up precisely during that Christmas vacation when Kanani and I fled from military school, following which my father had spent some time in jail. In the wake of his release, the brassiere firm ran in the local newspapers an impressive display ad defending and exculpating him in the murky business. All these machinations of his may be finally coming home to roost.

Because of Dad's being canned, household finances get much tighter. As a money-saving measure, we all move to a smaller fifth-floor apartment in Edificio Penélope just a minute's walk down our same street, with a grocery store and a barbershop at its front entrance, both run by immigrant Italians.

Now our father turns to the import-export schemes that had served as his wherewithal during the years before his ill-fated corporate stint. He looks into selling rice, for instance, though I don't know if that project ever materializes. When he secures the local distributorship for a couple of new U.S. products—a replacement zipper gadget and a brand of foldable, plastic rain bonnets—he enlists my brother and me to peddle them door-to-door. I sell maybe two dozen of each to interested schoolmates and teachers at the Colegio. A thirteen-year-old Kanani knocks on a few front doors, sales items in hand, but soon gives up on the enterprise.

In time our father gets involved in a textile venture with a partner named Méndez. Their small factory eventually becomes a provider of uniforms to newly democratic Venezuela's armed forces and police. As a perk, Kanani and I sporadically receive complimentary suits and slacks.

The firm also supplies horns and woodwinds from Selmer corporation—at the time perhaps the best-known U.S. manufacturer of musical instruments—to the Venezuelan military's marching bands, though I doubt if Bell padre ever sets eyes on, let alone handles, any of the instruments he peddles. Curiously, Selmer catalogs can be seen lying around the apartment; I ponder the irony of my antimusical father suddenly having musical interests. A casual request of mine for a cheap clarinet nevertheless elicits no more from him than noncommittal mumbles.

About the only kind company we'll find at home comes from the live-in maid, Remedios, and her spouse, Antonio, both of them in their late twenties or early thirties. They're among the many Spaniards who've left behind them the dead-end poverty of life under Francoism and harkened to the Venezuelan government's call for European immigration. Remedios and I will often chat at length as she labors about the house. She's as warm and attentive to Kanani and me as the circumstances permit. Her short, wavy-haired husband—the first man I ever meet who wears sandals—takes us out for neighborhood strolls and reminisces about his youthful, gullible belief in (Latin) America's vast wealth. Its streets paved with you-know-what.

Unfortunately Remedios will be summarily fired when Mary one day catches her spitting into the kitchen sink. We'll never see the couple again.

I continue with my reading, but much of what's on hand proves a bit less rewarding than what I've plunged into previously. My father has on his few bookshelves those best-selling business novels from the era: Cameron Hawley's *Executive Suite* and *Cash McCall.* Sloan Wilson's *The Man in the Gray Flannel Suit.* He also owns such sensationalistic fare as March's *The Bad Seed* and Metalious's *Peyton Place.* Crude, obscene phrases from the latter will forever spring into my head, since it's the first time I encounter such language in print.

My father also urges upon me his copy of Tocqueville's *Democracy in America.* I duly attempt it, yet am hardly ready for it, and soon quietly drop it, much to his irritation and disappointment. (Years later, in a hotel room in Strasbourg, France, I will finally read through Tocqueville's great classic, noting, curiously, that many of the positive things the Frenchman singles out about U.S. life are no longer the case, whereas some of the more negative, troubling, and bizarre aspects of America still remain strong. Few would agree, for instance, that Americans today demonstrate "a highly advanced political consciousness," as Tocqueville remarks; few on the other hand would contest his observation that "religious insanity is very common in the United States.")

Some of my more promising book glimpses come from my two piano teachers, who lend me literary fiction (Graham Greene, short story writer Philip Beaumont), humor (Thurber), and musical biographies (Geiringer's *Brahms*). From them I first hear of Joseph Conrad, whom I'll come to see as a kindred spirit of sorts.

Given our lack of home life, it's no wonder that Kanani and I become street kids, albeit mild versions thereof. Weekends I'm out with my peers till 3 or 4 a.m., driving, taxiing, motorcycling from house party to cabaret, and sometimes to brothel, often with a rum flask in my coat pocket.

One evening after work my father happens to catch me purchasing a bottle of Bacardí at the downstairs grocery store. He stands there and gives me a stern, silent look, then walks off in a huff as the Italian clerk grins wryly. Over the next couple of days I nervously await a response from Dad. A scolding. A concerned query. An anguished confrontation. He never once raises the issue. And I never manage to find out whether his silence on the matter was motivated by tolerance, indulgence, repressed anger, or mere indifference.

On weekdays I hang about with friends as much as possible, doing crossword puzzles, playing cards and poker dice. We also sit around on fences or at the Automercado snack bar, where we sip Cokes and goof off endlessly.

Kanani in particular revels in the excitement of being out on Avenida Miranda. He's dazzled by its array of street vendors, its bright-yellow hot-dog carts, its constant stream of automobile traffic at all hours, and especially its color-coded buses. He rides them so often that some of the drivers get to know him and let him ride free of charge.

He also loves the all-night, stand-up diners specializing in *arepas*, those soft, round, cornmeal crumpets that can be stuffed with any of two dozen kinds of prominently displayed meats or cheeses. Kanani with his friends, and I with mine, will often huddle around Avenida Miranda, munching on the *arepas* we've bought at El Punto Criollo— a legendary neighborhood spot on the corner of Avenida El Parque— and talking late into the night. (*Arepas* show up frequently in García Márquez's fiction. When I revisit Caracas in 1982, following a fifteen-year absence, I'll note with dismay that the *arepa* bars, including El Punto Criollo itself, have been mostly displaced by fast-food franchises, though a McDonald's in El Rosal does carry the traditional Venezuela muffins for the old-fashioned.)

For some reason, Kanani has no key to Edificio Penélope's front door, which is officially locked after 10 p.m. He devises a means of regularly breaking in via the back way: from the top of a garbage can he'll clamber up on to the roof of a cinderblock toolshed. Next he jumps farther up to a ledge. Then he slithers through a window into the second-floor hallway, where he summons the elevator up to the apartment.

As of the beginning of our second year, Kanani had transferred out of Mrs. Hayes's School to enroll in ninth grade at Colegio Americano. So once again, he and I were schoolmates, though for the last time.

Sometime that same year, Dad stopped providing us lunch money as well as bag lunches. Owing, I suppose, to his financial straits. Whenever I'd suggest that he give us *something* for our midday meal— Spam, or crackers—he solemnly urged us to take pride in what we make on our own, berated me for spending my money on dances, and brought up the old chestnut about "initiative."

Well, I did show initiative of a type that had ancient precedent and Augustinian overtones: in a word, theft. I began stealing lunches from school lockers, a free enterprise roughly parallel to the seventeenth-century relationship between Pilgrims and Pequots. My new practice naturally caused first unease, then outrage at the Colegio. A couple of friends knew of my budding apprenticeship in larceny, and word eventually leaked out among pupils and faculty.

My own situation was somewhat relieved when a quiet, sweet-tempered classmate—diminutive, athletic, from the Country Club, yet generous and gracious in her instincts and utterly without snobbery— started casually handing me cheese sandwiches during lunchtime. Still, my experiment in testing the limits of God's seventh commandment continued, off and on, for the remainder of my senior year. To my credit, the future saint Augustine wasn't even feeling hungry when, at age sixteen (my age too at the time) he'd ripped off those pears and—just for the fun of it—fed them to the pigs. (I think of a cartoon by Daumier: a judge in formal French robes loftily, impatiently reprimands a skinny, scruffy-looking detainee, saying, "You were hungry, you were hungry. Look, I get hungry every day, and yet I never steal.")

Kanani for his part found an adult angel. One morning he was summoned to the school principal's office and went in apprehension. There he learned that an anonymous donor had left him a bag lunch. The mysterious donations continued regularly for weeks, unexplained. Finally at mealtime one day a classmate named Robert whispered to him, "I know who brings you those lunches."

"Who?" Kanani asked.

"Mrs. Buckley," Robert answered. "Only she makes those cookies."

Mrs. Buckley. Originally from Oklahoma of Cherokee Indian stock, she was copper-skinned, with genuine Native American features. She taught English at the school and was Kanani's homeroom teacher, and also sang contralto in the American church choir, where I'd see her at Thursday night rehearsals and Sunday services. (Seeking musical outlets, I'd come aboard myself as a tenor in the fall. I still associate the aria from Handel's *Messiah*, "He was despiséd," with Mrs. Buckley's performance of it on Easter 1959.) As the year rolled on, she began inviting Kanani to dinner with her husband, who worked for one of the oil firms, and their three children, ages nine to three.

Many years later, I'd find out that my own musical sponsor, Mrs. Williams, had sent to my mom, then living in New Mexico, a long and worried letter describing, among other things, Kanani's lack of direction. I quote from a relevant passage:

He has become a matter of concern to us because he constantly hangs around the streets till all hours and only shows up at home to eat or sleep when necessary. I've talked to Kanani a couple of times (he also washes my car every week for a little spending money) and yesterday I told him that according to law any 14-year-old could choose the parent with whom he wished to live and to act as his guardian. I asked Kanani if he would choose you or his father . . . He unhesitatingly chose you. So you're elected, which is as it should be . . . However, I'd greatly appreciate your writing Gene, maybe in my care, as to your plans for Kanani.

Mrs. Williams now goes on to present a tentative offer from Mrs. Buckley to adopt Kanani herself for the time being. After a sketch of the Buckleys and their background, she explains:

Kanani definitely needs supervision as well as a home where he can take his friends and where there is interest, comfort and affection . . . And she offers to give him a home—clothe and feed him, pay his school expenses, supervise his school work, give him love and affection with no strings attached. She would keep him until you want him or until he's completely straightened out. Kanani wants to see you this summer regardless of what happens—and I personally don't blame him too much for what's going on, but he must be *made* to knuckle down . . . Mrs. Buckley would want control here with no interference from Kanani's father except that Kanani could see his father whenever he wished. Needless to say none of this has been discussed with anyone—the decision is yours.

My mother's negative reply, which I would dredge up from among her papers shortly after her death in 1984, is also lengthy. And cordial, eloquent, complex. After profuse thanks to Mrs. Williams for her efforts on behalf of both Kanani and me, she continues:

Mrs. Buckley's offer is magnanimous. Please tell her I realize its full import, and although I cannot consent to it, I sincerely appreciate her wonderfully kind and generous gesture and extend my heartfelt thanks. And I am sure that Kanani will always remember her with great warmth and gratitude.

This is my responsibility, and I would not be worthy of my son's confidence if I didn't accept it while waiting for more favorable conditions. The boy needs me now. At the moment my finances would be the despair of Dun & Bradstreet, but I am sure that all things will work out.

Much of the middle portion of her letter is taken up with a detailed account of the endless legal hassles she's had to take on, through several courts in both Puerto Rico and Cuba, concerning her divorce, the custody of the children, and my father's unreliable support payments. She introduces the tangled subject in this fashion:

> I regret that I must write my son in your care, giving the impression of collusion, or the need for it—which added to the other information in your letter indicates an unhealthy emotional climate. I have tried since my separation and divorce from his Dad to maintain a united parental discipline, preserve the father-image I think essential for a growing boy, and to accept the fact that moral right transcends legal right, when the father arbitrarily insisted on retaining custody. Apparently there is no parental discipline to divide; the father-image is badly blurred; and the moral right has not been balanced by moral responsibility.

Following five extremely dense paragraphs in which she recounts the byzantine intricacies of these custody battles, Mom sums things up by saying, "It is lamentable that I must give you these very personal details, but I feel that you should know them, for the entire matter of Kanani's welfare may depend on legal terminology and interpretation of 'Custody.' Personally, at this stage of development, I consider the term a rank misnomer."

After responding with offers of hospitality to those previously tendered by Mrs. Williams, my mother ends, "In closing, let me again thank you for your tremendous effort, interest, concern and kind wishes for me and my three children."

Today I realize our Colegio teachers saw us as exactly the deeply troubled, mixed-up kids we happened to be. They were trying to help out in any way they could. In my case, when the summer job at Miss D.'s agency came to its inevitable end, I somehow landed a one-to-two-hour-a-day gig at a European import-export firm in the Sabana Grande business district. My immediate supervisor, a Swiss fellow named Chesaux, fit to a T the image of a classically cultured, well-mannered European, and had some kind of sideline in art and art books. So, following school, I'd head out to the one-room office, where I'd run messages for him and his elder boss, and sit around sipping excellent roast coffee (which I'd just then discovered) while waiting for my next assignment. Monsieur Chesaux was very kind and attentive; we had many enjoyable conversations at work and in his car when he'd drive me home. I've since deduced that the school principal, Mrs. Mirc, must have been the force behind this exciting job adventure.

Despite the care of our teachers, and in spite of our frenzied partying and motoring, and my own working of sorts, 1958–59 was not a good year for the Bell boys. Lacking moral support at home and any core of identity within, we floundered aimlessly.

During my first year at Colegio Americano I had worked diligently, remaining a model pupil. My scholarly achievements, however, were not much appreciated at home. Dad felt that I should do more than stay about the house studying. "Why d'you sit around home so much?" he would bark. Show some initiative." He even exhorts me, "Why don't you try playing a musical instrument or something?" an inexplicable suggestion since he'd ignored my earlier request for a clarinet.

In the second year our academic performance crashed. I earned my worst grades ever. Kanani slid into an anomic slump he wouldn't pull out of till senior year in college. (Sometimes I'd recruit friends of his to give him pep talks. The results were always nil.) In order to cope, each of us developed some bizarre if classic buffoon-behavior patterns, a time-honored way for outcasts to gain attention and construct a public role. Yet since I was often picked on by friends because of my array of vulnerabilities, at the same time I'd also turned defensive and prickly, flaunting a chip the size of a brickbat on my shoulder and responding sarcastically to whoever attempted to offer me comfort. This latter trait lingered on, as a festering residue, well into my university days.

As I look back now, it isn't hard for me to see why kids lacking in spiritual sustenance, either from family or community, can end up channeling their strengths into illicit and destructive (often self-destructive) actions—can find in, say, gang life a sense of belonging. Kanani and I simply felt unwanted at home. We knew the town, the language, and culture of Caracas. But we were still aliens in Venezuela; we spoke fluent English and had U.S. antecedents. Yet we were also aliens among the Overseas-American crowd. We were thus doubly disposed to feeling "alien-ated."

My music, to an extent, furnished me an anchor, but Kanani, alas, was hopelessly adrift in the rougher rhythms of a Third World metropolis. A bit of bad company amid our peers easily could have pushed us over the edge, shaped us into something out of *Los olvidados* or *Pixote* or *Salaam Bombay*.

Some of my tougher cohorts in fact occasionally raised the challenge of hurling rocks at a house window, any house window, as we roamed the streets late at nights. Only once did someone in our group go beyond the verbal challenge and offer a physical response ... Bull's-eye! The glass shattered into bits. We all ran off, laughing, feeling heady with our bold deed. We never tried it again, though.

The year comes to a strange, unforeseeable climax starting one night in late April or early May. I and two swarthy, English-speaking Venezuelans named Joe and Nelson are returning from a party. Walking slowly along Avenida Miranda, we notice some green leaflets strewn about the sidewalk. Nelson picks one up. We eye it, shiver nervously at its left-wing, antigovernment rhetoric, and discreetly let the paper waft back onto the ground.

Following a quick *arepa* snack, we tumble into Joe's big black tank of a car. He drives up the hill and pulls up in front of my apartment building. After a few minutes of idly sitting and chatting, we see a lone automobile barreling up against the clearly posted traffic signs at the end of the narrow street. By reflex action we all shout, "One way!"

Suddenly the unknown car brakes at our side. Two white men in suits emerge and order us out. We comply passively as they search Joe's jalopy and its trunk. Finding nothing, they direct us into their official-looking auto machine. Cutting across a large swath of the city, they enter a drearier, older area in the Western sectors, unfamiliar to us, and finally they chug up a hill, the approach to a large, formidable structure that we recognize as a notorious prison.

It's all happened too fast for us to feel scared. We think maybe we're being booked for drinking. Or a traffic violation. Next thing, we've entered a yellowing office furnished with five brown desks.

I'm seated across a desk from a man with wavy, black hair, and am trying to digest his unexpected question: "So, tell us about those subversive sheets you've been handing out."

"Subversive sheets?" I shoot back, bewildered.

"Yeah," wavy-hair elaborates, "we've been following the three of you in your white car these last few hours. Watching you distribute those subversive sheets."

"But we were in a black car!" I exclaim. The discrepancy makes no dent in his cross-examination, which continues in this fashion for about a quarter of an hour.

In time they have us standing side by side, a couple of yards from each other, our backs to the door. We spend the rest of the night on our feet, lights shining bright in our faces as we field the unvarying line about those subversive sheets. None of our detailed, identical, not to mention truthful alibis convince them, though. At one point I foolishly allude to the green leaflet we picked up and discarded on Avenida Miranda. The interrogators immediately jump on the admission as proof of complicity.

So we're under arrest. Indeed, *incomunicado*—I'll first hear the adjective that night, and it refers to us three. Almost as in a movie, tough-guy cops, nice-guy cops, and neutral, no-emotion cops, all in plainclothes, rehearse their individual styles on us. By the time the day's first sunbeams peep in, the drumbeat phrase "subversive sheets" has come to feel like a grotesque joke, eliciting English-language gags and giggles from our three run-down selves.

My father's business contacts with the police must have allowed him access to higher authorities. Sometime during morning work hours I get a telephone call from him and field it in a separate, wood-paneled office cubicle.

His opening words: "Well. So you spent the night in jail."

In fact they're the only words I'll remember from our conversation. I gather we talk about what he's doing on our behalf and what I feel regarding Joe, Nelson, and me.

The three of us can't be kept standing forever within that first office. So we speculate as to where they'll put us next. For a while we end up sitting next to a large holding pen for common criminals. On the benches right across from us are some hardened, scarfaced, street lumpen types. They could've walked right out of a grade-B Roger Corman thriller or a Buñuel classic. We wonder whether they're our cellmates-to-be, and realize we've got some rough going in store for us if that's the case. But instead we're sent on to a kind of barracks with long rows of bunk beds. (I'm uncannily reminded of military school.)

Early on, a short, jolly fellow, sporting a moustache and a checkered sports coat, drops by and joins us in our area, sitting on an adjacent bed. Smilingly, woefully, he informs us that he too was busted in the police raid. He tries engaging us in conversation. Nelson immediately sees him as a probable undercover agent. In English, he warns Joe and me of his suspicions. We ignore the guy.

The next couple of days consist largely of the long and endless boredom of just waiting. And also the periodic interrogations in which I'll relate again and again our movements that fateful evening: Party. Walk. *Arepas.* And the drive up to my street in Joe's (black) car. I remind them that I, as a foreigner—as an American, this time—residing in Venezuela, have no desire to get mixed up in local politics.

On the morning of the third or fourth day, Joe's mother shows up in that front, wood-paneled office. In our presence she forcefully, tearfully pleads with the officials, in the grand manner of those mamás familiar to us from Latin soap operas and Mexican films. My father is somehow there too. Later, in private, he'll express to me his scorn for such melodramatics, his view that the pathetic woman only made things worse for everyone.

Still, it looks as if the first steps toward our release are under way. By early that afternoon, Dad is driving me home—and still raving about Joe's mom. He continues to do so back at the apartment, with Mary.

I'm just grateful to be out again.

On our return to society we find that our misadventures have become the talk of the town. We bask momentarily in being the focus of attention. Many times over I'll recount the ins and outs of our story to schoolmates and neighborhood people. Other folks in turn share with us their tales of police absurdity. A twentyish Venezuelan at the Automercado soda fountain tells us about some friends of his who were arrested at a street corner. When confronted by their interrogators, they were informed, "A crime occurred on that very street corner last week, and criminals always return to the scene of the crime."

On a more sinister note, we hear of indigent foreigners languishing in prison for months, even years, for no particular reason and with no benefit of trial.

Nelson gets a further taste of these injustices when he's asked to vacate the rooming house where he had stayed since September. (His parents live in Maracaibo, on the coast.) His landlord of course knows and very much understands that the guy was an innocent victim, fully exonerated and so forth, yet he still feels that Nelson's continuing tenancy might ultimately bring adverse consequences and be bad for business. I help him find a new place nearby.

The entire episode has happened not under the military dictatorship but a recently elected, mildly reformist, civilian administration. Years later, I'll learn from Nelson that our case had even come up for discussion at a cabinet-level meeting headed by President Betancourt.

By June I look forward to finishing at Colegio Americano even more than I'd once longed to flee HMA. I hate my whole life in Caracas; I hate the school and a lot of my schoolmates, I hate the silly romances (and my own lack thereof), I hate the apartment, the town, and of course I hate the loneliness and isolation. All of it further compounded by the ten thousand and one typical growing pains of teendom.

Among the few details I'll recall from our graduation ceremony is our singing the hymn "Be Still My Soul," taken from the middle portion of Sibelius's *Finlandia*, in the school choir. My dad doesn't attend, though my piano teacher, Mrs. Langmead, is probably present.

Despite my churning resentments, I get terribly dewy-eyed and sentimental at the reception. Dispense hugs left and right. Repeatedly air my desire to meet with this and that person in our afterlife up in the States, where most of us are heading for college.

My brother and I go on to spend the months of June and July in a dazed and confused fog, marking time before our departure. There are the inevitable long farewells to assorted friends. One evening, in passing, I wistfully mention to my father how much I'll be missing those guys and girls. By way of reply he asserts, "Well, soon you'll realize that high-school friends don't matter all that much." Sipping at his suppertime beer, he elaborates, "Granted, you never know when somebody might be a business contact. But mostly they don't count for much, really."

At some other point he expresses serious concern about our forthcoming daily life with Mom. "Every time you spend time with your mother, you boys come back about as neurotic as she is" is his somber, weighty pronouncement.

Still, Kanani and I look forward to our ultimate destination of Santa Fe, New Mexico, where Mom had moved with Valerie in 1958. We've had no plans, no projects as to our Stateside future, but we long to start a new life up there with our mother and sister, our beloved next of kin—blood of our blood, flesh of our flesh—whom we have not set eyes on in nearly two years.

Since Kanani's and my latest departure from our first home, our distant island paradise, our lost Puerto Rico, Mom had been able to phone us just once, concerned about the alarming news accounts of street violence during the overthrow of Pérez Jiménez. (International calls back then were complex and pricey.) Ever the devoted mother, she worried about the safety of her two sons, wanted our assurances that all was well.

She wrote frequently, though, and most recently was describing with ardent fascination the folk arts of her newly adopted home state, notably the wooden statuettes known as *santos* that were used for religious worship. Our family friend Steve she would mention on occasion, and discreetly, presumably her way of keeping their romance more or less secret—and of remaining extracautious about men, given her tragically destructive experience with my father.

Meanwhile, in a letter written sometime around school graduation, she reports that six-year-old Valerie is saying, all excited, "My boys're coming home soon!"

Dad feels, however, that Kanani and I should do some traveling "on our own." Instead of arranging a straightforward flight schedule, he fashions for us a complex, northwest-bound odyssey. First by steamer from the Venezuelan port of La Guaira, with overnight stops in San Juan and Ciudad Trujillo. Final destination of our sea journey in La Habana, where we'll be met by Mary, who'll be flying there to visit her family (Kanani's and my step-aunt and step-uncle, the occasional weekend hosts from our unlamented HMA days).

From Havana by mini-plane to Key West. Then Greyhound buses from south Florida all the way to the New Mexico state capital.

There may well be money-saving reasons for this choice of itinerary, I've inferred.

A few days before our departure, Dad gives me a typewritten letter with neatly numbered bits of father-to-son advice, à la Polonius. One item reads, "Don't trust people," followed by a couple of lines' elaboration. His final entry exhorts, "Don't ever leave the United States. It is the greatest country in the world."

On the afternoon of our last drive to La Guaira—the harbor this time, not the airport—he hands me about two hundred dollars in pocket money and explains how to make a collect call, in case anything goes wrong these next two weeks. Near the gangplank, by the water's edge, he smiles, for once radiating fatherliness and charm, and he actually embraces the two of us.

Despite some zigzags, my brother and I were at last going home to the States.

Part Two: American

Reentry is a significant event for the Absentee American; the experience may be vividly recollected decades later. Respondents described reentry as difficult, painful, turbulent, or traumatic . . . The experience is often referred to as a shock . . . In professional literature on the subject, this transition is generally referred to as euphoria, irritability, hostility, gradual adjustment, and adaptation.

—CAROLYN D. SMITH, *The Absentee American*

Not Yet at Home in El Norte

> [P]ersons living as foreigners in the host culture may have an
> unrealistic sense of their ability to fit easily into the home
> culture or a culture they believe fits them. Actually moving to
> the place where they anticipate being at home may result in
> the painful experience of either not being accepted by those
> in that community or being shocked to discover that they do
> not fit in or even want to fit ... Belonging nowhere and
> everywhere is a normal, predictable result.
>
> —DAVID POLLOCK, "Where Will I Build My Nest?
> The Multicultural Third Culture Kid," in
> Carolyn D. Smith, *Strangers at Home*

WHITE WAITING ROOM, says the sign, unambiguously.

COLORED WAITING ROOM, says another, farther down the hall.

Same goes for the restrooms, the game rooms, and most everything else at Greyhound bus stations in the Deep South. It's all black and white. White versus black. At each and every southern depot where Kanani and I come down from the bus, we'll encounter these signs, time and again, without fail. The constant reminders of state-enforced racial segregation, and the attendant oppression and intimidation, are among the greatest shocks to our newborn Yankee souls as we first travel across the U.S. of A.

Peeking inside the plate glass windows of the Colored Waiting Rooms, we'll often see scared-looking parents, sitting around with their little kids, waiting.

My brother and I initially feel some bewilderment as to which of the bathrooms and other facilities we can rightfully use. Does our yellow-brown, Asian skin qualify as "colored"? Do our overseas, middle-class origins count as "white"? Cautiously, we venture into the white-designated areas anyway. After two days we enter them by force of habit.

Our concerns are by no means unfounded. During a lunch stop in Little Rock, Arkansas—a bastion of violently aggressive, prosegregationist militancy—Kanani is stealthily followed into the white bathroom by a trio of (white) teenaged roughnecks. The warriors hang about in silence as the boy completes his number-one business. Then, as he departs the urinals, the brave threesome surrounds him threateningly. Thinking fast, Kanani addresses them in rapid-fire Spanish and sashays swiftly toward the door (his hands unwashed, unfortunately), leaving the three courageous toughs thoroughly nonplused.

Several times, on buses, I'll note the occasional white passenger who chooses to ride long hours standing, rather than sit next to a colored person.

The SS *Satrústegui*, on which Kanani and I had set sail for Phase I of our journey out of Venezuela, is a medium-sized Spanish vessel. Owned and run by an outfit called Iberian Lines, its employees all hail from Spain. ("Ah, Spain," exclaims the ship's on-board barber to me as he trims my sideburns. "The most beautiful country in the world! *In the world!*" Clearly a point of disagreement with my father.)

Being out on the open seas arouses within me sensations both exciting and serene. Among my favorite activities is to sit alone either on stem or stern of the ship at night, contemplating the spumy-white, disembodied wake below, and the big black dome studded by thousands of stars above. I feel as if I'm floating in space, directly experiencing the vastness of the universe. An astronaut somewhere above the high seas, heading for his earthly destination.

The ship itself is clean and institutional, with a pervasive smell of varnished wood—its prime building material—plus the expected trappings: Deck chairs. A collective dining hall. A bar-cum-lounge where people sit playing cards. A night-time Latin band. Love affairs. Kanani notices quite a bit of gambling, drinking, and carousing on board, and even a woman carrying on amorously with some of the men on the upper deck.

Any passenger ship is a self-contained world. Such a fact has spurred many a prime scribbler or filmmaker to set their narratives in these makeshift communities. In the case of the *Satrústegui*, many of our co-passengers are Cuban expatriates who for economic or political reasons left for Venezuela in the 1950s and are now casting feelers towards a return to their rapidly transforming native land. One of them, mustachioed and bespectacled, is a well-regarded pop-music composer and pianist. Another, stocky and curly-haired, with classically dark, Latino good looks, turns out to be a professional singer of boleros. The two frequently pair up and jam together on the dining-hall piano, much to my awe and envy.

Early on I'll meet a lovely, charming Venezuelan girl called Marta Lilia, an eighteen-year-old medical-student-to-be at the Universidad Central de Caracas. Like so many others on board, she's traveling with immediate kin to visit relatives in Havana. We spend much of our five-day, pan-Caribbean cruise together, watching the sea, breathing in its salt air, and talking of many things. Countries compared. Jokes remembered. Our distaste for Mexican ranchera music. Our respective futures. Over time I develop a chaste and innocent little crush on her.

Following our softly radiant parting of the ways at the port of Havana, we'll go on to correspond regularly for some four or five years thereafter. It's a sweet little movie romance that, like so many good things (and unlike the similar romance in Richard Linklater's film *Before Sunrise*), has to reach its end when, in the mid-1960s, she finds herself a serious boyfriend in Caracas, after which I'll never hear from her again.

The *Satrústegui's* first stop is San Juan, where we're scheduled to dock for the better part of the day. My brother and I debark and take a cab in order to catch a final glimpse of the family home on Mallorca Street. To our surprise, we find an American couple living there, a Protestant pastor and his wife who purchased the place from Mom just before she and Valerie had packed up and left the island for good. The couple invite us in for a brief moment; we feel odd, knowing it's our house no more. Then Kanani and I walk about our old neighborhood streets and chat, also briefly, with childhood friends, not realizing it's the last time we'll ever see them.

Our ship was originally slated for a similar day's visit at Ciudad Trujillo, capital of the Dominican Republic. For unspecified reasons— later, we'll learn, because of a secret landing by the U.S. Marines—the stop is canceled. Instead we watch Hispaniola's verdant north coast roll slowly by and, within days, arrive at Havana harbor, where Mary is supposed to be awaiting us. The abrupt change in itinerary, though, will have some unforeseen consequences.

Kanani and I nervously come ashore, scanning more than once the crowd of anxiously expectant kin. Our stepmother is nowhere to be seen, even though we had wired her from the ship. Our fellow voyagers— including Marta Lilia and her little sisters—go their literally merry way. Their large numbers slowly, steadily dwindle. Kanani and I are soon the very last ones left. We try calling Mary's relatives, but there's no answer. And there we are, seated by ourselves in an empty Cuban customs hall with our bags and boxes.

In recent months, meanwhile, the revolution has been gearing up. The system hasn't yet moved toward full-blown Communism or even socialism. But there's nationalist and populist fervor aplenty in Castro's impassioned speeches, sentiments that in turn are resoundingly seconded and applauded by large sectors of the Cuban people. Earlier that year, the public trials and executions of numerous Batista thugs had already given the *guerrillero* government a bad press in the United States. The momentum of events has led to growing diplomatic tensions between the new régime and the good Yankee neighbor to the north.

And here we sit, two gringo teenagers, traveling unaccompanied, and with no one to meet us or claim us. The port authorities now voice their suspicions. They wonder just what we're doing there all alone. Repeatedly they question us as to our citizenship. Our native fluency in Cuban Spanish perhaps raises some uncertainties.

One customs employee casually asks, "You're rich, aren't you?"

"Us, rich?" I answer. "Nothing like that." After all, we're middle class, I've always known, though at the time it doesn't occur to me that any American is likely to be considered rich until proved otherwise.

We're shunted from desk to desk. The questioning drags on. Finally we're taken into custody. And before we know it we're being transported aboard a small launch, under a bright tropical sun, to some kind of offshore detention center.

The place, clean and spare, isn't a dungeon or a jail. It even has attractive Spanish arches and an outside garden for walks. Still, my brother and I find ourselves in a situation uncomfortably resembling house arrest. "What a mess," Kanani remarks earnestly, nervously, a number of times. Owing perhaps to my own previous experience as a detainee in Caracas, I'm less fearful; in fact I'm oddly numb about it.

Finally, at some point Mary shows up and singles us out as her charges. Never have we felt so relieved at seeing our stepmom. During the final bureaucratic negotiations for our release, she gets into a dispute with one of the uniformed gents concerning Cuba's "drift toward Communism." The middle-aged fellow cordially responds and explains that, actually, the new land reform law is a means of fending off Communism. But there's no common ground for a discussion, and Mary probably lacks much knowledge as to either the concept of land reform or the actual law.

Once freed, Kanani and I are taken by taxi to spend the night at that unpleasantly familiar green stucco building in Miramar. This time, though, we're lodged not in our erstwhile private, empty "home" upstairs—where Kanani had once wept bitterly and uncontrollably, where we'd spent many a loveless, desolate weekend furlough together—but rather with Mary's sister and brother-in-law, on the ground floor. Again, it's the very last time the two of us will set foot inside that sad place or see those accidental kin, our step-aunt and step-uncle, who'd served as dutiful sponsors during our biweekly leaves.

To pass the time, that afternoon I'll take a bus—the same blue, chug-chug bus my brother and I used to ride, with much relief and anxiety, as cadets-on-leave—to pay a casual visit to the military academy. It is dusk as I arrive, the only noise that of the ever-twittering crickets. As I stroll through the mute, chiaroscuro grounds I encounter Argüelles, the fortyish, balding deputy headmaster, and Saker, stocky and extroverted, a stellar ex-student and greatly admired campus personality in my time, who'd graduated the same year of my departure. They're lolling about outside the deserted dining hall.

We chat, exchange amenities, update our bios: my life as a gringo Venezuelan, now on a Statebound, homebound journey; Saker's engineering studies at the University of Oklahoma, where he has actually met a couple of older Caracas schoolmates of mine.

The political situation comes up. "Something big is happening in this country!" exclaims Argüelles to me.

"We're going to make the world tremble!" remarks Saker.

In our time, in fact, the school had harbored its fair share of Fidelista sympathizers. And here I was, witnessing these sympathies within a changed light, on a different stage: Castro's cause is no longer a remote and shadowy underground movement but the party in power.

(Years later, I'll hear that HMA was shut down by the revolution, its physical plant presumably nationalized. Saker, the ex-student, will appear briefly in the *New York Times* in the late 1960s, in a single-paragraph news item about his having been a staffer at the Cuban U.N. Mission, and, just recently, deported from the U.S. by the Immigration Service. No details were provided.)

Next day, in the departure area at Rancho Boyeros airport, having said all our good-byes, Kanani and I sit around waiting for our Florida-bound flight, when who should strut in but another former HMA schoolmate! We exchange greetings. A handsome, cocky, bantam type, he's one of the guys who'd been kicked out in the child-sodomization case. Now he sports olive-drab wear, an automatic weapon, and a wad of bills as he refers, with characteristic nonchalance, to the revolution. (Today, as I write, I wonder how he viewed the socioeconomic changes. Back at HMA he had been more of a partygoer, stud, and good-time-Charlie type than the kind of political devotee you would expect to morph into a *miliciano*. Also, given the anti-homosexual policy later to be adopted by the regime, I can only assume that the guy's youthful misadventures had been stricken from his past record.)

An hour after leaving Cuba our mini-plane touches down at Key West, the first of many upcoming stops in our country of citizenship. As we deplane, we overhear a conversation between two well-dressed, thirtyish American businessmen. "Well, *that's* one ordeal that's good to be over with." Yeah," says the other, "I wouldn't go back to Cuba if they *paid* me!" Some Cuban passengers give the gringo twosome dirty looks. My brother and I understand none of it and in fact are indifferent. Besides, Cuba is the past; that little exchange is our final encounter with Cuban concerns for a long time.

And now—not precisely as immigrants yet definitely not returnees—we are about to embark on our adventure in seeing the U.S.A., beginning with the former Confederate portions.

The interstate highway system is still in the planning stages, so the roads we'll ride on scarcely differ from the two-lane thoroughfare that takes us, via local transport, from the southernmost Florida Key to the Greyhound bus station in downtown Miami. There in the pinball-machine room I'll first hear a grown adult male spew out, upon tilting his game, the angry interjection "Oh, shit!"

Our tickets consist of a long string of some fifteen to twenty coupons—the number of times we'll have to change buses before reaching our last stop in faraway New Mexico. We're hauling our belongings about in a loose assortment of old suitcases and cartons. Somewhere along the way, in a southern state some night, we over-hear one bus driver comment tersely to another, "Two kids." (Years later, I'll wonder if the uniformed employee was voicing surprise, per-plexity, or concern—or merely describing the obvious. Still, that both Kanani and I happened to appear younger than our actual years must have made these "two kids," journeying alone, seem even more of an oddity to those long-distance drivers.)

Meanwhile, the coldly efficient impersonality of the company clerks, diner employees, and bus operators comes as an unpleasant small jolt to us, our first little shock before the racial ones. And the vast, geomet-ric spaces, the dreary bus depots, and the general aura of loneliness leads me to remark, as we see the scenery flashing by, "I don't like what I've seen so far of the States." "Me neither," Kanani agrees.

Some folks on the buses are friendly enough. One extroverted, gray-ing lady, when I tell her about my forthcoming musical career, sug-gests jokingly that, for stage purposes, I expand my last name to "Belloni." And there's the dapper, bespectacled, early-thirties chap in a gray suit and necktie. Intense-looking, he coincides with us on a lot of consecutive buses and remarks quietly to me during a rest stop, just after we've used the urinals, "You kids seem to be on a long haul." I explain to him our overseas travels and weird land itinerary. Eyebrows raised, he shakes his head in disbelief.

Our odyssey takes us through the endless, flat expanse and elusive horizon of Texas, on into the more varied, multihued, rugged country of eastern New Mexico. In Albuquerque the sheer length of Central Avenue amazes us until, from downtown, we board our final bus, going north. Early on I'd wired Mom about our arrival; now we feel puzzled at not finding her at the Santa Fe depot. We settle into its high-backed, dark wood benches for an uncertain wait. As it turned out, Mother, believing Albuquerque to be our terminus, had first driven down there with Valerie and Steve. Having figured things out, she then drives back. When at last she stands at the front door of the station, Kanani sees yet cannot recognize her. Me, I'm just finishing a pinball game, at which point little Valerie cries out, "There they are!" and runs toward us in her white dress and patent-leather Mary Janes, beaming, jumping up and down, and hugging each of "her boys" enthusiastically even as Mother and Steve give us their warm welcomes.

After two years without seeing them, we "boys" feel deliriously elated and happy. (The memory of that sudden reunion and what it meant will remain among the most vividly joyful of my life.)

Time to settle in. The first dwelling my brother and I will know in El Norte is a small, modest frame house with pink stucco trimmings, situated at the outskirts of a village called Española, an important junction halfway between Santa Fe and Taos. (The town's name means simply "Spanish," so we remain coincidentally linked to the Hispanic world.)

Steve continues with the U.S. Forest Service, doing duty in various workstations scattered about the state's northwest. Mother works for a spell as a freelance reporter for the *Santa Fe New Mexican* (where her immediate boss is budding novelist Tony Hillerman).

Picking up from where we'd all left off in P. R., we three siblings and our mom ease into a family routine of sorts. Kanani, Valerie, and I get involved in the usual kinds of brother-sister activities: games, jokes, roughhousing, and tiffs. Steve drops by regularly and joins in our four-way Scrabble games. We're kept further company by Kanani's dog, a lively, border collie half-breed whom he's named, simply, "Dog." At one point Valerie stares at the frisky mutt and suddenly remarks, "He's smiling!" We all laugh uproariously, except Valerie, whose feelings are hurt; she sulks and cries.

The nature of Mom and Steve's ties is a mystery topic that none of us hears addressed. When I ask her casually in the kitchen one day if she had moved to New Mexico because of him, she grins slightly, says no, and explains that she'd wanted us all to stay connected with the Spanish world, and of course there were the newspaper jobs . . . So I'll be a wee bit surprised when, just a year later, in November 1960, a letter from her starts out telling me to hold my breath: she and Steve have just gotten married!

But that happy ending is still in the future. Meanwhile, despite financial straits, Mom soon finds me an inexpensive, secondhand upright piano and has it placed right by the dining table. It's my first personally owned keyboard ever! Excited, I plunge into daily practice, working feverishly on Mozart and Chopin in preparation for auditions at university. (I also pick out show tunes by ear; Mom wonders as to their advisability, given the inferior status of the nonclassical arts at that time.) I'm nervous about my future in music school, and I say so in the letters that I'll write to Caracas ex-classmates over the next couple of months.

Still, for my pan-Caribbean days I feel little or no nostalgia, and not just because of the inner pain I routinely associate with those years. After all, we were "down there," supposedly, only in passing, preliminary to our yearned-for, definitive, authentic existence up north. On the other hand, once I've departed Española and enrolled for good at an out-of-state campus, I will lie in my darkened dorm room late at night and actually try summoning up wistful feelings for my brand-new life as a New Mexican. But alas, I cannot. Something in me has lost the old habit of homesickness, is now incapable of missing places and even the people—my mother, my siblings—that matter most. Though I'm not aware of it as yet, my ability to nurture continuous, lasting attachments has suffered, and I've become deeply damaged as a result. Add to that Dad's legacy, and my own lack of stable, constant family bonds or community ties over a minimum four-year period ... well, I'm woefully unequipped to function normally as a feeling creature.

But my grasp of this whole pattern is still decades in the future.

In the meantime, Dad and I exchange letters about once a month. Sometime that year, I'll complain, both to Mom and to my former teacher Mrs. Williams, that the man's letters to me consist almost solely of "sermons, sermons, sermons!"

Back in Caracas I'd already been accepted by the University of New Mexico. Then, in light of my mother's home in Española, I'd gone on to request classification as a state resident, so as to pay the lower, in-state tuition fees. Despite vague doubts raised by the admissions office about my eligibility, I was nonetheless prepared to enroll there come September.

Sometime in early August, though, I received word that—thanks again to Mrs. Williams's help and contacts—I had been awarded a full tuition-and-fees scholarship at the University of Arizona. At the time Mom's money situation was uncertain. I also knew that I could not count on my dad for any consistent financial help toward my studies. And so for sound financial reasons I seized on the offer and went on to spend my next four years enrolled at that more distant campus, of which at first I knew nothing, other than its having a good music department.

One unfortunate result of this windfall was that, while my brother and sister continued to reside in New Mexico and would attend the university there, I'd have only intermittent contact with the state's physical beauties and rich blend of cultures. At least, when vacationing in Española and other towns to which Steve, Mom, et al. subsequently moved, I did go (and today still go) on family outings to the deep-red ridges and purple-streaked, undulating plains, to mute Indian ruins and enigmatic petroglyphs, and to adobe chapels in ancestral settings where the villagers still employ Cervantine turns of phrase. These quasi-magical spots our caring stepfather would now help us explore under an enormous blue sky.

The land was Steve's life. A son and grandson of humble Hispanic farmers and shepherds from the state's north country, he had served in the Navy during World War II and then availed himself of the GI Bill to study forestry in college. Upon graduation he joined the U.S. Forest Service and slowly fashioned an entire personal vocation out of his primal ties to the land of his youth. In time he came to know every butte, mesa, and layer of soil, every variety of spruce, pine, sage, or cactus, and each and every indigenous site of his surrounding milieu, all of which he negotiated on foot, horseback, bicycle, skis, and motorized transport. To this day he feels happiest and most comfortable when out on an open, rural expanse, preferably desert. We were uniquely privileged to have him as a guide to our special new homeland.

In addition Steve now served as an attentive, affectionate father to his newlywed's trio of kids. Kanani and Valerie especially received from him the selfless and unconditional support for their growth and education that is often taken for granted as part of family life. Kanani as a college student actually took to referring to Steve as "my father." Still later, when a twenty-three-year-old Kanani came perilously close to "falling through the cracks"—the result of adaptation problems aplenty, followed by fatherhood at age twenty-two—Steve helped place the struggling new parent in a wage-paying position with the recently founded U.S. Job Corps. In time Steve also assumed with great relish and much joy the role of grandfather to Kanani's son Sebastian Estevan (the middle name directly in Steve's honor).

Because of my own early departure for college, by contrast, I gained only off-and-on experience of Steve as family man. It was a chance circumstance that left me without a gradual transition to a more suitable father image. My psyche, lacking in the day-to-day exposure to Steve as an actively committed dad, instead ended up unnecessarily haunted by the troubling memories of my biological father as male parent. And so I grew much angrier, more bitter and resentful about our gringo dad down in Caracas than my little brother ever would be, while Valerie hadn't so much as been faced with Bell, Sr.'s presence. Today, as I write, we regard "grandpa Steve" (our current term of endearment for him) as the good father who saved us all, who gave Mom and her three lost children not just a livelihood but a life and love.

At that time, though, I was scarcely in a position to understand Steve's cultural and personal universe. I had first of all to deal with my recent identity shift from Hispano-Caribbean to Anglo-North American, and I also had a very different world of my own to make. These processes would absorb much of my spiritual energies over the next few decades. As I boarded the bus for out of state and waved a wistful good-bye to my whole family, it wasn't so much a college town that I'd embarked on as my next stage in a complex, nonlinear, secular pilgrim's progress.

Now at the university I meet students, dormmates, and professors. They inevitably ask "Where're you from?"

And I reply, almost unthinkingly, "From Venezuela."

Unlike anywhere in Latin America, here the answer draws a blank as my fellow gringos randomly confuse the place with Argentina or Perú or Brazil. To my surprise and chagrin, Stateside issues of *Time* don't even carry a section called "Hemisphere," which, in the magazine's south-of-the-border edition, had been a weekly department. New acquaintances, meanwhile, remark on my accent in English, something that I'd never even been aware of. My recent provenance invites occasional friendly humor: a first-year twosome takes to dubbing me "The Caracas Kid," presumably their way of assimilating me to the more familiar Cisco Kid. In other recurring jokes, people ask if I'm a Latin lover, or they say that I *don't* exactly look like such a macho type. Or they wonder if I've been involved in any of those crazy revolutions down there.

Realizing that my previous country of residence means almost nothing to my northern listeners and has no prestige or standing among them, I end up saying little about it other than to the Latino students with whom I sometimes hang around on campus. Looks like I've got to learn how to repudiate that side of me. Besides, I'm an American, aren't I? After all, that's how I've always thought of myself! And, as a lifelong U.S. citizen who speaks the lingo fluently, I feel little of the caution, timidity, and uncertainty that typify the usual greenhorn's approach to his new country.

So, blissfully unaware that some of my Hispano-Caribbean customs—linguistic and otherwise—might be out of place here, I cling to them unthinkingly. No translation, no transitions necessary, right?

One afternoon, during the first few weeks of term, I'm walking through the music practice-room corridors with a fellow freshman named George. A tall, leggy, female classmate of ours comes galloping down the stairs.

I greet her casually, "Hello, cute one."

George looks at me, amused and bemused. "You're crazy!" he remarks, shaking his bespectacled head.

On another occasion, in the same area, I catch sight of a smart sax player, Tom with the carrot-colored hair.

Walking by, I say to him, spontaneously, "Hi, redhead."

Replies Tom, "Hi, blackhead," and then adds, with a smile, "Aha! Gotcha on that one!"

My salutations simply replicate old Spanish formulas. "Hello, cute one" directly translates from *"Hola, mona!"* or *"Hola, guapa!"*—each of them acceptable, normal greetings for Latina addressees. Similarly, "Hi, redhead" is verbatim English for *"Hola, pelirrojo."* Among Spanish speakers, of course, to salute someone by his or her physical traits isn't necessarily inappropriate. To Anglophones, though, it can sound aggressive or strange— "crazy," as George said. It's like my initial bewilderment when, back in Puerto Rico, my playmates would address me as *"chino"* or *"japonés."* Now my American friends are bewildered by my greeting them the same way, with adjectives.

Meanwhile, the crueler and more thoughtless aspects of Latin sociability have remained as part of my conduct, and earn me no credit from my peers. Talking with Bill, another guy from my classes, I allude to a passing girl who has a serious complexion problem as "sandpaper face."

Bill says, "That's nasty."

He's right, of course, although less so for Spanish ways. The "sandpaper" epithet is my Englishing of *"papel de lija,"* which in Latin America you might apply—along with other metaphors like "waffles" or "pineapple"—almost neutrally to an absent third person. English speakers, on the other hand, would shun the usage as impolite. But I won't get around to making sense of my college friends' reactions till years later, when my contacts with them lie well in the past.

At any rate, my Hispanic identity begins receding temporarily, or at least is losing its immediate relevance as I plunge into the study of music. Carolyn Smith in *The Absentee American* points out, "Returnees who are able to become members of a group with shared goals, such as a sports team, gain immediate access to friends and group acceptance." Obviously my music, from the start, fulfills a similar function. Whether singing in symphonic choir, casually accompanying vocalists and instrumentalists, or attending the constant stream of recitals that is part of everyday music-school existence, I'm able to use these means to gain immediate, if back-door, entry into an American life that more verbal, bookish studies and tasks might not have provided, and in which I probably would have felt somehow out of place. Nevertheless, there's some illusion involved. I'm not resolving my identity conflicts, merely postponing them for the time being.

Still, all I'd ever wanted to be is a musician, and here at long last such a possibility looms within my reach. I feel an inner thrill as I first walk down the music building's halls and hear live melodies emanating from its practice rooms, catch glimpses of piano students busily working on their Bach or Beethoven, overhear juniors and seniors talking about thirds and sixths and octaves just as regular folk might discuss bus routes or the weather. I thrill, quite simply, at now *living* in the world of music as my chief focus, my way of life.

And I'm amazed when I meet and befriend a few select music majors who share my passion for the art. One of them, Mike, is a native Tucsonian, tall and wavy-haired, a good pianist and cellist who'd always felt marginalized from his bourgeois family, precisely because of his artistic inclinations. (A war orphan—a fact that may explain his prickliness—he is attending the university on survivor benefits.) Another friend, Chris, is an Air Force veteran and father of three, who in his teens in segregated Tennessee discovered opera on the Texaco Saturday afternoon broadcasts, and since managed to become fully conversant with musical theatre from Mozart to Menotti. He's also a talented stage actor, a ham, and just incidentally, my first African-American friend. Years later Chris will tell me of the many small racial indignities he'd had to put up with from certain fellow students and even faculty members. ("You and I, Gene, we were the music school's mascots," he'll remark to me in 2003.) With both Mike and Chris I'll chat at length about the classics as I'd never been able to before.

Meanwhile, the piano beckons. I practice on my instrument up to four hours per day, and even more than that on weekends. My obsession derives in part from the simple joy of finally being a legitimate, developing pianist of sorts. But there's also a vaguely fearsome sense of having monstrous amounts of catching up to do, because, unlike most of my peers, I haven't had the advantage of ten years' musical training.

Up through my senior year I'll make rapid technical strides, performing such moderately difficult works as the Chopin C-minor Nocturne, the Bach E-minor Toccata, the Beethoven Sonata in D opus 10, and Brahms's Intermezzi opus 118 and B-minor Rhapsody. As already was the case in Venezuela, my mental-musical-visual system allows me a fast preliminary grasp of the compositions and vastly facilitates my ability to get them up to speed.

On the other hand, because of my late start, serious classical performing is simply out as a career possibility. In order to get *really* good, sad to say, you need to have been playing since childhood. Which means that I've got to find my proper path in the musician's life. Public-school music (choirs, orchestras, bands) is a mystery to me. Before college I'd never even heard of it; only following years of U.S. residence will I begin to grasp its noble role and function. So, among the various music-major options I first pick theory and composition. By my junior year I've become well versed enough in the theoretical part for one of my teachers to hire me as part-time grader for the weekly written exercises in Harmony I class. On my own time, and for class assignments, I compose. The dozen pieces that I complete—chamber movements, art songs, piano miniatures, jazz arrangements, satires—aren't all bad and show some technical ingenuity. Coming from no specific grounding in any musical experience or tradition, though, my creative activities go nowhere. I've simply no starting idea, even a mistaken one, of where I might belong as a would-be composer.

The marching-band subculture that largely dominates music-school life at a large, state university offers me few attractions. Besides I don't play a wind or percussion instrument, and I can't make head or tail of the football games where the bands do their halftime shows. Meanwhile, the assorted vanguards—serialism, neoclassicism, and the like—then enjoying élite respectability require a cumulative knowledge and proficiency that, with my novice status in the field, I still lack.

Finally in my sophomore year I switch to musicology. Once again, I throw myself wholeheartedly into this next enterprise. Week after week I check out my full allowable quota of classical LPs from the town library. Scores dutifully in hand, I listen to pieces repeatedly, playing the recordings even as I cook and eat. In consequence I get to know quite intimately some of the oddest, weirdest corners—medieval masses, lesser Italian madrigalists, organ composers from before Bach's time—of Western musical history.

Partly guiding me through this self-training process is James Anthony, my first intellectual mentor, a journeyman musicologist on the faculty. A native Rhode Islander perpetually in love with Paris, he will later become known for his scholarly work on the French baroque. A fine piano teacher and a man of broad culture with a constant wry smile, he serves as an inspiration at a time when I'm in urgent need of such a figure. Like Mrs. Williams back in Caracas, he also seems to intuit my psychological troubles. Over a two-year spell he'll support and indulge, well beyond the call of duty, my imbalances and incompleteness, and make helpful efforts for my sake that I'll finally appreciate only years hence. Studying with him is my ritual initiation into the traditions of intellectual disciplehood. I like the relationship, the feeling. I like what it represents to me as an eager young apprentice in a field not yet fully my own.

Music, however, isn't my whole life during those years. Other, discrete social circles exist as well. One of them is the foreign students' association, particularly its Latin American segment. For reasons I'll never know, a lot of the Latins on campus are in fact from Venezuela. They've come for study at the university's highly regarded engineering school. During my first couple of years I spend long hours with my "fellow Venezuelans," chatting in dorm rooms, telling jokes in Spanish at the snack bar, and going to the border town of Nogales, Mexico, where we find comfort in our temporary return to the Hispanic world.

Later, in my junior and senior years, much of my free time is spent socializing with the minuscule, bohemian, semi-Beat element around campus. Though small in numbers and visibly marginal, the bunch includes some of the school's best and brightest as well as a wide range of cultural types. A bearded local sage. A pretty boy from L.A. Assorted folk singers. A dazzling piano virtuoso. New York sophisticates. Some extremely bright small-town women from the state's hinterland. And the inevitable professional students and dilettantes. Just as one sees on the occasional TV report, the crew really does sit around smoky tables talking about Sartre, Shakespeare, religion, the Algerian war, Fellini, and Paul Klee. In short, they're at home in the wide world of ideas and art; through that variegated crowd, I find out that the life of the mind can have an everyday existence, earthly uses, and a human face.

Looking back, I now realize that, given my lack of native ground, classical music always seemed to offer the promise of a rich yet culturally neutral universe to which I could aspire. (Reading books on science had provided similar solace in Cuba, but I'd eventually run up against my ineptness with the nuts-and-bolts procedures of lab work.) The symphonic classics became my country, so to speak. Rooted though they may have been in the Europe of their origins, they were still sufficiently abstract, foreign, and universal for me to find in them a refuge.

What's curious is that Kanani also turned to music in his college years. He became an accomplished folk singer-guitarist and song-writer, and even wrote a delightful song about me, entitled "My Brother's Hat." From 1967 to 1979 he played the coffeehouse circuit, until the groundswell of Reaganism swept aside that sensitive, precariously poised subculture and his performing career along with it.

As a sophomore at Española High, which he'd started to attend just before I left for college, Kanani felt immediately bewildered by the social scene. For example, he found himself completely unable to make sense out of the year's first all-school pep rally, a ritual that neither of us had ever so much as heard about in our previous life.

His school's student mix comprised three ethnic factions, none of them his: 1) the local Hispanics, profoundly suspicious of outsiders—of Spanish-speaking foreigners particularly—and not at all disposed to displaying their identity, other than on occasion in extravagant ways, like the *pachucos,* the colorfully appareled Mexican-American gangs of the time; 2) the Anglos, mostly lower-middle or working class, rural, provincial, and WASP, and either cowboyish or Southern Baptist in culture, though a bit more accepting than the Latinos of Kanani, whom they initially referred to as "that South African"; and, 3) the various Native American groups, then as now another, separate country.

Kanani's general approach was to attempt to fit in, somehow, with all of them. In fact, over the next decade or so, his survival strategy would be to refashion himself constantly. In college he'd go through numerous phases: dandy, cowboy, philosopher, folkie, Latino. Not surprisingly, he strongly identifies with the protagonist Zelig of Woody Allen's disquieting, comic film by that name.

In high school he did next to no work. The rudimentary level of the material taught in class offered him few challenges. He muddled through with C's, scarcely opening his books. Because he did geometry Spanish-style, the school authorities initially set him back a course. Unlike his experience at HMA, though, the blunder was soon caught and rectified. One class for which he studied seriously was anthropology, in part because its cultural-relativist assumptions spoke to his own deracination. As an adult, he would read extensively in the field.

There existed a more banal reason for Kanani's lagging academic performance: nearsightedness. Starting in Cuba, it had become necessary for him to get up and stand close to the blackboard. He seriously needed eyeglasses, but our father had done nothing to correct the deficiency. So I'm surprised when, being met by Kanani and Steve at the Santa Fe bus station for my first Thanksgiving break, I find my kid brother enthusiastically wearing spectacles. Now at least he's able to see. Today, Kanani, all grown up and a natty dresser, owns some eight pairs of eyeglasses, in a wide range of designs and colors that match his varied wardrobe.

I take a lot of luggage with me on that first trip home. Besides clothing, toiletries, and piano scores, I bring all my classical LPs inside a sturdy, handsome box previously crafted and painted for me by Steve. I also drag along a duffel bag brimful of paperback books. For extra reading, just in case. Mother and Steve burst out laughing when they see it. Curiously enough, I will in fact eventually read most of those volumes. For weekend travels in my adult years, I'll scale down my expectations and pack a mere five books. (Again, just in case!)

From my very start at the university, there are hints of larger matters that will concern me for the rest of my life. First is English composition. Or rather my lack of skill in it. Surprisingly, I've placed into the more advanced level of the universally required (and much-feared) freshman comp class, perhaps because of my halfway-decent English vocabulary, gleaned in part through Latin cognates as filtered through Spanish, plus the scattered reading I've done over the years. Alas, it's not enough. My initial essay for the class comes back covered start to finish with instructor's pencil marks. And a grade of D minus.

As the weeks roll by, I arrive at a scary realization: due to my disjointed past schooling and my weak training at Colegio Americano, I know next to nothing about writing in English—about its standards of organization, argumentation, diction, and clarity. Now I pay the price as I tremble over weekly assignments and wonder whether I'll ever manage to write adequately, let alone feel comfortable with writing.

Oh, my God! I've got to improve my prose! I grudgingly recognize the grim fact. And I set out to tackle it in every way possible. One means is simple, all too simple. If my sizeable vocabulary is what got me into a higher-level class, well, why not build upon that store? Over the next few years I'll look up in the dictionary any unfamiliar word that I encounter, then jot down the definition in a notebook I keep in my front pocket. As a junior and senior I'll even win prizes in a vocabulary contest sponsored annually by the school.

On the negative side, my writing becomes a turgid and opaque tangle of big, strange words. At least six or seven years will go by before I finally start being able to write with anything like due simplicity, native rhythms, and personal style.

Some of my writing problems are cultural in origin. The sin of a comma splice comes as a surprise to a kid schooled previously in a language that, by custom, uses few semicolons and relies a lot on commas for punctuation. The same goes for run-on sentences, which are quite common in Spanish but a no-no in expository English. The Spanish language likes and even highly values long, winding sentences. Contemporary English prefers short, fast-moving ones. Then there are the small habits that have got to be cleaned up. In Spanish, one writes out centuries with Roman numerals, for example, "in century XIX." My composition prof is perplexed when he sees that usage in one of my papers.

More important, though, I've no real experience of U.S. daily life, while (save for music) much of my personal background is unusable, even incommunicable, for ordinary comp purposes. (In the words of Ruth Hill Useem and Richard Downie: "When [Third-Culture Kids] come to their country of citizenship—some for the first time—they do not feel at home because they do not know the lingo or expectations of others, especially those of their own age.") My ignorance of current U.S. affairs further compounds my writing problem. Among my first assigned essay topics in class is "Federal Aid to Education," a mysterious, unheard-of issue to me. And since I'm in no position even to begin finding out why Washington should or should not help fund the nation's schools, for my paper I write about the evils of television instead.

(I must confess that, ever since I did start getting a handle on American politics, many of its higher-level debates have struck me as artificial—like the arguments over states' rights that were marshaled against antiracist activism and legislation in the 1960s, or the bizarre, theological hairsplitting over "the federal deficit" that became a prime-time scholastic spectator sport in the 1980s.)

At times I begin to feel ever so slightly disenchanted with a country I'd long heard idealized by my father, my mom, and my Caracas schoolmates. On the personal level, I'm surprised at the casual rudeness of the many Americans who, following a lengthy conversation, will simply walk off without so much as a formulaic "good-bye." (Years later, I'll find this very same behavior satirized in Dickens's *Martin Chuzzlewit*.) In another incident, I see a lost notebook in a classroom, with the owner's name and dormitory address on it. The girl at my left, I'm aware, lives in that same dorm, so I suggest maybe she could take it back there as a little favor. She answers, "Why should I? I don't even know who she is." Similarly, in the cafeteria, a classmate and I are sitting down for lunch, and I notice an abandoned briefcase on one of the chairs. "Looks like someone left his stuff here," I note. "Well, that's not my problem," says the classmate. Neither of us does anything about it.

At the university, frats and football rule the roost, setting much of the campus tone. Over the years I'll have my share of nasty encounters with the Greeks and their kind. From their expensive cars they'll taunt me out on the street or occasionally grab me by the arm as I ride my bicycle. Once I observe a trio of them kick a parked bike (not mine), and hear a voice from among them bluster, "Well, it was in my way!"

In a particularly sordid incident during senior year, a mob of half a dozen frat guys drops by my place to beat me up after word has reached them that I dared speak ill of a "brother" of theirs to a female classmate whom we both knew in common. They force open the door to my apartment and cause minor damage to a brick path. Luckily I happen to have been out at the time of their social call.

My friends in the "Beat" crowd, on hearing about the incident, fantasize about getting guns and mowing them all down. Or getting into the frat kitchen and poisoning their soup. Fortunately, we lack the means to do so. It never occurs to me to take them to court for breaking and entry.

Still, although fraternities can resemble street gangs in their actions, there are significant differences. They have more money, for instance.

Then there's my dorm roommate in sophomore year, a gross gringo such as only the most dogged anti-American propagandist might have dreamt up, so extreme and stereotypical is he. Tall, lanky, with a blond brush cut and a couple of pimples in his sunken cheeks, his lower-than-C grade average has earned him suspension from his frat. Yet he continues to believe passionately in the Greek system. A business major who imagines himself a high-placed insurance man some day, he looks upon his humanities requirements with indifference at best and likes bragging to me about his latest sexual conquests. Geography not being his forte, he refers to Venezuela et al. as "Mexican countries." He has a special animus against "camel jocks"— the racist term for Arabs—as well as the standard prejudice against "niggers," whom he thinks belong "in their place" in Harlem.

"Rinky" is his preferred pejorative. Nonfrat people, he feels, are "rinky." My classical music (which he compares to "a bunch of howling cats") is truly "rinky." And my finding such- and-such a woman smart or a good conversationalist strikes him as pure "rinky-dink." (In frat-boy parlance at the time, the requisite term of praise for something or someone is "bitchin'!") He regularly, loudly greets my guests with a vigorous handshake and such jokes as "Hi, Seymour Butts here!" or "I'm Dick Bender!" Eventually some fellow students take to teasing me as "the man with the crude roommate." Though not particularly malicious, and in certain ways he's even a nice guy, he serves as an unwanted initiation into the fabled vulgarities of U.S. life.

Discrimination happens. To me as well as to others. Both in small-town New Mexico and at the university. I find myself shunned now and again by women, or, more accurately, by the prejudices that have shaped them. In Española, a tall high-school senior of Anglo stock has accepted me for a movie date one July evening. When I ring her bell some days later, the girl opens the door and informs me matter-of-factly that her dad (whom I can see, standing sullenly in the background) has forbidden our date. She blurts out a fast good-bye and closes the door. I feel perplexed more than hurt.

In my university classes there's the occasional pretty woman who silently ignores my attempts at small talk. In the case of at least one snub, a dormmate of the snubber and a personal friend of mine confirms the brush-off as indeed an instance of bigotry, though whether owing to my dark skin, Asian features, Hispanophone origins, or undefinable foreign accent she doesn't say.

Such incidents, while not frequent, are disquieting enough when they occur. Back in Latin America, I'd been teased to my face as a *chino*, a *japonés*, or a *gringo*; and though I may at times have been shunned by fellow Latinos because I didn't have all my marbles firmly in place, my racial and cultural makeup hadn't ever been directly at issue in gaining acceptance.

It takes me far too long to understand that, in the Southwest, the term "Mexican" is actually a loaded word, a pejorative. The more benign, colorless "Spanish" is the preferred designation among both Anglos and Latinos. ("Hispanic" and "Latino" haven't even entered the everyday lexicon as yet.) In my earlier Caribbean incarnation at HMA, I'd met exactly one kid from Mexico. So now the many Mexicans and Mexican-Americans whom I see in the halls or at the library strike me as new, exotic, and strangely fascinating. Sometimes I'll inquire of a Hispanic or brown-skinned student, "Are you Mexican?"—and feel an air of discomfort descend on the conversation.

Ironically, in many cases the term "Mexican" is only remotely applicable to them anyway. Because immigration from across the border in the early sixties is not yet a massive phenomenon, many Latinos and Latinas I meet in both states are the strictly local, mixed-blood descendants of Iberian colonizers and their indigenous consorts, and so have roots going back to three centuries of imperial Spanish rule. The lands where they've been born and raised were officially Mexican only between 1820 and 1848, after which an aggressive United States took them by conquest and treaty. (My stepfather, Steve, is of that stock.)

So many confusions . . . Mexico . . . Mexicans . . . New Mexicans . . . "Spanish" . . . and all the rest of the terminology. They're just one more instance of my own Hispanic background being less than helpful in my efforts at adjusting to my quasi-immigrant status and Anglo-American circumstances.

Political and social topics still stand as something distant and opaque to me. My chief preoccupations during the second half of my undergraduate career revolve around my future and my mind. On one hand I've taken on the goal of becoming a musicologist. I entertain romantic notions of unearthing manuscripts in the dark corners of old Europe's churches, of putting my bilingualism to work by studying Spanish Renaissance composers so as to "fill a gap" in the field. And then I dream of passing on the beauties of Bach and Mozart, the complexities of Bartók and Stravinsky, to bright young students at a small college somewhere in the Midwest or the East.

On the other hand, musicology and music have begun to look like dead ends. The thought of spending long stretches with the bloodless artifacts of forgotten third-rate composers, of fussing over a host of aridly technical, pedantic problems, terrifies me.

There's also the matter of my complicated, slightly pained relationship to the art's practical side. Granted, I've made considerable progress on piano and have performed a little bit in public as soloist as well as accompanist. And I've picked up the rudiments of jazz, serving as a so-so keyboard man for local combos, even playing the occasional gig at a bar or a dorm dance.

But I face a problem that inevitably confronts late bloomers in music: uncooperative hand muscles. The hard truth is that, for almost any postchildhood beginner on an instrument, a major obstacle will crop up in developing your fingers to a point where they'll sail smoothly through fast runs—something that, to talented early starters, evolves naturally. It's a bit like acquiring a foreign language in late adolescence: no matter how rich and full your grammar and lexicon grow, the chances are you'll always make mistakes and speak it with an accent.

About the only renowned pianist I know of who first took lessons in his teens is Paderewski, a lone instance that at least provides grounds for hope. Also, at summer school in Boulder, Colorado (where I actually study briefly with composer George Crumb), I meet a late-starting pianist who, for two straight years, had holed up in a cheap apartment, practicing five hours a day and sustaining himself with table-waiter jobs. His efforts paid off; in time he became proficient enough to play with chamber ensembles and avant-garde musical groups in Europe.

Though I consider such an option, economic factors and the military draft pose some serious disincentives. And alas, I know that on any music-department faculty, public performances are part of the job, and that my piano skills need major advancement if I hope to function as a self-respecting practitioner within the field.

So some frightening decisions lie ahead.

Finally, and most tellingly, in my junior and senior years I'm discovering the universe of words. Verse. Prose. Theater. Thought. The final pages of *Crime and Punishment* move me deeply, putting me on a twenty-four-hour high. I start exploring Joyce, Beckett, and Camus, delving into Ibsen, Strindberg, Shaw, and Ionesco. I feel almost physically the verbal textures of Baudelaire, Yeats, Eliot, and particularly Keats (my mouth drools over the foods described in "The Eve of St. Agnes"). I fall in love with the intelligence and wit of Jane Austen. I test the philosophical waters by sampling Plato, Hume, Mill, Nietzsche, and especially Bergson, whose *Introduction to Metaphysics* allows me a first awareness of my intuitive side. And I check out recordings of Shakespeare's plays, which, text in hand, I listen to religiously, committing to memory the occasional line or short passage.

Music begins to seem too much a self-contained world, like mathematics or chess. While I continue practicing on piano and enlarging my musicological knowledge, I take every opportunity to study a literary repertoire that looms larger, fresher, and richer in possibilities.

Still, feeling ready to do something with my (however uneven) musical background, in senior year I apply for graduate study in musicology at Harvard, Columbia, and Berkeley. Come April, all three send me acceptance notices. None offer financial assistance. These partial rejections are a blessing in disguise. Had I received from any of them even minimal aid to do musicology, I probably would have continued and then ended up trapped in a subspecialty whose limits I found confining, in an art where I felt unfinished and incomplete. By the summer after graduation I've decided to go on to Berkeley—a state university, with relatively low tuition—and, once I'm there, I can switch to literature.

Confronted with a whole new field, I keep on reading—the Greek classics (Euripides arouses my sympathies), Russian novelists, modern

English poets (I learn much of them by heart), the existentialists-absurdists who dominate much of literary talk at the time. I still lack a structured grounding of any sort in a national literature, though, and this accidental gap will cause a lot of drifting and uncertainty in my studies.

When Mom and Steve see me off at Grants, New Mexico, on the long, sleek, Santa Fe Chief train, I start on my first railway trip ever, California-bound, and on a mental and spiritual journey whose dimensions and dangers I can scarcely imagine. Luckily there are moral supports plus an unexpected source of financial aid to see me through. Mike and Chris, my music-school buddies, had graduated and moved to Berkeley a year earlier. They and their new friends now meet me at the East Bay rail terminus at Richmond, and in the ensuing years they'll provide much-needed company on the lonely edges of the "multiversity."

As I venture into various campus offices the next few days, among my tasks is to request the out-of-state tuition waiver then available to graduate students having 3.5-plus grade averages. My attempt succeeds; all I have to pay at registration is the "incidental fee" required of every matriculant, which in those pre–Governor Reagan days stands at a mere ninety-six dollars per semester.

Meanwhile, I find an inexpensive studio apartment on a quiet, tree-lined street near Piedmont Avenue, between Dwight and Derby. Over my next two years there—and with no phone—I'll scrimp by on food-service jobs, federal loans, the rare piano gig, and occasional small checks from Mother and Steve.

And I begin taking an array of courses in Spanish and English literature.

Ah, Berkeley!

No place in the continental U.S. has marked me as deeply, as decisively. Both university and town surpassed any expectations I'd arrived with. The experience, day-by-day and long-term, was to prove exhilarating yet also depressing. I lived through some of my most formative highs and lows there, both as a mind and as a man of feeling.

First, there was the atmosphere—the air, literally—a dry, cool freshness unique in the world. Temperatures seldom went above 80 degrees F. in summer or under 40 in winter. Save for the rainy season, December to March, the everyday climate was sunny and crisp.

The campus itself, located on a hill that rose first slowly, then steeply, had a unique and spectacular beauty, with its central, inclined greenswards, its gentle rivulet traversed by wooden bridges, its grove of eucalyptus trees, and its distinctively American style of architecture (in contrast with the revival Gothic or faux-English red brick of the older eastern campuses). Over the university grounds just beyond the main library and Wheeler Hall, there rose the needle-sharp, gray obelisk of the campanile, whose bells rang out rhythmic arrangements of Bach and Tcherepnin's keyboard miniatures for all denizens at dinnertime.

And there was Telegraph Avenue, perpendicular to the Bancroft Way exit of the UC campus, and onto which tens of thousands of students, profs, and other employees poured forth daily amid the wide array of shops and crafts vendors, the record businesses blaring offbeat classical strains, the fully stocked yet homey bookstores (Cody's for new stuff, Moe's for used paperbacks, and other more specialized shops), the Mexican restaurant La Fiesta, which served savory flautas and tasty huevos rancheros such as my palate had never known, and, kitty-corner, farther down, the Caffé Mediterraneum, split-leveled, which—with its varying-sized marble tabletops and its mingled aromas of freshly roasted coffee and inexpensive Greek fare—functioned as chief gathering spot for local Bohemia of all ages and persuasions.

On this five-block stretch you witnessed a constant parade of people of every look, shape, and style. You walked and participated in a cosmopolitan carnival, a human Babel casually enriched by the presence of the several thousand foreigners who swelled UC's ranks. Next door to the Mediterraneum was an all-night laundromat whose machines were creatively labeled, in pairs, TRISTAN/ISOLDE, ROMEO/JULIET, and the like; there, during my initial year or so at Berkeley, after the library had closed at 11 p.m., I'd often settle in and study (without any wash), simply in order to be near the endless street life and to put off for a spell the cramped solitude of my apartment (as well as the temptation to lie down and sleep).

At the core of Berkeley's many attractions was its earnest, high-power intellectualism, detectable at every level and in every corner. Being at a place that counted so many serious, even great minds among its members was a genuine treat. (I mean, Pulitzer Prize winners and Nobel laureates were actually out there, walking those very paths!) Students and amateur scholars, young and old, sat about the vast open-air Terrace or the smaller Bear's Lair basement, urgently, passionately discussing books, music, politics, science. Among my passionate literary interlocutors was Ellen Goldensohn, daughter of a New York medical-school professor and herself a graduate student in English, who later would become the editor of *Natural History* magazine. And I'll never forget a late summer afternoon in 1964 when I accidentally heard a deep-voiced, thirtyish sage in chino pants and sneakers commenting on and eloquently declaiming from California poet Robinson Jeffers to some rapt listeners casually seated about one of the Bear's Lair's round tables.

In similar fashion the music crowd, with whom—via my college chums Mike and Chris and the latter's wife, Mary—I'd become friendly, lived and enjoyed their classics simply as part of everyday existence. (Someone once called a get-together in celebration of Anton Bruckner's birthday.) Fine jazz could be heard piping into the student center lobby's loudspeakers. (Pianist Vince Guaraldi's *Black Orpheus*—an album I once saw him play from in a small café on Grove Street—was a much-favored LP at the time.) And the *Daily Californian,* a thick newspaper better in certain respects than many a larger city rag, featured everything from real-world and campus news, to opinion columnists (syndicated as well as in-house; right, left, and center), to knowledgeable and intelligent editorials (dealing with issues beyond that of dorm food), to informed and witty coverage of cultural events about town. (I contributed a few modest apprentice pieces—on Resnais's *Last Year at Marienbad,* on a Schubert concert—to its pages.)

There was a certain magic in being surrounded by so much intelligence and intelligentsia. But it was intimidating as well. The reading lists and writing workload in my various literature classes proved to be longer, deeper, and more demanding than anything I'd known previously. Back at my first college, it would've been unheard of for a student to have to write three ten-page papers in a humanities course at any level—which, at Berkeley, was the norm. In addition, due to my musical studies and my patchy background in writing, my prose in both languages still lagged. During my first semester a young Chilean instructor named Vicente Urbistondo twice took me aside to praise my "good ideas," yet also advised me to work at making my sentences cohere internally and connect logically. (I've remained ever grateful to him for his gesture, and wrote him a letter of thanks in the midnineties.)

To complicate matters further, my Spanish had grown rusty from four years' disuse. It was now stagnating at a native high-schooler's level and had gotten steadily debased by forms from English. My class papers were an inconsistent brew of Caribbean fluency, inappropriate gringo additives, and the most rudimentary literary turns of phrase.

My problems multiplied as I took on the study of English and American literature. Because of this second late start of mine, I was still at the ABC stage in my knowledge of the canon. The sensation as I first read, say, *Henry IV, Tom Jones,* or *Moby-Dick* was joyous, roughly akin to what I'd experienced during my piano apprenticeship back in

Caracas. Wanting to know more of those joys, I eventually enrolled for work toward the M.A. in English. In the course of the year I encountered special pitfalls, among them my still-evolving, as-yet-uncrystalized relationship to the language, which on occasion adversely affected my grades.

An infinitely larger problem than my own untutored skills was the problematical institution of "English" itself. Rather than an enclave of Bohemian literati, gathered about to enjoy, learn from, and be moved by poems and novels (as music folks normally do with sonatas and symphonies), what I'd walked into was a giant, entrenched corporate enterprise that had its own corporate language, style, tone of voice, and hand gestures. Whosoever preferred not to absorb these tribal ways might find survival difficult. The great books were filtered and sometimes obscured via a vast, bureaucratized clerisy whose own correspondingly vast critical canon every novice needed to know and respect simply in order to gain access to those priestly offices.

Besides its overwhelming size, there was the stifling insularity of the department and the field. Many an English grad I met knew little about authors outside the standard British or American ones. Some frankly boasted about never reading "foreign" books. Their world—baroque, complex, sophisticated—had its overtones of smugness, the result of their hegemony within the lettered halls of academe. (Most educated Americans, when they think *literature*, tend to think "English.")

So, with just a semester's course requirements and an oral comprehensive remaining toward my M.A. in English, I decided to abandon the field and transfer into Spanish instead. In the process I picked up my first teaching job as assistant for an intermediate grammar section.

Here, in Berkeley's smaller, cozier Hispanic halls I at least felt comfortable. I had a native's knowledge of the language (which, in the past two years, I'd made active efforts to improve upon through word lists and other exercises). And of course I knew something about the culture through personal experience. In many ways I date the beginnings of my legitimate entry into American life—as a salaried professional, doing something I felt right with and believed in—from that year.

Yet there were disappointments of another kind. If the English edifice was Alexandrian and baroque, the Spanish colony, just a few floors up within the same Dwinelle Hall, was latter-day underdevelopment. Since tons of basic documentation remained—and still remains—to be done in Hispanic studies, with whole archives as yet uncatalogued and key collections still unexhumed, many of my Spanish professors at Berkeley adhered steadfastly to a nineteenth-century, positivistic notion of literary research, conceiving of it as a purely paleographic enterprise—analyzing manuscripts, comparing editions. One eminent scholar—a nice, bright fellow who at various moments kindly encouraged me—saw Freud as a "new idea," whereas, in English department circles, psychoanalytic theory had attained a status of quickie shorthand and facile formula. At one point the same professor actually dictated to his graduate level seminar a list of seventeenth-century epics, complete with places and dates of publication. (No such bare facts would have taken up an English professor's class time, which would more likely have been spent on arcane analysis or discussion.)

Spanish literature itself had me in another dilemma. From my studies I grimly recognized that—due to imperial Spain's protracted decadence, then Generalísimo Franco's stultifying dictatorship—the country's larger literary tradition, generally speaking, wasn't on an equal footing with that of England or France. Lope de Vega and Calderón, while eloquent and indeed great poet-playwrights, weren't Shakespeare. The Spanish eighteenth century, acknowledged as a cultural low even by Hispanists, had no authors the equal of Pope or Dr. Johnson, let alone anyone remotely comparable to Britain's comic novelists or France's radical philosophes. And the Spanish Romantics, save for Bécquer, qualified mostly as airy bombast.

Friends and acquaintances I'd made in English at times questioned my having pulled out of the field. A few even mocked me, saying, "Lope de Vega?! How's he doin' these days?"

Yet I also knew that, besides "only" Cervantes and Lorca, there was a range of Spanish-language authors every bit as good as their foreign equivalents. Regarding verse, Góngora and Quevedo in the Renaissance and a host of poets in the twentieth century—including Latin Americans like Neruda, Vallejo, and Paz—could hold their own against the best full-time lyrists elsewhere. Concerning fiction, Pérez Galdós would have earned the renown of Dickens or Balzac had he written his novels in English or French. (Years later I'd also read Clarín's *La Regenta,* and find it in some ways a richer, fuller account of illicit passion and its consequences than is Flaubert's lofty and Olympian *Bovary.*) Over midafternoon coffee, in the autumn sun at the Terrace, I sometimes tried conveying these points to my friendly carpers from the English fold, but there was no convincing them. The unequal exchange furnished my first conscious glimpse of the phenomenon of culture serving as an informal extension of national-state power.

At any rate, I found a solution to my dilemmas by moving once again, this time into comparative literature. The change allowed me to combine the best of both Spanish and English, along with some French courses. Besides, I'd already spent most of my life comparing cultures, so it amounted to a logical choice. "Comp lit" helped put me academically where I happened to be culturally: neither in "English" nor in "Spanish" but somewhere in between the two, yet also above, outside, and even critical of both.

The word "Berkeley" naturally brings to mind "politics," the radical, left-wing sort. Berkeley in fact was where I experienced the beginnings of my political education. No place in the U.S. could have been a more appropriate place for me to start. Owing to my quasi-immigrant rootlessness and my intense four years in the world apart of musical study, at college graduation I was a political ignoramus who thought of politics merely as what took place inside government buildings. And other than entertaining some vague notion that a Scandinavian-style arrangement, combining basic economic security with democratic freedoms, seemed the most sensible solution, I had no idea of how actually existing societies were governed and held together.

My years in Berkeley helped me first see that there was considerably more to politics than the hairsplitting debates between Republicans and Democrats, or the then-reigning formulas about freedom vs. "totalitarianism"—that politics was also collective movement in society.

The levels of activity at Berkeley proved as much. To enter south campus from Telegraph Avenue on a weekday was to be faced by dozens of card tables, where individuals from groups covering the ideological gamut from Maoists and Trotskyists to assorted conservatives (libertarians and Edmund Burkeites as well as John Birchers) displayed and distributed their respective literature, alongside single-issue forums ranging from the Fair Play for Cuba Committee and Save the Grand Canyon to more colorful organizations such as the Sexual Freedom League, with their taste for scandal. I also recall an ad-hoc initiative opposing the change to all-digit telephone dialing, then just entering into effect. Crowds milled about the various tables, where discussions often turned heated and lively.

In addition there were the idiosyncratic freeshooters, among them Jerry Rubin, whom I met and chatted with once at the laundromat and who showed me—and many others—that political activism could be fun (among the campaign points in his unsuccessful bid for mayor of Berkeley was a promise to legalize marijuana). I also enjoyed the legendary Lenny Glazer, a street philosopher who used to stand on some randomly chosen spot near the card tables and, in his residual New York accent, reel off irreverently funny orations skewering official pieties and extemporizing on any topic that occurred to him at the moment, from the limits of Lyndon Johnson's War on Poverty to Zionism to the larger matters of human history. And of course there was Mario Savio, whose forceful voice often filled the quad, and whose eloquence and simple honesty became the most vivid symbol for all that was positive about Berkeley radicalism. (His untimely death in 1996 would cause in me, and in numerous others I talked to, a profound sadness.)

I spent many long hours on the sidelines of those impromptu groups, watching, listening. Getting an education every bit as valuable as what I was picking up in my courses. Feeling at times like the witness to an ongoing philosophic dialogue where grand ideas were being tossed about from one speaker to another. During the summer of 1964 the two hot topics—nationwide and at Berkeley's card tables—were the Barry Goldwater presidential campaign and the civil rights movement. I took note of the many uncompromising, well-scrubbed conservative spokesmen who, in the name of property rights, and darkly invoking the specters of possible Nazi or Communist tyranny, argued doggedly against *any civil rights legislation whatsoever.*

The Watts ghetto riots of 1965 sparked much passionate talk among the black students and other urban brothers who used the campus as a kind of social refuge. In a particularly memorable exchange from late that summer, some African-Americans of different ages got to informally debating, well past sundown, whether or not all whites were no good and not to be trusted. Suddenly, a carbon-skinned fellow in his midtwenties, fiery and articulate, grabbed by the shoulders a skinny, tender-looking, long-haired adolescent white kid from among the onlookers, trotted the boy to the center of the crowd, and asked the hardliners among them, "Look at him! How d'you know for sure if *he's* a racist?" After a moment's troubled silence, the sounds of debate played on.

Among the high points of campus activism during those years— and of course a watershed nationally—was the free speech movement

(FSM) of 1964. A lot of erroneous facts and false notions concerning that event have since become common currency. Here are the bare outlines of the episode as I remember them:

President Clark Kerr, reportedly under pressure from the regents, decided to ban the political tables and leafletters from the south campus entrance area. In reply, activists of all persuasions, from left to right, repeatedly expressed their opposition to the ruling, and eventually some seven hundred students began a sit-in inside Sproul Hall, the university's Greek Revival administration building. Meanwhile massive, sympathetic, open-air vigils sprang up in Sproul Plaza.

Then the real fireworks began. Some days later, the chancellor of the Berkeley campus, Edward Strong, called in the state police and had the sit-inners forcibly removed and arrested. In protest, FSM leaders called a student strike. The campus population by and large paid heed, skipping classes, walking picket lines in many cases, and bringing classroom routines to a halt. The arrested students were soon released on bail, the ban was officially lifted, and activists once again set up their card tables. Meanwhile Sproul Plaza had become a major venue for speakers and demonstrations, and would remain so for years.

At the time I was too much caught up in my own problems to be more than a sympathetic (and awed) observer. But almost every night during these events, I stood around the Sproul Plaza–student center area, listening to the speeches and feeling drawn to the human phenomenon I saw taking shape before my eyes.

Among the countless events that filled those few months, two particularly stand out in my mind. The first serves as an instance of the positive ways in which a committed collectivity can respond, spontaneously and intelligently, to an ominous challenge.

It was a pleasant October night, during the sit-in phase of the free speech movement, before the arrests had yet occurred. Protesters were assembled in a vigil in front of Sproul Hall, listening to orators and the occasional folk singer. Suddenly, from down Bancroft Way there descended a horde, hundreds strong, of fraternity and sorority types shouting, "Beat the Beatniks!" and thirsting for blood.

They took their position on the edges of the gathered vigilers. Right-wing Greeks and left-wing protesters began a tense standoff. A leader from the frat faction was now offered the mike. From the podium he delivered a vague, stumbling oration, made up largely of clichés and punctuated by rounds of applause from his cohorts. When he finished and rejoined his brethren, the Greeks' catcalls and threats of violence only grew in pitch. They were answered by countercatcalls and equal threats from the vigilers. The atmosphere became charged and dangerous.

The situation was saved by a little miracle. Out of nowhere, an FSM speaker made a very brief statement—barely more than a sentence—to the effect that responding to violence with violence only brings people down to the level of their provokers. His FSM audience, knowing immediately what was meant, turned absolutely silent. To the vicious insults and verbal assaults coming from the frat boys and their little sisters there now came from the radical side . . . no answer at all. None. Absolute, stony silence.

Over the next few minutes the provocations became sparser and more isolated. Finally the Greek mob turned around and shuffled back to frat row, their defeated tails hanging between their legs. Perhaps for the first time in their lives, their group thuggery had failed them.

The other FSM-related matter that's stayed with me has to do with the misleading, not to say dishonest, local press coverage of the events. From my own experience and that of fellow students, I knew that the strike had been spectacularly successful. Many profs had canceled their classes, and attendance at those that were actually held was notably thin. Yet the San Francisco dailies ran headline after headline proclaiming such false news as "STUDENT STRIKE FIZZLES," followed by reports baldly asserting that UC-Berkeley students had ignored strike calls by FSM leaders and dutifully gone to their class-rooms instead. In addition, loaded terms like "CAMPUS WAR" were employed in describing the conflict. A few months later *U.S. News and World Report* alluded darkly to the Berkeley "riots" that had "torn the town apart." These of course were outright distortions of what had been overwhelmingly peaceful protests, the violence and the threats having come exclusively from the police and the frat boys. Reading those false headlines and fabricated news items provided me my first direct experience of the degree to which the famously "free" and "objective" press will simply lie whenever it suits them to do so. The lies about those events haven't stopped, either.

Anyway, in the wake of FSM, what was already a vibrant and stimu-lating milieu became in the ensuing years a place of intense ferment, with daily speakers from every point of view featured in Sproul Plaza. On special occasions, on those very steps or just behind the Bear's Lair, you could hear Norman Thomas, Norman Mailer, or Isaac Deutscher speaking out against the Vietnam War, and such luminaries as Martin Luther King, Jr., or Stokely Carmichael orating on racial justice. Then, around sunset, when the political theater had subsided, the air was filled with the cross-rhythmic beat of drumming bongo ensembles.

During my first twenty-three years of existence, I haven't liked myself a hell of a lot. Dad has inculcated in me the sense that my interests hardly matter and that I'm not much good. And my difficulties in figuring out where I belong, first as a musician, then as a literary per-son, generally as a mind, and ultimately as a gringo (or Latino, as the case may be) have long been pressing on my soul. Finally, an angry side emerges that frankly hates my mixed identity. Negates as not-me my Hispanic past. Denies within me those overseas lands where I'd once lived. All so I might be the American boy I've always been taught I really am.

My inner battle becomes further complicated, and more anguished, as a result of the first viable, lengthy love relationship I'll experience with a woman of my choice. (In my two former extended liaisons, I'd been the pursued, not the pursuer.)

Anya (as I'll call her) is of European upper-class background. Refined and multilingual, she has a resonant British accent and a genuine love of classical music. She too is a lonely outsider in American life and, in her own way, is as confused about her national identity as I am about mine. For approximately a year, we'll provide each other passionate company as mutual first loves consoling each other's solitude.

Because of her cosmopolitan background, Anya is also the first among my peers of either sex to understand my multicultural past and urge me to acknowledge it. To make something of it rather than fight, reject, or mock it. A positive lesson that I take a while in learning, but for which, in the years to come, I'll be much indebted to her.

Still, her elegant poise masks a deep-seated childish streak. The two of us are both very immature emotionally, and the romance in time becomes enormously destructive. Essentially, she sets out to remake me into a cool, commanding copy of the European aristocrats she has grown up with. As she initially describes it, though, she's not out to alter my substance but merely to improve my public persona, to polish up the crude surfaces of a diamond in the rough.

So, in her view, I need to cultivate a lower, deeper voice, and speak more slowly and deliberately. I've always talked fast, a legacy of my upbringing in the Caribbean, where rapid-fire speech is the norm. But now, when ordering a hamburger at a diner, I should express myself authoritatively, with a slow, commanding baritone, "Give me a hamburger!" and put behind me my habitually requesting, in a shy, diffident tenor, "A hamburger, please." Also, I'd best curb my enthusiasms while in good company. Steer clear of controversial topics. And not get carried away by wildly eccentric notions. And my punning's got to stop! Those who like word play, Anya insists, are socially lazy types who simply can't engage in adult conversation.

Being very much in love with her, I take Anya's counsel seriously and try to measure up to her desires. I start controlling my speech, sounding more and more like an English professor. I pay for several months' singing lessons, with a view to deepening my voice and giving it greater power. And, when we're out with our circle of friends or with Anya's mother, who lives in town, I now dwell on innocuous subjects. Harmless gossip. The weather.

And yet, the greater my efforts to change and, in Anya's words "grow up," the less I seem able to please either her or myself. What once started out as a seemingly well-intended Pygmalion project becomes instead an onslaught on my very being. In time her didactic enterprise assumes the form of attacks on me in public. She mocks my foreign-sounding English phonemes in front of our friends. To my complaint one afternoon about her mockery she replies dismissively, "Oh, Gene, don't be primitive." At one point over dinner she characterizes me as "a wide-eyed adolescent" and "still a teenager." And when I bubble with enthusiasm over the beauties of the Alhambra palace in Granada, she mimics my voice, saying breathily, "For Gene, everything is wonderful! Wonderful!"

On another occasion we're discussing our respective literary researches. When I mention my impatience with details—for which Anya, incidentally, has an eagle eye—she snaps back, "Then how *do* you expect to be a scholar?" And so, in negation of my own bent for big-picture sorts of questions, I take to reading specialized articles in the academic journals.

By the spring of '66 I'm well on my way to being reduced to a shadow of my true self. At the same time I live trapped and tangled in the fear of Anya ditching me should I fail to mature.

Then, I go to Europe.

My inner struggles acquire new content and added intensity as I go on to spend that entire summer in the Old World. Six weeks' study at the Sorbonne. Touring here and there in France and Switzerland. And, finally, going westward to Madrid, where Anya will join me for a month's rail travel through the peninsula.

The European experience is my first time spent outside the U.S. since Kanani and I touched down at Key West seven years earlier. And it comes both as a revelation and a shock. Living day to day amidst the Old World's historical layers and cultural density has a predictably major impact on a restless young mind that has cultivated an interest in six centuries of music and three millennia of literature, a mind that, moreover, has been at odds with American presentist thinking and philistine Babbittry.

The smaller, pedestrian-scale urbanism still predominating in the older continent, by comparison with the automobile-based spread of America's western cities, furnishes an attractive lesson in the organization of social space. And of course Europe's civilized air, that indescribable feature we generally refer to as quality of life, makes it clear that America's notorious crudity and uncouthness are neither natural nor a worldwide norm, but the local product of a specific way of life, aspects of a national character that have developed within a particular time and place.

For the moment I'm too naive and confused to take into account Europe's sinister and equally potent legacy of continental warfare and overseas conquest. Nor am I willing to grant that American roughness of manners has its upside in the country's genuine democratic ethos, its greater openness, its acceptance of more popular and plebeian styles and values, as opposed to the greater rigidity and closed barriers of old, élite Europe. No, what matters to me right then is that, in experiencing a culturally richer, socially more mature civilization, I'm dramatically reminded of my foreignness in U.S. life. Over the years, after all, I've been told that America's my country. As a consequence of my seven straight years in the States, uninterrupted by any visits abroad, I've gradually, unconsciously absorbed the idea, preached to me by my dad and then trumpeted from every last little U.S. corner, that "America is the greatest country in the world."

For the first time in my life, I recognize that I don't fully belong in the U.S. of A.

My month in Spain—where I've the benefit of some personal friends whom I visit, and so can see beyond the Franco dictatorship's confining orbit—inevitably returns me to my Spanish-speaking past, now within a deeper, ancestral sort of setting. Save for visits to Mexican border towns, I haven't set foot in a Hispanic country since 1959. Now I find myself surrounded by Spain's Spanish, the original Hispanics.

While thoroughly enriching in themselves, my travels with Anya won't do us much good as a couple. We return to California that September with her barbs at their fiercest and my soul at its nadir. I hate myself, think myself worthless, and frankly say so to relatives and friends. In a phone conversation with Mom regarding my desperate inner state that early fall, she notes, calmly yet earnestly, "It sounds as if someone has been dwelling exclusively on your bad points and ignoring your good ones." I hear only the words, not the store of experience informing them.

Soon after our arrival in Berkeley, Anya puts our romance on hold. Tells me, as usual, that I've got more growing up to do. Meanwhile she starts going out on a regular basis with Pepe, a Cuban guy in our department who's got all the characteristics she's been attempting to impose on me: a deep, mellifluous voice—he's an amateur stage actor—and a surface aura of self-confident authority.

The first few months of our slow breakup I spend wandering in the typically limbo-like pain of an abandoned lover. For a couple of months, hoping to "mature" for Anya and for myself, I even waste money on a psychiatrist, who, save for an occasional echo, says scarcely a word in response to my outpourings. A man who, I later realize, is simply unable to see into this patient's cultural-identity problems.

Still, the time spent away from Anya's daily put-downs affords me the opportunity to reconsider what she's been saying about my alleged shortcomings. Gradually, tentatively, with an increasingly powerful sense of discovery and relief, I begin to realize that almost all of the faults she'd systematically denigrated in me are, in fact, my very best traits. What Anya had dismissed in me as "wide-eyed" and "primitive" was actually part of a passionate, energetic, enthusiastic approach to life that clashed with her own extreme prudence. My penchant for eccentric, unsanctioned topics was the mark of a restless mind that sought alternate worlds and fundamental truths beyond the humdrum, banal, and bourgeois. My not adhering to the rules of polite society stemmed from a healthy, creative nonconformism. My acknowledged problems with the demands of small, ordinary detail were the largely technical downside of a Platonist preference for general ideas, as opposed to Anya's more Aristotelian bent for hard fact. Or, to put it in terms developed by Jung and elaborated on by Harriet Mann: my difficulties with nuts-and-bolts matters were the remediable side effect of a visionary, Intuitive sort of temperament that contrasted with Anya's own Sensation-based ability for close observation. So I'm not so bad after all . . .

Finally, my love of word play could be construed not as laziness but as a symptom of my deeper, artistic fascination with the expressive medium of language. This realization comes to me in one fell swoop on a quiet afternoon in the spring of '67, after having spent several weeks on such thoughts. I'm relaxing alone on the living-room sofa of my Dwight Way flat . . . when suddenly I remember those light farces that I'd written and directed as a middle-school kid in Puerto Rico. I dwell momentarily on my taste for putting distinctive, often funny questions in my students' Spanish-grammar tests. And then, I'm casually blurting out loud, to no one in particular, "Well, I'm a writer . . ."

Miraculously, I now understand what Socrates had meant by his exhortation, "Know thyself!" some twenty-five hundred years ago. But there's more. For the very first time in my life I actually *like* myself, and will continue to do so from then on, regardless of any future temptations to backslide into self-hate.

In an exquisitely ironic way I owe to Anya my newly gained self-knowledge and self-love. Had she not zeroed in so accurately on me with her criticisms of my key traits, I might never have had occasion to reinterpret her assessments of my character and turn those opinions inside out. (I'm reminded of an aphorism by Nietzsche: "We are despised for our virtues.") And, had I not loved Anya, I would not have learned so much about myself. Love, it seems, really can save people.

This unexpected landfall in self-discovery is additionally reinforced by a one-week Christmas visit to Caracas. I fly down at the behest of my dad, with whom I've been exchanging some angry and bitter letters over the previous year. He now sees a need for us to talk face-to-face. As I arrive once again at La Guaira Airport and descend Pan Am's movable steps, the pungent smell and sensations of thick tropical air, filled with the sounds of countless crickets in December, immediately transports me back to my childhood.

The trip is my first to Venezuela since departing for the U.S. in 1959. At my father and Mary's apartment we now argue over the Vietnam War, the free speech movement, Communist China, and Dad's alleged reasons for not having gotten me piano lessons. (I was too specialized in music, he claims, and besides, finding piano teachers is the wife's job, and so should've been Mom's responsibility. And so on and so forth.)

In spite of the endless disputes, the visit has some profoundly salutary effects on my soul. Being in Venezuela I can hear Caribbean

Spanish spoken all around me. Can see, sniff, and walk about the sites of my midadolescence. Can take in the Hispanic folk carolers and other Christmas Eve customs. Can chat at length with friends and schoolmates from that era. This helps fashion within me a long-overdue balance between my past and present, between my Latino and U.S. sides. On my return to Berkeley, friends remark on my changed aspect, telling me, "You look great!"

My new self-awareness has a major intellectual component as well. For a class I had enrolled in that fall on Spanish-American narrative (under the Chilean writer Fernando Alegría), I chance to read *The Lost Steps* by Cuban novelist and musicologist Alejo Carpentier. And I find myself thoroughly smitten! For one, the plot of Carpentier's novel—which tells of a classical musician, originally raised in South America of foreign parents, and currently residing, none too happily, up in the States—bears an uncanny resemblance to my own case history. More importantly, I instantly recognize *The Lost Steps* as that rare sort of great book in which romantic adventure, cultural concerns, personal passion, and literary art all magically coalesce into a wise, luminous scripture.

Soon thereafter I'll go on to read Borges's already legendary fables. Plus Julio Cortázar's recently published *Hopscotch*—which has caused a minor international sensation—along with his short pieces, then much in the air as a result of the critical success of Antonioni's film *Blow-Up*, which is based on a Cortázar story. And I discover the Mexicans Juan Rulfo and Carlos Fuentes, and the Peruvian Vargas Llosa. Meanwhile, unbeknownst to me, at that very moment, García Márquez's masterwork *One Hundred Years of Solitude* is being published in Buenos Aires.

In short, I've become actively aware of the narrative flowering then taking place in Latin America. And it's at that point that I realize I can play a genuinely useful role as intermediary between these living authors and their U.S. fans. I can bring my knowledge of the two major languages and cultures of the Americas to my future teaching and writings.

Well, it seems as if, at long last, I've staked out for myself a clear and specific mission in U.S. educational and intellectual life. Around this time I make a couple of writerly resolutions.

First, I'm not going to churn out volumes that'll be glanced at exclusively by six or seven other specialists. The great Latin American writers, I feel, deserve better than the precious, overwrought machinery that too often ends up smothering many classic authors. After having been both intimidated and bored by the elaborate verbal juggling acts, the high-wire jargon, and the fiercely abstract roaring beasts of American academic criticism, I've now become simply bored with much of the stuff. Literary criticism, I sense, could and should be readable, meaningful, enjoyable, and even fun.

My second resolution is that I'll now write either about good authors or about authors whom I like. I've already spent too many long, dreary hours laboring over third-rate composers or overrated scribblers who've had little to say to me, and I hope to spare myself a repeat of that soul-deadening task. Finally, to the occasional snobs from English who still question my working in Spanish, I can now respond that the best living novelists and short-story writers are, in fact, the Latin Americans, next to whom Updike and Bellow seem cranky and old-fashioned and the French *nouveau roman* writers icy and unfeeling.

In the first half of 1966–67, in the wake of my return from Europe and before my personal self-discovery, I'd been teetering on the edge of personal collapse. The second half of my final year at Berkeley, by contrast, will be my most fortunate few months ever, culminating with the day in May when I receive by mail the award of a three-year, government fellowship to work toward my Ph.D. in romance languages at Harvard University.

I feel a bit as if the Coast Guard has come to rescue me from shipwreck on some stormy island. Aside from the obvious benefits of Harvard itself, there's my newly growing need to get away from Berkeley—from the visible reminders of my past madness, from Anya and her many unpleasant associations, from Berkeley's musty Spanish department (later to be much revitalized). Even from comparative literature, a field that, though a fine thing in principle, in practice means the expectation that you'll give yourself wholeheartedly to the higher academic theory and criticism, to crit for crit's sake. Given my budding commitment to writing general-interest sorts of criticism, such a reading diet attracts me only in measured amounts and for my own purposes.

Harvard comes largely as a relief. A few years earlier the august institution represented to me the life of the mind at its highest, a special world where knowledge and thought were respected and revered. Now, having since studied in three advanced disciplines and completed a combined master's in comp lit at Berkeley, I've fewer naive illusions or anxieties about the nature of graduate work at élite, highpowered universities, where the pursuit of learning does have its dry and even joyless side, and is in some measure about training for professional advancement and an academic job. As I'm currently envisioning it, Harvard is a place that'll be better than Berkeley in some ways and less good in others.

Still, it's tempting to think everyone out there knows about, indeed is in awe of, the admittedly famous school back east. A chastening reminder to the contrary crops up when I need to contact the Harvard admissions office on a bureaucratic matter, and I dial directory assistance so as to get hold of the renowned institution's telephone number.

"Cambridge, Massachusetts," I say to the operator, "for Harvard University."

"How do you spell that, please?" she asks.

"H-A-R-V-A-R-D," I say.

The sound of a phone buzz a whole continent away is followed by the Boston operator's answer and then the local operator's request: "Cambridge, please, for" [slowly and emphatically] *"the Harvard University."*

Telling my friends about the little episode only adds to my general sense of well-being. I've never felt so simply full and right as I will between January and August 1967. As a crowning moment, I even get from Anya a beautiful letter apologizing for her rough treatment of me. I'll save it indefinitely, for decades in fact. I'm entering a new and very different life-stage. Not just professionally but also personally and spiritually. And oh, do I enjoy the sensation!

After years of aimlessness and confusion, I receive, in April, my M.A. diploma in comparative literature, signed by the new governor, Ronald Reagan.

Meanwhile I try new things. I paint houses; I peddle an antiwar newspaper, the *Vietnam Observer*; I attend the Sunday rock concerts at Provo Park; I become enamored of the Beatles's Sgt. Pepper album and of Country Joe and the Fish; I hitchhike up and down California; I travel to Mexico City by combined bus and train; and I take an intense three-week job, in San Francisco's Mission District, as a bilingual interviewer for the legal aid branch of Lyndon Johnson's antipoverty program, receiving a troubling glimpse of the multifarious ways in which America's poor are preyed upon and cheated by loan sharks and used-car hustlers. I also reestablish ties with old friends, spend time with my family in Grants, New Mexico, and, as usual, do all the reading I can, gobbling up Samuel Beckett's uniquely poetical and comic fiction, savoring the prose style of Nabokov (whose three-page taxi-driver scene from *Lolita* I type out and then carry about in my shirt pocket), feeling the excitement of first encountering John Barth's homage to Borges in his soon-to-be-influential essay, "The Literature of Exhaustion," published in that August's *Atlantic Monthly*.

And I finally start seriously writing fiction of my own. Three short stories—"Report on a Concert," "The Hidden Shape of Things," and "The Revenge"—are actually first conceived and drafted at my Dwight Way apartment in 1967 and will slowly make their way, a full thirty-two years later, into a little collection of mine, *The Pianist Who Liked Ayn Rand: A Novella & 13 Stories*.

Getting a late start as a writer of any kind, I'd eventually realize, has its own obstacles. The problems are not so much physical as social, namely, the lack of literary friends and contacts that you make and grow up with when in college, when there are campus magazines and newspapers that allow you to serve a public apprenticeship. Without that experience, you're all alone with your rough drafts.

Despite the difficulties that face a late bloomer—first in getting good enough, then in finding a willing publisher—I've always had some narrative project in the works since my graduate-school days. A new short piece. A novel. A satire. This memoir ... Whatever their ultimate intrinsic worth, I know that I've developed more fully as a critic and essayist as a result of the thousands of hours I've spent crafting fictions. At least I know something about what it's like to give flight to your imagination and harness its energies, know a little bit about the struggle to create verbal worlds where previously there had been none.

Over the years I'll have occasion to read theorists of satire. Having also written—on inspiration and with much perspiration—a satirical novel and a number of shorter spoofs, I can say that I know for a fact that many high satirologists haven't the foggiest idea of what they're theorizing about.

Whether it be rough-drafting or close-crafting, invented fiction or factual essay, the writing habit will serve as my little realm of freedom, my newer way of simply being me. In the rough-and-tumble of the everyday, I'm often stuck with how others (mis)perceive me, and also with my scattered, divided selves, my own pained feeling that I don't fully belong, and my shyness and awkwardness as a person. When I sit down to apply words to a page and slowly build them up toward a final edifice, by contrast, I'm constantly correcting and rectifying mistakes and thereby fashioning a more solid and identifiable self. Whereas, as Norma McCaig accurately points out, "many global nomads report a sense of powerlessness and devaluation when reflecting on their upbringing," my writing, in some measure, is where I'm that much less at the mercy of those who've wanted me to be what I am not, who've even wanted me not to be at all. Writing, I discover, allows me to be normal, to evolve and exist as a useful and productive citizen of both Americas and of the world.

I love Berkeley and the Bay Area, and always will. On any later trip back to the West Coast, I'll make it a point to include them in my travels so I can go nosing about in my old haunts. Berkeley is where I began to grow, where I first miraculously started to become a somewhat sane creature after twenty-five years of being crazy.

By 1967, though, I'm finding the place too small for my drift at the moment, am feeling uneasy with the rah-rah, anti-intellectual current in greater California that seeps its way even into Berkeley's most dissenting elements.

I check in at my eastbound flight, entitled to a half-price discount thanks to the smudged youth card in my hand (borrowed from a Costa Rican buddy, a future spokesman for Nicaragua's Sandinista government). Before that day, I'd moved on to new places—Caracas, the Cuban military school, Arizona—as a result of other people's agendas, whether benevolent or malign. And ironically I'd initially ended up at Berkeley by default, because it was a closer trip from New Mexico and was also cheaper than the big Ivies. Now, for the first time in my life, I hold inside me the quiet expectation that—for the moment, at least—I'm venturing onto a path and a vocation of my own, conscious choice.

Trying Another Coast

*The culture shock of the move [for young returnees] can be
compared to a roller-coaster ride—initial excitement followed by down times, occasional pockets of excitement and
then down again (when they're sure they'll never fit in).*

— KAY BRANAMAN EAKIN, "You Can't Go 'Home'
Again," in Carolyn D. Smith, *Strangers at Home*

Oh, the temptation to conclude this narrative on the upbeat note of
the previous paragraphs!

A classically happy ending: our quasi-immigrant boy riding off into
the sunset (the sunrise, actually), ready to enter Harvard's mythic
realm. His recognizable first step toward making good in this
America. (Jetliner takes off majestically over the bay. White letters
unfurl: "THE END.") A standard final scene in countless exemplars of
the American Romance of Immigration. A tale told many times over
in our high-school textbooks and autobiographical success stories, in
TV dramas and glossy mags . . .

Yet once the immediate practical hurdles of settling in another
country are overcome, the battle for adaptation has barely started and
is never quite done. And however much you feel you've entered
American life for good, some event, big or small—a war, a scuffle with

the authorities, a disappointment or a slight—may present itself at any time to put that desired sentiment in doubt.

When that happens you'll hear your other identity whisper the nagging question, "Is this your country? Do you belong here?" As the 1970s slogan notes, *"La lucha continúa"* ("The struggle goes on"), and any plateau of satisfaction and serenity you reach is yours to savor only for the time being. A new and better life is neither an equipoise nor journey's end but rather the safe haven of the moment, with forthcoming rough rides and troubles all its own, though undoubtedly new, and maybe better, ones.

Many an immigrant to these shores might eventually choose—as in fact many have chosen—to return to the Old Country, though this documented pattern is scarcely touched on by the media mythologies that shape U.S. thinking. Even less do we hear about the many immigrants who arrive with almost nothing and, far from Making It Big here instead lose what little they have, the uncounted undocumented aliens who sink, succumb, and even die. There must be millions of such cases, ignored by the mythmakers and known only to their relatives, if they have any . . .

Luckily, my own story, albeit no fairy tale, will have a happier if somewhat ambiguous finale. By the time I enter Harvard in 1967, I've got my Berkeley M.A. in comp lit in hand, plus a fair knowledge of what graduate school's about. So from the start I'm able to maintain a somewhat ironic attitude toward the rococo world of doctoral-level literary study. Thus protected, I go on to spend four fruitful years enrolled there, teaching some brilliant undergraduates and finding the place fascinating in an anthropological sort of way. Yet I'll never develop for Harvard the affection that I've continued to harbor for Berkeley.

Of course, there's no question as to the overall intellectual quality of the place, which is evident everywhere I look: In the professional polish, wit, and leftism of the *Harvard Crimson* daily. In the humane depth and erudition of lecture classes given by scholars such as H. Stuart Hughes in history and Gregory Nagy in classics. In the lively, intense conversations I overhear at Lehman Hall, the university's student hangout, or at nearby off-campus spots like the Café Pamplona, Cambridge's oldest coffeehouse, founded by an expatriate Basque woman in 1957, and—with its marble tables, stucco walls and Iberian dishes—an evocation of her old Spain.

I'm especially fortunate enough to find a personal mentor in Raimundo Lida, an Argentine émigré professor from the Perón era. From early on he encourages whatever modest talents I have and provides much-needed friendly attention and support. At the same time he urges me to cultivate intellectual discipline and rigor and not to depend merely on flashes of intuition. Without his warm and wise counsel, I might conceivably have remained caught up in a sort of higher dilettantism.

In addition, during my last year at Harvard, Dwight Bolinger, the well-known linguist and a wonderfully sweet, gentle man, offers me ideological company and professional encouragement, to the point of (unbeknownst to me) recommending my name for a summer job at Middlebury College language school, where, in 1972, I will meet my wife-to-be, Audrey.

Much of what I learn at Harvard, though, comes independently of my academic studies (however invaluable these may be). I continue to read a lot on my own, especially in twentieth-century vanguard literatures—European, American, and of course Latin American. I also actively memorize soliloquies from Shakespeare, long stretches out of Beckett's *Endgame* and *Waiting for Godot*, and lyrics by poets ranging from the canonical Castilians Góngora and Quevedo, the French Symbolists Verlaine, Mallarmé, and Rimbaud, on through more recent Anglophones like Pound, cummings, and Stevens.

Outside of class assignments I compose practice essays on Latin American authors and labor further at my fiction. For my slow apprenticeship I find major help from two very receptive creative-writing professors: Theodore Morrison, who gives his blessing to my bent for fantasy (while criticizing my proclivity for overwriting), and Monroe Engel, who, by contrast, suggests I work instead at being less abstract, at filling my narratives with more real-life things and people. Each turns out to be right in his own way.

These good moments are spread over a four-year period. Alas, the inner serenity I possessed when first arriving at Harvard proves short-lived, shattered as it is by events personal and political.

For starters, the ever-conflicted relationship with my father comes to an unseemly end just five months later, in January 1968, when he, Mary, and my half-brother, Hal, pay me a few days' visit in my new surroundings.

In the previous six or seven years, Dad has evolved into something of a religious fanatic, preaching to me at length about God and country in his correspondence, and sending me Bibles as birthday gifts. One such volume, a New Testament, is inscribed, "My dear son, In these four gospels is the good, and all else is evil and badness." Also, as the Vietnam War expands, he keeps urging me to join the army, even though he himself had slipped out of the draft in early 1941, thanks to my mom-to-be's efficient string-pulling. He and I thus share even less in common than was the case in our Caribbean years. Meanwhile his continuing high-handed treatment of Kanani and me scarcely helps sustain my filial affections.

I've long considered breaking ties with him. Friends in Berkeley, though, had cautioned me against such a drastic step, warning me about the dangers of subsequent remorse and guilt. Their advice stays with me; I've decided to continue to put up with the situation. He's my father, after all!

Yes, he is. The same old Dad. During his brief Harvard sojourn, he and I will argue, more harshly than ever, over religion, politics, the war, the Soviets, China, Scandinavia, school-board decisions, blacks, intellectuals (who, in his estimation, understand nothing), foreign automobiles, the existence of God, and other jovial topics.

At one point Mary declares, "I'd rather see my son, Hal, *dead* than have him become a Communist!" Dad seconds her.

I might well have put the whole unpleasant encounter behind me were it not for Dad's parting actions. As we sit side by side in his rented car, exchanging good-byes at the Conant Hall front doorsteps, he now unfolds—with quiet, fatherly regard—an outlandish series of claims against my mom. First, he says that, in Puerto Rico, she had been conducting an affair with Dr. Ravitch (the fellow who'd gotten her out of the mental hospital). Second, he tells me he has come to the unfortunate conclusion that my sister, Valerie, is not his daughter.

Feeling too shocked and revolted to respond adequately to such slander, I ask him why he's telling me this stuff now, so many years after the alleged events. Blandly, softly, he replies that he simply thinks I ought to know.

It's an accusation too insane and a lie too big for me to dignify with any counterargument or denial. Upset and sad, I beg the man not to repeat the story when he visits Kanani, who is still too young, too pure to be hearing such things. Otherwise, the rest of that meeting will remain a blank—our final farewell, handshakes, hugs, whatever. No subsequent memories. This is my last time in his presence.

Shaken, that same night I go rushing down to my current, girl-friend's place. Disoriented, incoherent, I barely make it through her doorway before spewing out to her the weird, farfetched charges I've just heard from my father's lips. But I make the mistake of saying that he should "forgive" my mother.

" 'Forgive?' " she snaps back. "I mean, do you believe in the double standard?" Not knowing what to make of this response, I take my leave and head back to the dorm to sleep everything off. Next day, over coffee, I tell a woman friend—a thirty-year-old fellow student from Mexico and a mother of two—who expresses her unmitigated horror, saying the Spanish equivalent of "What a bastard."

The man this time has left me no choice; I cannot maintain ties with someone so completely spiteful and destructive. Soon thereafter I write him an extended and wrathful letter in which I sever our bonds for all time. A week or so later I'll find out that he did in fact proceed to restate the same odious libel to my twenty-two-year-old brother, then living with his first wife and infant child in rural North Carolina, on his Job Corps assignment. Kanani too, in a curt and formal note, has terminated the filial relationship.

As for my mom, for several months I don't know how to deal with her. Sure, we write, we chat over the phone, but my soul has been successfully poisoned for the time being. When I tell her about the breakup just days afterwards, I say it was because of the many disputes, without letting on as to the real reason why. I'm battered by a welter of confused emotions: fury aplenty, yet also shame at what my father said, shame at not being able to stop him or do something about it, shame at not defending my mother when immediately faced with the calumny, even shame at my accepting the "double standard."

There's a new installment at year's end. On a Christmas visit to my mom in New Mexico, she tells me that, during the summer, she received from my father in Caracas a letter besmirching her past conduct as wife and mother, and now asking her to change Valerie's last name, for the same supposed reasons. Sitting at her sewing machine that sunny afternoon, she remarks soberly, "He must be a very sick man to be going around writing things like that." And now I tell her about what he'd said to me last January. Kanani for his part already reported to her his own episode some months ago.

After Mom's death in 1984 I'll find among her papers the offending letter—unctuous, lofty, smug yet "concerned," all two pages of it. The indictment seems to have come from nowhere, other than some obscure itch to settle old scores. I quote from the relevant passages.

Dear Carmen,

I take this opportunity to clear up the question of [Valerie's] fatherhood, something that obviously should have been cleared up years ago, and would have been except for my stupidity and even fear of the truth . . .

There is no point in holding grudges or resenting at this late date. Let's let bygones be bygones. At least that is the way I feel. But I don't see the point in Valerie carrying my name any longer.

I suggest that you figure out a way to change Valerie's surname and to clear up the fact that I was not her father. By searching and trying hard you will find a way to do this. Naturally I expect you to do this with a great deal of delicacy for Valerie's feelings. None of this is her fault and it would be a pity if she should be hurt by this new truth. But in the end she must become aware that I am not her father. I'm afraid it's up to you to tell her how, who, what, where, and when. And if you find that this is difficult for you then I suggest you try to imagine how difficult it was for me to accept the fact that I was cuckolded in my own house and in my own matrimonial bed.

Yours,
[His full name]

The very sight of that letter, as I copy it decades later, numbs me with disgust.

Meanwhile, back at Harvard, to my surprise the break with my father also produces in me not guilt but a sense of exhilaration and release. I feel as if I've sloughed off an entire life's burden! Have rid myself of my least favorite human being! It's sheer joy! The intense jubilation, though, will in time produce a wrenching, sad legacy. From then on I adopt a policy of extreme rejectionism toward anybody who hurts me in any way. What solution could be better, really? It worked for my father, right? So why not for everyone else? More rejection, more! Whoever slights or negates me won't get so much as a peep from me. That unforgiving, sweeping category, alas, will come to include my mom, brother, and sister, and a wide array of friends, colleagues, and lovers.

My uncompromising stance, unfortunately, will seem to be further vindicated and hardened by a double whammy seven months later, when my girlfriend (she of the "double standard" question) cheerfully ditches me for a sociologist from—of all places—Venezuela. ("Please trust me," she earnestly asks while informing me of her change of heart.) The bitter filial breakup, the abrupt and unromantic jilting: the two events will remain long associated in my mind, during and long after Harvard.

During my remaining years as a student I'll become possessed by nonstop rancor, anger in the extreme. While informing only a few close friends about Dad's sordid last words as my true motive for breaking with him, I'll also take to lashing out at anyone on any seeming provocation. At women, at roommates, at America. At some faculty members, at my family ... The rage will eventually assume political form as I refocus it onto the injustice of the Vietnam War and pour forth my transferred passions into countless letters to the editor (some of them published). Meanwhile, in my personal life—both with friends and with myself—I'll often single out my ex-lover as the prime reason for my hates, and I even flirt openly with misogynistic attitudes. As part of my revenge against femaledom, I'll juggle five, six, seven casual affairs and sex-flings at once in the following year, even as I make it brutally clear to each of the good women that I've no affection to offer them, that indeed I want to be "incapable of love."

But I'm fooling myself all of this time. Blindly, profoundly fooling myself. I cannot, will not see that ultimately I'm in the grip of an uncontrolled fury against my father.

Decades later, I will have the benefit of long, soul-searching conversations with Denah Lida, the widow of my late, lamented Harvard mentor Raimundo—and, let it be said, among the most delightfully wise, sane, and life-loving individuals I'll ever know. Passing time has brought us a bit closer in age and allowed us to become friends, and in our monthly chats she and I will often look back on those troubled years. On more than one occasion she'll remember her husband and other faculty associates wondering, "Why is Gene Bell so angry?" Ah, well . . . Even I could not have given a fair answer, had they asked me then. I would've chalked it up to romantic mishaps or the horrible war, both of which no doubt aggravated my state. In the longer run, though, my father had put me on a private warpath of my own. Had disabled my soul, crippled my affects. Had transformed me into a seething cauldron that chronically gave off sparks and smoke and steamy waters of resentment and ill will.

In the meantime, back at Harvard, the intellectualism I find there does at least provide some basic training for my modest skills as mind and scrivener-to-be, a familiar enough if narrow stream on which I can drift and sail at will, hither and yon. As a way of life it may serve only as an extended, intense, and even rewarding distraction from what most matters on this earth, but, as things stand, I've got this twin aftermath of an ex-dad and an ex-lover to deal with inside of me. Seeking to avoid a replay of family and romantic pain, I now decide to live solely through books, to set all my feelings aside, to let my head lead my existence and exclude most everything else. And while I'll be lucky enough not to revert to my self-hatred of yesteryear, I'll resolve my long-standing problems of the heart only by becoming a hermit part-time, a recluse by default who, to any degree possible, summarily rejects whatever might possibly hurt him.

Seeking company around Cambridge in the wake of my two breakups, I check out of my joyless Harvard dorm and start rooming in a large apartment near Central Square with some student radicals doing graduate work in Asian history. A random move, it turns out to be a lucky accident, perhaps the most crucial extracurricular compo-nent of my 1960s education. My roommates are all in some measure involved with antiwar activities, and they're passionately questioning the tired, Cold War dogma of their academic discipline, as is also hap-pening in many fields and on hundreds of campuses across the land. Never will I learn so much directly from friends as I do via my three years cohabiting with Jim, Jon, Tom, and Kung, though the knowledge I gain is profoundly unsettling and, in the short run, inapplicable.

Our long conversations at 8 Amory Street, in which I hear them talk geopolitics as casually as most people discuss the day's weather, and my social life with their group, in which we mingle drink and dance and more geopolitics, soon prompt me to borrow from their ample personal libraries in history and politics. And so I devour books by the revisionist U.S. historians who are reinterpreting the Cold War. I steep myself in Noam Chomsky's hard-hitting, encyclopedic polemics. I dip at length for the first time into the foundational Marxian texts and the sociological classics of Max Weber and of C. Wright Mills. I study Marcuse and other reigning sages of the time. I gobble up left-liberal and radical magazines and any underground press items that drift my way. And after about two years I become more conversant with such issues as how societies are put together, and why empires behave as they do. Indeed, I'm spending more time on politics than on the exquisite verbal flights of literary theorists, though I'm still faithfully reading fiction and poetry.

And I consume hundreds of articles, books, and leaflets about the war in Indochina, each item feeding what will eventually grow into an obsession. My mind becomes hyperinformed about the Vietnam conflict as I read more than enough about the "free-fire zones" where U.S. policy is to "kill anything that moves," or about the Air Force bomber pilots who frankly admit to enjoying the job of unleashing their payload and watching their megaton bombs drop and explode. The horror and disproportion of it all fills me with a powerless rage, as does the systematic distortion in the press. In a key instance, the news reports will regularly imply that the term "Viet Cong" designates the regular army of North Vietnam. In this way they obscure a more unsettling reality, which is that the National Liberation Front—the actual, official name of the "Viet Cong"—is a *South* Vietnamese guerrilla uprising, with local roots and grievances. This error would persist well into the future and be repeated in standard dictionary entries. Similarly, the media backgrounders will conveniently forget that the U.S. intervention openly violates the 1954 Geneva Accords—the legal, international peace treaty that had ended the French neocolonial war, described the North-South line in Vietnam as "strictly provisional," and called for nationwide elections. The elections were cancelled when the Eisenhower administration created South Vietnam.

Back in Berkeley I had seen how the local press, even with reporters directly on site, could print flagrant lies about the free speech movement. Now, at Harvard, I am witnessing the obfuscatory process on a grand scale, with a fictional version of a remote, brutal war being disseminated day by day and imposed on the public by sheer repetition.

At the age of eighteen I'd thought of professors as free individuals dedicated to the life of the mind, seeking pure knowledge and wisdom. I imagined them somehow standing above petty machinations, outside society's sordid power struggles. I'll still retain vestiges of this notion when I arrive at Harvard. Eventually, through my radical roommates and the climate of the times, I become aware of the top academics from the Ivy League and elsewhere who actively work with the Defense Department and the State Department, helping them pursue the Vietnam War, as well as of those who publish work that creates public support for such policies. A good part of my political education thus consists of realizing that American university campuses aren't just ivory towers (though portions of them are more or less that) but founts of information and advice for our society's corporate chieftains, state power brokers, and military brass. Meanwhile, elsewhere on the verdant campuses, in the more modern buildings that house the physical science departments, select researchers thoughtfully devise ways of making deadlier and more destructive weapons, big and small.

Anti-imperialism is at the time the leading banner among student leftists, who demonstrate against U.S. overseas economic control and against U.S. firepower in particular. Well, as a red-blooded son of U.S. empire, with direct experience of some of its everyday doings in the Caribbean, I respond with zeal to the battle cry. Still feeling too alien to get much involved in any of the radical organizations, though, I stay on the sidelines while attending every peace demonstration I can. I also aid in distributing the occasional batch of leaflets. Give a few talks to school and hospital groups. Do some political canvassing in Boston's Latino district for a Congressional antiwar amendment. Help edit the *Bulletin of Concerned Asian Scholars*, the dissenting journal with which my roommates are associated. Play piano for a couple of political theater productions. Compulsively write lots of angry and irreverent letters to the editor. And publish a handful of political articles in an alternative weekly that will eventually become the *Boston Phoenix*.

At this point I begin entertaining serious thoughts of emigrating to Europe, where I've repeatedly felt quite comfortable being a complete foreigner, away from my neither/nor identity and its array of confusions back in the U.S. (Many Overseas Americans often express strong yearnings to live abroad again.) It's an added incentive that, at this alienated time in my life, the American tourists whom I meet casually Over There tend to deal with me as if I were a foreigner, rather than as their compatriot.

One afternoon in 1971, an American family sits across from my table at a Parisian café.

To pass the time, I ask the father, "Where're you folks from?"

"Uhm . . . United States," he answers, slowly, just a bit condescendingly.

"Oh, what part?" I inquire further.

"Uh . . ." (*Slowly.*) "Long Island." (*Pause.*) "Have you heard of it?"

"Yes, I have," I say, and let the exchange drop.

On another occasion I'm chatting with an expatriate librarian at the U.S. library (since gone) on the Rue du Dragon, raving about the militaristic drift back home.

A blonde student who's standing nearby intercedes and asks, earnestly, perhaps accusingly, "Have you ever lived in the United States?"

"Yeah," I reply, "I studied in California."

"Well, you see," she muses, "I love the United States so much, I get upset when I hear Europeans criticizing it."

In the wake of such incidents, for a while I take to presenting myself as an Asian living in Paris. Several times, when Americans address me with the "Where're you from?" query, I answer pointedly and curtly, "Vietnam."

I watch their faces change expression. Then I go on to explain that my rural village was wiped out by U.S. warplanes.

My American interlocutor sometimes reflects, "Well, there've been atrocities on both sides."

I guess I relish the role of secretly being an Overseas American once again. And I start setting my sights on eventually reliving that condition, literally and openly, day by day. Before taking such a step, though, there's that Harvard doctorate I must complete in order to put my prolonged life as a student safely behind me. Somewhat apprehensively, I go job hunting. The 1971 academic job market is a depressed one, the first major downturn after two decades of broad, unprecedented growth. Somehow I land a position as instructor at one of the younger, more respected campuses of the State University of New York (SUNY) system. There will I teach and, I hope, write that thesis.

It'll be my very first, year-round, semipermanent, full-time, fully salaried and fully perked, honest-to-goodness situation of employment in this work-obsessed country, the United States of America.

Life in (and outside of) the Heartland

[Many Adult Third-Culture Kids] do not feel central to any group . . . this is the "nowhere" side of feeling at home everywhere and nowhere. For a few this feeling lasts a lifetime.
—RUTH USEEM and ANN BAKER COTTRELL,
"Adult Third-Culture Kids," in Carolyn D. Smith,
Strangers at Home

I am alone in my one-bedroom, garden apartment in Binghamton, N.Y. The ground-floor rental unit comes equipped with electric heat, heavy suburban-style furnishings, and textured wall-to-wall carpeting, linden green in color. My portable record player and small radio both date back to Harvard graduate-school days. I've no TV set. No phone, either. No one can reach me here unless they come knocking. I'm about eight months into my instructorship at one of the best of New York's state college campuses.

It's four years since I broke with my father. Told him I never wanted to see him or have anything to do with him in my life. Never, ever. Warned him I'd return his letters unopened. My brother, Kanani, rejected him as well, though with more distaste than anger. And in that same year, 1968, a girlfriend ditched me for another guy, soon after I'd decided to fall in love with her. It was my third, perhaps fourth experience in being classically jilted in about as many years. My ongoing fury at my male progenitor, along with my self-enforced, antiromantic, Miss Havisham-type isolation, have all combined into a larger, rejectionist impulse that long ago took on a life of its own, and has brought harmful, even destructive consequences for me, my friends and casual lovers, and my more positive and loving next of kin.

It's an unhealthy dynamic that will be further exacerbated by my angry opposition to the unending U.S. war on Indochina. "The War that Will Not Go Away." So reads the front cover of an issue of *Newsweek*. Regular army troops from North Vietnam and their southern guerrilla allies in the National Liberation Front have recently launched a spring offensive. The U.S. responds with a massive air assault. In terms of munitions and aircraft, I read repeatedly, these are the biggest aerial bombardments in history. By now the U.S. has dropped over Indochina a tonnage tripling the total unleashed by all sides in World War II.

Since 1969, the endless war has had me in a constant, bitter rage. I've read dozens of books, hundreds of articles dealing with the conflict and its background. Can't get informed enough about it. Can't do all that much about it, either, except vent my rage to myself, to others.

In 1970 I'd read a field report from the kingdom of Laos by a well-known French journalist. B-52's, he noted, had been bombing that peasant country's southern half around the clock for months, years. Everything in southern Laos was destroyed, he observed. Those inhabitants who hadn't fled to the city were living in forests and caves, simply to avoid the ceaseless rain of U.S. bombs, he said. Few things in my life had ever struck me as so monstrously unfair: these professional military men, flying thirty thousand feet above their "enemy" targets, thoroughly protected by radar and by distance, far, far away from any antiaircraft fire. And killing, burning, and maiming with impunity. Never hearing the alien cries or smelling the charred flesh.

I would sometimes mention the massive bombardments of Laos to Americans I'd meet. Many would say, "Well, that's just your point of view" or "There's two sides to every question" or "Who's to say what's really going on over there?" Or they'd claim the war was a good thing precisely because I could protest against it, assert that in fact we're fighting a war over there just so people like me can have the right to "rap" against the war at home.

The French reporter's article and Nixon's invasion of Cambodia had prompted me to make a despairing call to my mother. From her home in rural New Mexico she insisted that we Americans were fighting in Southeast Asia to preserve our way of life. That night I felt a frustration as great in debating with her as I did when talking with other, regular gringos. Toward the end of our discussion, I asked if she might look at a recent article by Seymour Hersh in *Harper's* on the infamous My Lai massacre.

To my surprise, she read it soon after and wrote me an anguished letter, saying she was "*appalled*. In fact, that's not the word for it. This is not war. This is barbarism." In my lonesomeness and fury, though, I never followed up on her conciliatory gesture. Will not so much as go visit her for three more years, until 1973, when I'll drop by to see her on my way to Mexico City.

Following Mom's death in 1984, I'll look back with guilt at my shortcomings as a son. My failure to respond actively and positively to her letter of support and solidarity will weigh heavily on my soul, fill me with sadness even as I write this page.

Back then I hate my father. I hate the war. I hate the bombings. I hate defenders of the war and all their stupid arguments. (There's a four-by-six-inch card taped onto the wall next to my Formica dining table, inscribed in crude block letters, "AMERICANS ARE STUPID.") I hate the town I live in. And I hate my Ph.D. thesis advisor back at Harvard.

"Gene, you're so full of hate," says one of my casual girlfriends around that time, repeatedly, with an incredulous laugh.

Still, I've got a social life. I go to people's houses—colleagues', friends'. Play classical or jazz piano with local acquaintances. Hang around the campus snack bar with graduate students or undergraduate leftists. Sometimes I'll shock someone by stating that if some midwestern farmer voted for Nixon and then had a surprise visit from a tornado, well, he got what he deserved. Hadn't he favored the bombing of farmers and babies in Southeast Asia? Hadn't he sent mass-murderer Nixon the clear message, "GO BOMB!"?

Later, in the 1980s, I'll find myself in disturbing company, when Reagan at a White House press conference is asked how he feels about a hurricane that has just laid waste to Nicaragua, then governed by the Sandinistas. The president's terse reply: "Delighted!"

Back in 1973 I'll even go so far as to say, calmly, with a straight face, "I hate gringos." I fantasize idly with literary friends about writing a novel called *Hate,* my own version of such one-word classic titles as *Hunger* and *Nausea.*

Binghamton, New York, has traits that make it special. During the 1920s it served as a regional operating center for the Invisible Empire, Knights of the Ku Klux Klan. Local lore claims that workers themselves would drive any trade-union organizers out of town and feel pride in doing so. In addition, Binghamton was home to a strong contingent of supporters for George C. Wallace, the right-wing, third-party contender from Alabama, a kind of protofascist who astutely appeals to Middle America's murkiest, most provincial prejudices and resentments. At a nearby drugstore in 1972, I overhear middle-aged lady clerks sharing in their grief and sorrow for George Wallace the morning after the attempt on his life by a lonely, troubled young drifter.

Binghamton is one of several "test-market" towns where giant corporations launch new products before "going national" with them. There are nine shopping malls here, more per capita than in any other small town

I know of. The population includes a variety of white ethnics, whose group psychology, I gather, is to buy their way into the American dream. The mass-consumption society at its most expertly engineered and refined.

One of those fabled plazas is located a few steep blocks from the apartment where I live in 1971–73. So I'll often walk, bike, or drive down to the mall, if only to get out of the house. I drop into a Discount Records outlet or a tiny bookshop. Chat with the clerks. Find some break from my constant loneliness and anger. During my two years in Binghamton, I'll buy many more LPs than I normally would have. It's a way to spend spare time and dollars. Fill the empty weekends.

On Sundays the enormous mall parking lot is superbusy. Jam-packed and alive with huge cars. A strange new sight for me; the states where I'd previously lived had local blue laws restricting Sunday commerce. At the various Vestal Plaza megastores I see whole families strolling through the overstocked aisles, observing, touching, holding, and occasionally buying the merchandise, just as, in another era, they might've attended an open-air band concert or simply gone for an afternoon walk. There's even an auditorium at the mall, for civic events.

During my student days, I'd never so much as seen a modern, suburban-style shopping mall, let alone set foot inside one. In fact I scarcely knew of their existence! Three decades after my Binghamton stint, and a few years after first drafting these words, I'll come across the following passage in Carolyn Smith's *The Absentee American:* "To Absentee Americans, especially those who have lived in Third World countries, the affluence of America is overwhelming . . . With surprising frequency returnees comment on how they feel about going to supermarkets. 'I am still, to this day, overwhelmed by supermarkets where they sell everything,' says [Peter] Nelson. Another returnee adds, 'I am astounded by the huge parking lots surrounding the shopping malls which always seem full. Can this many people actually be in need of purchasing this many new things?' "

On a similar note, Clare Kittredge, who grew up as a Foreign Service brat in Europe, Southeast Asia, and the Middle East, and more recently has been a contributor to the *Boston Globe*, writes in an essay, "Growing up Global," "Consumption, unconscious waste, the size of supermarkets, are all shocking to children who have grown up in countries where people make the most of limited resources." These were precisely my reactions to the megamalls of Binghamton.

Since I lack a home phone, sometimes I'll breeze down and use the Plaza phone booths, in the late hours, well past closing time. All night long the store lights and the parking-lot lampposts stay brightly lit while the soothing Muzak sounds play on. My telephone talk done, I'll amble about the glass-bound alleys and peer into the shiny shop windows, feeling like the only person left on the planet, marveling at the unreality of it all. It's an America I'd once intuited only vicariously, from the safety of liberal weeklies, sociology studies, and left-wing books. Never, as a gringo kid attending schools in the Caribbean, could I have envisioned this sci-fi world or imagined it in my future.

After the gregariousness and sociability of graduate student life, the intense loneliness of adult existence here in Binghamton comes as an unsettling shock. Outside my job, human contact is relatively scarce. People seem to live within private cells—ranch or bungalow, red brick or Cape—of their own choice. They seem to live within their own heads, also. Or at least *I* do! Granted, I've aggravated things by not having a phone, not calling on my mom, not . . . et cetera, et cetera, et cetera. During my near-decade in various U.S. cities I could always at least go walking idly. Here in semisuburbia, by contrast, you stand out when strolling on the sidewalk—assuming there is a sidewalk.

At first I try taking bike rides around a brand-new, middle-class tract-housing development that borders my apartment complex. The sensation I get isn't terribly comforting. The uniformly straight and empty streets, the cold aluminum siding, and the general human desolation make the landscape less than hospitable to this aimless, small-time cyclist, as if I'm moving through an Edward Hopper painting, one of his familiar gringo subjects, trapped in a hotel room or downcast in a diner, staring out amidst the shadows into a vast distance, longing for company. Walking and shopping. Classroom, office, the mall. What there is, there's plenty of. Otherwise there seems to be little else.

Death and destruction have been raining from the skies. Entire villages have been wiped out. The week's fatalities number in the low three figures. Thousands, driven from their homes, are languishing in shelters.

Indochina?

Not this time. I'm still in Binghamton in 1972. Hurricane Agnes has battered the Northeast, especially central Pennsylvania and southern New York State—Binghamton included—with full force and devastating consequences.

It's their punishment for Nixon, for Vietnam! Oh, yes, they're finally getting just what they deserve. That's what I tell a few trusted folks around campus, some of whom, perplexed, ask me if I'm for real.

Suddenly, the satirist in my soul feels a gust of inspiration. The Muse descends. I see in these occurrences a chance to give certain people in my life a taste of their (of his!) own medicine. Assuming the voice of a right-wing curmudgeon, spouting in extreme form some of the garden-variety ideological clichés my father once taught me, I write and send off to the town newspaper a letter to the editor. My own "Modest Proposal" à la Jonathan Swift.

To the Editor:

I'm absolutely sick and tired of reading all these bleeding heart reports about alleged flood victims. If these people are having such a rough time, they can show some private initiative and rebuild their homes on their own.

I made everything by my own efforts, and frankly I do not like having to pay taxes out of my hard-earned salary so that these crybabies can mooch off a government handout. All this flood-welfare is a step toward socialism, and I'd just as soon have no part of it.

(signed)
Jonathan Swifte
Binghamton

To my amazement, the mock tirade soon appears in the evening paper. Then come the rebuttals. A flood of them (so to speak). A dozen or so attacks on Mr. Swifte run in the daily. In one of the more humane ones, a woman writes: "I have sat here and read the letter from Jonathan Swifte in disbelief at least five times, and I still can't believe it. I'm sorry, Mr. Swifte, but I can't believe there are such heartless and callous people as you make yourself out to be . . . Where is your compassion?"

To her credit, she adds, "Don't we have enough with this horrible war, drugs, diseases without cure, etc? When a tragedy such as this strikes, can't we feel for the other person?" Her letter ends: "What an awful world this would be if we didn't help one another in time of need. Please, God, don't ever make me part of a selfish world."

In retrospect, I can say I like this person. Another letter, also from a woman, takes a tougher stance: "You are sick and tired? You can bet they're sick and tired of cleaning mud and slime and dirt from their homes . . . They should show 'private initiative'? Of course they have private initiative or they would have had nothing to lose in the first place . . ."

My favorite reply, from a man, starts out: "While being a conservative who is opposed to much of the socialism being thrust upon us, I am totally disgusted with the letter written by Jonathan Swifte about flood relief . . . I was in Elmira the day after the flood, and in Corning the following day. While I've never met any 'alleged' victims, there are plenty of real ones available." The angry Republican goes on to cite one heartrending tragedy after another. Property losses, job losses— though no deaths. Still, they're hurtful instances. Any of us could have been one of those victims, myself included. And I tremble still as I read through his examples. For his final reflection, the indignant conservative notes: "I applaud any . . . efforts made by state and federal governments to assist these people . . . along with [funds from] private individuals . . . Maybe they should start one for Mr. Swifte so he wouldn't have to pay his share of one for these 'crybabies.' If he is a self-made man, I thank God I was created."

I feel a wee bit scared. If my address (which I'd included in the original of my letter) chanced to leak out, I could end up faced with an angry mob. So I'm nervous while at home. A knock on the door makes me jump. Luckily there's no phone to ring and add to my tensions. Still, I do tell a few people around town, show them the letters, both mine and my respondents'. Some of them laugh, knowing just what I'm up to. Others are bewildered. "You're crazy!" exclaims a sharp young leftist, a close friend of one of the local victims (and whom I also know a little from activist groups). And there are those who don't get it at all. "I mean, do you believe what you say in that letter?" a slightly older, former student of mine asks, bewildered.

Yet all the same, both then and now, I feel a strange little thrill as I ponder my outrageous words and the righteous outrage they elicited from straitlaced, upright, solidly conservative citizens, now faced with the duty to defend . . . government spending! A "costly social program"! Welfare, of sorts! I even draft a rebuttal to my rebutters:

To the Editors:
  I am shocked by the hysteria people have shown in their
vicious attacks on me. Isn't this a free country, a democracy?
Don't I have the right to say what I want?

It simply doesn't make sense. Here we spend billions fighting Communism halfway around the globe. And yet we let the Communists sneak in through the back door by allowing tax-funded flood welfare.

As I see it, if somebody chooses to build his home next to a river and the river floods, well, that's his problem. Why should I have to pay for his stupid mistakes?

The attackers and their alleged victims should read America's greatest writer, Ayn Rand. A wise lady, she might teach them a few lessons about what it means to depend on yourself, not on others.

(Signed)
Jonathan Swifte

Eventually I decide against sending my reply. But the entire episode makes me smile, even guffaw. It will remain among my happiest and most fulfilling moments in my life as U.S. citizen and scribbler. I've taken some of the hoariest, most predictable, mainstream superstitions and thrown them back in a few self-satisfied faces. And I watch my rugged-individualist readers getting hot under the collective collar about it, seeing red at viewing their own reflex, clichéd thinking in its weirdest and most grotesque form.

Were I in touch with my father, I'd have sent him a copy of the "debate."

Years later, I'll find out that Ayn Rand, ever true to her principles, really does oppose disaster relief. As her heroine Dominique Francon notes in *The Fountainhead*, "Compassion is a fine thing. It's what one feels for a squashed caterpillar." Rand's followers, I assume, feel the same way. Will Alan Greenspan and Michael Milken kindly speak up?

I'm sitting on my living-room sofa in Binghamton, reading a note from my brother. He, his wife at the time, and their six-year-old boy are living in Hartford, where Kanani just started a job teaching college art. He suggests a get-together now that we're both stationed in the Northeast. I don't answer the letter. He won't write again that year. And because I'm phoneless, he can't call me.

My isolation remains nearly total.

Besides, I'm still pissed at him and even more pissed at his wife. I'd phoned him in May of 1970, when we were all students, to vent my rage over Nixon's invasion of Cambodia. Kanani wasn't in at the moment. So his spouse and I got into a sharp exchange. Her chief argument: you see, Gene, you have the right to rap against the war, and that's precisely why we're over there, so people like you can rap against things like the war.

Well, I answer, maybe a lot of those other folks don't want the right to rap. Maybe they want land, rice.

That's so materialistic! she argues. There's more to life than just feeding your belly! And what about the threat of Communism?

Those Vietnamese peasants pose no threat to us, I say.

Oh, you're right, Gene. You're right, she replies sarcastically, dismissing me with a few contemptuous words. All very angry and heated, on both sides. In the wake of that exchange in 1970 I'd decided never to call on them again. (Years later, I'll base a climactic dialogue in my first novel, *The Carlos Chadwick Mystery*, on that clash.)

Things were further aggravated when, in reply to the article I'd sent them regarding the secret, round-the-clock U.S. bombing of northern Laos, Kanani mailed me a note that started out, "Looks as if it's propaganda now I get. You probably think I don't read anything." Following an explanation of his principled, aloof, noncommittal stance, along with a routine report on home life, he ended his letter with the succinct mandate, "Send no more propaganda."

I've since sent no more letters of any kind. After all, our relationship had always been difficult and troubled, though in the course of time I'd come to see that most of it was my fault, actually.

Many years afterwards, my aunt Leila—Mom's younger sister—will inform me with mild amusement that, as a preschool toddler, I hadn't been exactly overjoyed at the arrival of child #2 in the Bell household. Later, in Umpierre, I'd hector the little boy at home after I'd been picked on by neighborhood playmates. Or, worse, sometimes I'd join *them* in taunting and bullying him out on those mean streets. On one occasion an older guy threw a ball directly at Kanani, out of sheer cruelty, eliciting from him a poignant wail, yet my eleven-year-old self did nothing.

Oh, I was definitely not my brother's keeper! My sole consolation is that I wasn't as bad a sibling as our father was a dad. Still, by the time Kanani and I had moved up to the States, the patterns were in place, the damage was irreparable. In El Norte our paths quickly diverged. I staked my claim on my alien past and on my taste for things foreign, aimed my studies in that general direction—even made them my life's mission.

As "the sixties" evolved, moreover, I'd assume a position that was passionately absolutist on the Indochina slaughter and on racial issues. One side's right, the other's wrong, and that's that. Kanani instead opted to stress his Americanism. He wanted to believe in the United States. He got variously involved with U.S. folkways and pop culture. Remade his cosmopolitan confusions into an anthropologically based relativism, which he took up as passionately as I clung to my absolutism. No single cause is worth defending, let alone fighting for, he would assert. The war? Indifference was his chosen, embattled stance. Racism? Hey, well, back in Puerto Rico there had been those who mocked him, Kanani, as a "chink." So who's right, and when?

And though each of us managed to develop musically, there was no overlap whatsoever in our tastes and preferences. I played classical and jazz piano, he took up folk guitar and song. I ignored most pop music, he followed it closely. (Even as I write, with so many of our differences patched up, his library has few recordings that I'd purchase, and vice versa.)

Back during our teens in New Mexico, our mom, our stepdad, Steve, and I would sometimes gang up on Kanani and ridicule his folk songs, his fancy guitar case, and his visionary, speculative bent.

Now, as I write, I see that what seemed like merely intellectual or political clashes inevitably took on the character of older- vs. younger-brother sparring bouts, bore the weight of our past rivalries, conflicts, and power imbalances. I still don't realize this while in Binghamton, though. Don't want to realize it.

Nor do I want to see how our parents' divorce, our many moves and displacements, our rootlessness and alienation have all had even more lasting and damaging effects on Kanani's psyche than on my own, keeping him in constant inner pain. As a survival strategy he's developed a superb virtuosic wit. An uncanny ability to produce a constant stream of one-line jokes, many of them corrosive, biting, sparing of nobody and of no single group, yet somehow not bitter, aggressive, or mean. It's the wrenchingly defensive humor of a chronic melancholic who prefers not to believe too much in anything. Don't take things seriously! That way they'll hurt you less . . .

Despite everything, "Kanani was very gentle," as Mom said casually to me just a couple of years before her death. These words would prove to be a slow revelation, a fruitfully evolving insight into my brother's delicate nature. He's a feeling person, the kind who puts special stock in family ties. He married young, fathering a baby boy at twenty-two, when he himself was still directionless. Yet being a parent was his own semiconscious way of creating the family that he'd so long lacked. The one subject he'll take to heart and neither mock nor evade is that of his only son, Sebastian.

And so, Kanani, believing instinctively in family ties far more than my misanthropized soul would permit, has reached out to me, made brotherly overtures that I'm unequipped to deal with.

Alas, it will take Mom's death in 1984 to bring Kanani and me together and enable us to refashion fraternal bonds, to engage in serious conversations instead of intellectual shadow boxing and verbal tiffs. But that is almost a decade and a half away from my time in Binghamton.

Why am I in Binghamton?

Or in this America, for that matter?

Both to myself and with others I am already fantasizing, idly but frequently, about taking off and settling in Europe. Joining the expatriate ranks. Maybe landing some teaching job in France, or Germany. I've actually sent out application letters to a few universities, though with scanty results.

Four longish experiences have I had in the Old World thus far. Spent those six weeks studying French at the Sorbonne, followed by my Spanish tour with Anya. Drove from Amsterdam through Eastern Europe with a pair of Harvard grad students in 1969. Hitchhiked up and down Italy with a *petite française* in 1970. And, on a more recent night in Paris, in 1972, I even found myself the intended object of seduction by the flamboyantly gay Franco-Cuban novelist Severo Sarduy.

And I liked the usual European stuff. Better, crunchier breads. Tastier, subtler cuisine. Stronger beer and coffee. Beautiful, aged façades. Exhilarating street life. Human scale ... Plus the cultural density. Greater and visible appreciation for things artistic. Streets named after writers and composers. A deeper feeling for life. All that history! Everything more livable, generally.

But what I most enjoyed was my status as total and complete foreigner. Not having to feel my way through the neither/nor limbo that is my perpetual lot here in the States, where I'm neither gringo nor Latino.

"Where're you from?" Europeans would ask me Over There, on a train or at a café.

And I would answer, without hesitation or complication, "From the United States."

Plus there was the relief at not finding myself constantly surrounded by imperial power! Not having to deal, day by day, with the official saber-rattling rituals, along with all the convoluted Orwellian apologetics emanating from every little U.S. corner, high or low. Being a child of empire, I fight the empire inside and outside of me both. And I consider fleeing it.

Sometimes I yearn vaguely to be a citizen of a small, developed, democratic country, like Switzerland. Or a marginal one, like Canada or Costa Rica. Where your nation's sphere of influence ends, and the rest of the world begins precisely at its natural or political borders.

Most of my regular socializing in Binghamton takes place in the company either of a few foreigners or with Americans intimately involved with foreign products. Music, languages, books from elsewhere. Overseas news. Or else with left-wingers, which in Binghamton might as well be foreign. Or else with Latino university students. I drop in at their gatherings, still being young enough to mingle on the sidelines of their circle. My competence in dancing merengues and salsa surprises them. A brief return to my Antillean roots . . .

Yet my sights are ultimately set not on going back to the Caribbean past but—once I'm done with my Ph.D. thesis—on heading for old Europe. Where I can lead a culturally richer literary life and, as the expression goes, "write."

I do lots of writing at my Binghamton desk, some of it promising, some of it less so. And I read, by the pile, item upon item. I've got time to spare, after all. Weekends are long. I've no married life, no kids. No

TV set, no telephone. Contacts with my mother and stepdad and brother and sister remain minimal. Relations with women are sporadic, problematic, at times anguished.

Among the reading materials I plunge into are two or three dozen U.S. journals and magazines; Latin American novels and verse (much of these brand-new), politics, too; volume after volume from Time-Life's Library of Art (among the better offspring of that creepy conglomerate); Cold War "revisionist" histories; Marx and Engels; Vietnam (still!); books on Nazi Germany and related topics; French novels; European novels.

From American literature I restrict myself to quasi-outrageous avant-gardists like Pynchon and Barthelme; brilliant bad boys like Mailer and Henry Miller; transgressors like the Beats. I can't abide reigning figures like Updike or Bellow, representing as they do the official, center-right, U.S. mindset (along with what I then see as an antiquated brand of realism, a dogma I'll eventually outgrow). And there's Nabokov, whom I was once crazy about and will still savor on occasion, but whose cranky, ignorant, latter-day fulminations I now find disquietingly silly.

Why read all that stuff? What's it for?

Habit, compulsion, I suppose, are driving me, in part. But also some desire for transnational learning, maybe even wisdom. America is not the world, nor is Latin America. I don't want—I never did want—to be an academic specialist, duly gleaning every last grain from one's own little subfield and that's it, no more.

Plus, if I end up in Europe, I might as well have read their authors, too.

No doubt there's life outside of Binghamton, beyond this U.S. of A. If only I could find some way to get there . . . Maybe with those books I can.

In Binghamton, I hardly know where I belong. Social life among the faculty is very much nuclear-family oriented—a fact of U.S. life that, I'm only now realizing, is more the rule than the exception. If you haven't got a nuclear family in tow, you're more or less left out. I do have a couple of faculty friends. They invite me to their houses. Help make life bearable. Companionable. Connected.

More typical, though, is my amicable encounter with a well-known social-science prof. He and I have bumped into each other in the foyer of our office building.

"Hey, Bell, got a minute?" he asks. "How 'bout coffee at the snack bar?"

We head out. Queue up. Pour the institutional liquid into our institutional cups. Take our respective seats at an empty table amid the midmorning hubbub. The prof downs his stuff in just a few sips. Then says, "Well, Bell, time to go." He's up, we're off. Coffee is literally what the man had meant, not the three hours of aimless, amiable chatter that such an invitation would've conveyed in other countries.

Then there are the students, who are overwhelmingly from the Big Apple—Jewish or other white ethnics. Likable and bright, if at times proverbially New York-blasé. They've their own concerns, rooted in their original neighborhoods and boroughs, and not much in common with my own preoccupations (whatever those may be). The undergraduates coming from small or middle-sized towns in upstate New York are fresh, wholesome. Lacking in the cynical, hard exterior of the city kids, they radiate a charming, endearing innocence. To them, I must seem vaguely Martian.

Virtually no out-of-staters enroll at Binghamton, save for the sizable contingent of postgraduates, among which are a number of foreigners. There are actually more Europeans than Californians or Pennsylvanians here. Eventually, either they or the campus Latinos and I will find one another, hook up, keep each other frequent if casual and compartmentalized company within a somewhat desolate and melancholy milieu. Curiously, I'll maintain sporadic contact with members from all these groups over the years to come.

* * *

One Hundred Years of Solitude by Gabriel García Márquez . . . for the first time in my life I'm teaching the Colombian author's great book to my Binghamton students. And I'm happily savoring, relishing, and reveling in his wondrous details. In class, I often go overboard and spend inordinate amounts of time on the tiniest bit of trivia regarding his plots and characters.

It's my fond hope to write about him someday. He and the other novelists of the South American literary "boom," who started gaining world renown in the 1960s, have furnished my cultural mission. A desire to share with the regular, nonspecialized U.S. reader what I know about those dazzling and visionary artists. I want to serve as a useful guide to these authors' strangely rich and complex verbal artifacts. Be to them what Stuart Gilbert was to James Joyce, what Martin Esslin was to the dramatists of the absurd.

As I read up on García Márquez, I'll eventually find out he was working in Caracas during roughly the same set of years that Kanani and I attended school there. The thirtyish journeyman writer even witnessed from up close, as a salaried reporter, the fall of the military dictatorship of Gen. Marcos Pérez Jiménez. I'm amazed to learn that he got the initial charge of inspiration for *The Autumn of the Patriarch*—his densely difficult portrait of a Caribbean tyrant—as a direct result of his eyewitness experience in Venezuela.

At my Binghamton apartment, I write every morning. For at least an hour, sometimes three. I embark on a book I'd been wanting to write on the Latin American novelists, aimed at the common reader. I devour much of the existing criticism, scholarly and journalistic both, then pour out lots of prose from my ballpoint pen. I even come up with a general introduction plus a pair of chapters on Alejo Carpentier and Juan Rulfo. But I'm far from ready for such a grand undertaking. There's too much stuff to digest. And I don't have enough legitimate writing experience to enable me to bring it all to fruition. I've scarcely even reached the journeyman phase.

In the years since 1967, I've also produced a dozen or so short stories. The protagonist of one, entitled "The Hidden Shape of Things," has precise plans for the sculpting of a statue, yet lacks the training, technique, and wherewithal to actualize his grandiose artistic vision.

Another of the stories deals, rather clinically, with a fictive incarnation of my last girlfriend, she of the blithe jilting that had helped put me on my narrow, angry path of misogynistic and misanthropic eremitism. It's my way of getting a handle on, and maybe then exorcising, that youthful mistake.

I send the pieces to Arthur Orrmont, an agent in New York City. I'm pleasantly surprised when he finds them good enough for submission, as a collection, to trade publishers out there. So impressed is he with the lead piece, "A Report on a Concert," that he even attempts to sell it on the magazine circuit. The agent, bless his soul, believes in my potential and tries hard, with houses big and small, for two full years. All without success, though with some nice rejections.

The stories, I'll realize years later, are still immature. For the most part, their initial ideas are better than their overall performance. Or they're too much in the shadow of the era's leading avant-gardists. Time and again over the next decade and a half I'll return to those short narratives. Work at crafting them into something like satisfactory shape. Drop a few, add others. Expand the ex-girlfriend story into a section of a novel.

I've turned to writing, in some measure, because my musical hopes never fully panned out. To evolve into a respectably proficient musician after starting out late in life, as I've noted above, is close to impossible. I cling to the knowledge that there are beginning authors who are well into their seventies.

In my classes on literature I spend a lot of time on political and historical topics. This goes against the reigning formalist doctrine that sees all art as a pure and all-sufficient realm, completely divorced from society. From people. From life.

My thesis advisor and major professor at Harvard—we'll call him Pierson—was wont to deal with Latin American novels about war and revolution as if the books were isolated constructs. Any talk of the bloody wars and real revolutions that had actually prompted the writing of the novels was ruled out by him as irrelevant to literature. He is actually reputed to have said in faculty meetings, in echo of Field Marshall Hermann Goering, "When I hear the word 'sociology,' I reach for my revolver." Any mention of psychology—of Freud, say— would elicit a like reaction from him.

As part of my youthful rebellion against not just Pierson but the entire prevailing formalist orthodoxy, I poured out in 1969 a polemical attack on those high-flown dogmas. And made a plea for a more historically, socially oriented criticism. That essay then went from magazine to magazine. It was returned and rejected, if sometimes with supportive and friendly notes. In 1973 it finally sees print in *Science & Society*, a respected journal of Marxist studies.

Oh, but . . . what a shock! Reading my long essay on printed pages, I'm utterly embarrassed at the crudeness of both my thought and my style. I am in fact aghast at most of the thing, even if it does contain some useful and neglected information. I'm learning one of my first serious lessons as a published writer, this discrepancy between personal typescript and the editorially sanctioned version in printer's ink. What looks good on one's bond paper might actually sound awful as it sits, forever, between the spine and covers of a legitimately bound volume.

Apprenticeship in writing, I am dimly beginning to realize, is a lengthy and painful process.

The war has moved into high gear, with blanket U.S. aerial bombardments up and down Vietnam, plus the mining of Haiphong harbor, something the militarists have been dreaming of for years. Again, in terms of sheer scale, these are the biggest conventional airborne operations of the century. No firebombs are used, though. Still, a Soviet ship in Haiphong is accidentally hit and sunk. And the Parisian legation in Hanoi is reduced to rubble by our highly sophisticated ordnance. The French chargé d'affaires is killed as a result of the action. The U.S. is out of control and behaving very dangerously.

The usual mass rallies are held around the Binghamton campus. With chanting crowds. Angry leaflets. And fiery, eloquent speakers. A couple of Latino students see the whole antiwar movement as a "white" issue, unfortunately. But others show real courage. Deciding to take action, several dozen Binghamton students—including a few of my Latinos—along with some committed profs now descend en masse onto the town courthouse, staging acts of civil disobedience. Accordingly, they all get busted. Once booked, they can choose between doing time in prison or paying a modest fine.

As I hear about it, I consider joining in with them. I also think back on my own episode with involuntary incarceration back in Caracas. And I finally opt not to repeat the experience, though wondering whether my inaction is appropriately prudent or simply cowardly.

Meanwhile I've been doing research for my Ph.D. thesis. And I've written a preliminary chapter on Alejo Carpentier, the Cuban author whose novel *The Lost Steps* helped me refocus my life a few years ago in Berkeley. (By pure chance, Carpentier had also drudged in advertising in Caracas during the 1950s, just when Kanani and I were living there as troubled pubescents and teens.) My chapter analyzes the novelist's works from the point of view of his Marxist beliefs.

In the summer I'd mailed the typescript to Professor Pierson, my graduate advisor at Harvard. We'd subsequently agreed to discuss the chapter in his Boylston Hall office on the Tuesday before Thanksgiving break.

Now it's the day after our meeting, following my six-hours' return drive in wet snow, my first such terrifying experience on a slippery highway. In my recently bought VW Beetle I'd actually gone into a tailspin when, during snowfall, I'd been foolish enough to press on the brakes while on a bridge. (By sheer luck there were no cars behind me.) I'm feeling even more shaken and distraught, however, as a result of a blowout I had yesterday with the renowned Professor Pierson.

Our encounter went something like this:

PIERSON: Well, Mr. Bell, this could be a possible essay in a literary journal. But I wonder about your premises. Really, does Marxism have anything to do with literature?

ME: Well, it may or may not. But for a novelist who's a Marxist, it's directly relevant, no?

PIERSON: And where do you get the idea that Carpentier is a Marxist?

ME (*a bit taken aback by the question*): Well, umm, uh (*stumbling a bit*), the man's an active participant in the Castro regime. And also a member of the Communist Party.

PIERSON: So? What does that prove?

ME: (*Not knowing what to say, I single out a few instances of Marxist thinking in various Carpentier texts.*)

PIERSON (*sucking on his cigar*): That is not Marxism, Mr. Bell. Marxism is about proletarian revolution. And nowhere in Carpentier do I see the proletarian revolution.

ME: Well, sir, then how about Carpentier's short story, "Like the Night"? It depicts four young soldiers on their way to war: a Greek headed for Troy, a Spaniard for the colonies, a French boy going to New France, and a twentieth-century American ready for a landing in Europe. They're all very gung-ho about war. And they accept their leaders' rhetoric about the nobility and glory of the upcoming struggle.

Toward the end of the story, though, we're back on board the ship with the Greek lad. And he overhears a cynical old veteran telling a dumbstruck crowd that, actually, fellas, Helen is perfectly happy in Troy and that her nocturnal shrieks of delight are an embarrassment to the court ladies. No, my friends, says the wise and aged warrior, this is simply a war to get rid of the Trojan competition and then sell more Greek pottery in the east!

The young man looks out at the wine-dark sea, and weeps.

PIERSON (*with a cold stare*): And what, pray tell, is Marxist about *that*?

ME: Oh, it's the economic interpretation of history, sir. You know, the idea that wars have economic causes.

PIERSON: Oh, really, Mr. Bell. Look, Homer says that the best soldiers are well fed and have their bellies full. And Homer was no Marxist!

ME (*beginning to see that this conversation's at a dead end*): Well, sir, uh, I think maybe this isn't working. Maybe I'd better change my thesis topic. Try something else.

PIERSON: Oh, no, Mr. Bell, you must not do that. You are a free agent. You can write anything you want. I'm not anti-Marxist. Harvard isn't anti-Marxist. If you were to abandon this topic, you would go around saying that I am anti-Marxist, which simply isn't true.

ME: Well, what am I to do, then?

PIERSON: I want you to demonstrate to me, once and for all, that Carpentier is a Marxist.

ME: But I already have.

PIERSON: No, I'm sorry, you have not.

(*Our voices rise. Our tempers flare.*)

PIERSON: At this point, Mr. Bell, I wonder, perhaps you should find yourself another thesis advisor?

(*I storm out of his office, watching his face peek out the doorway as I hear his last words.*)

PIERSON: Don't worry, Mr. Bell. Getting a Harvard Ph.D. isn't everything in life.

The episode doesn't end there, however. Later that month I write a long letter to Carpentier himself and send it to his cultural attaché office at the Cuban Embassy in Paris. I recount to him my experience and ask the great writer, whose Marxism I had simply taken for granted, if he could possibly help me out and resolve the confusion by letting me know if he considers himself a Marxist.

His reply comes dated 14 April 1972. It's three double-spaced pages long. He leads me through several of his works, pointing out their Marxist content. Moreover, he emphasizes, "I would like to remind your teacher that I spent several months in a Havana prison for my Marxist activities, which since then have been inseparable from my life." In his next-to-last paragraph he sums up, "You may inform your teacher that I am a Marxist in my attitude, activities, and in the functions I discharge in my daily life."

Well, I fancy, I have won! This is it, the document that vindicates me and my analysis! I send off a photocopy to Pierson with a short cover letter.

Pierson's reply arrives a few days later. He starts out by congratulating me for having obtained the Carpentier letter, which, he grants, "has great documentary value." But, he says, in the end, what does this prove? Only that Carpentier *says* he's a Marxist. So what? He, Pierson, could cite to me certain Argentine novelists who, during Perón, were card-carrying Peronistas yet who meanwhile wrote non-Peronist novels. Rule #1 of every good literary critic: don't always trust an author's self-characterizations, Pierson says.

Ah, well. That takes care of that! Pierson's response, I grimly realize, forecloses any hope for further exchange on this issue. (Over the next few years, though, he'll distribute and use copies of the Carpentier-Bell correspondence for discussion in his Harvard seminars.)

What's next? What the hell, I've got to find a new topic, one that's safely formalist. Pure literature and nothing else . . . As luck will have it, I soon come across Tzvetan Todorov's recent *Introduction à la littérature fantastique*, a clearly and elegantly argued look at the various themes, techniques, and devices of fantastic narrative. Todorov furnishes me the set of categories that I can apply to a few "big" Latin American fantasticators. Over a five-month period I write a semifinal draft of my first chapter, on Borges.

To my relief, Pierson finds my new tack "acceptable." On with the dissertation! I complete it, all 480 pages of it, in twenty months, while teaching full-time at Binghamton and, later, for a year at Yale.

Someday I should write a letter thanking Todorov! He helped me get my Ph.D., saved me from sinking into the morass, the incompleteness of what is known in academe as ABD, "all but dissertation."

Now it's a deliciously warm afternoon in Binghamton. I'm standing just a few feet outside my apartment door, where I'm enjoying the summer warmth, the June air filled with the flamboyant sounds of house finches and song sparrows, the pungent aromas of family meals being grilled over hot charcoal, the brightly shimmering bars of sunlight streaking through the fresh, green foliage.

I'm in my final stretch in this upstate town, which I'll be leaving within weeks to take on a year-long position at Yale I just landed at the last minute. And I'll soon be preparing some snacks for a weekend visit from Audrey, who had been a graduate student at Middlebury College summer school when I taught there a year earlier. We were housed in the same dorm there, on the same floor, where we met for the first time in the hall, near the laundry room.

We began a rocky, off-and-on romance. Things are smoothing out in recent months, though. She's five foot one, brown hair, brown eyes, Polish-American, from a small town near Buffalo, spent a year in Spain and France shortly after getting her B.A. degree, currently teaches sixth-grade social studies near her hometown, and is a sweet, affectionate person.

We haven't any idea as to our common future yet. In August she is scheduled to depart for Holland, where she is to start a teaching job at the American school in The Hague—for how long, she doesn't know. So we're both at a kind of crossroads.

Audrey represents something new in my life. Before, most of my serious girlfriends had been, in some measure, versions of my dad: charming yet cold and distant, smart yet verbally and emotionally abusive, controlling yet uncaring. Or they'd used me for their purposes and then, being unreliable, abandoned me, in certain instances more than once.

Meanwhile I'm beginning to sense—without being able to articulate it or think it through—that, in choosing or being chosen by such mates, I'd been punishing myself for Dad's treatment of my mother. That, by allowing them to do unto me as he had done to her, I was, in some convoluted way, expiating his personal sins. Conversely, in the past I thoughtlessly—and foolishly—held at bay some saner, more balanced women who'd offered me simple, straightforward, no-strings-attached warmth and affection.

My father's legacy runs deep.

Now, perhaps, I am finally ready to respond to more intimate and humane sentiments. Audrey and I spend several weekends together that summer, going on excursions to a lake resort here, and to Montreal there, as we sample new kinds of ethnic cuisine and talk about the upcoming changes in our lives. When we say good-bye at Boston's Logan Airport that August, for the first time in five years I'm able to pronounce, however gingerly, the word "love."

I also depart Binghamton, not so much saying good-bye to the place as simply fleeing, skedaddling. I neglect to take my proper leave from several folks in the area who'd been very good to me. But though I liked the SUNY campus and many of its "citizens" of every age group, I wasn't ready as yet for a town like Binghamton, lacking as I did in the personal resources, the family grounding, the balanced affects, and the mature sense of appreciation for human ties that might have made my stint there livable, bearable. Instead I'd spent two years wrestling with my many inner demons, notably but not exclusively the mixed legacies of father, family, and ex-girlfriend(s).

Yale in this regard comes as a fruitful interlude and provides the discipline of a time limit. Over the next twelve months I'll teach six classes, complete my Ph.D. thesis, reinstate old friendships and start new ones, visit Audrey in Holland twice, and engage in a passionate exchange of letters with her. We'll write three or four times a week, and, with her superb eye for visual beauty, she'll fashion numerous unique, one-of-a-kind love-greeting cards using a combination of color inks, collage, typeface, and fanciful rubber stamps.

Still, because of my past history of disappointments, I fear the worst, more or less expect it to end, yet it doesn't. So I find myself genuinely, happily attached, without feeling the urge to flee, to hurt before being hurt . . .

Later on, when we settle into a lifetime as a couple, Audrey will gradually soften my hard edges and help "humanize" and "civilize" me, though without denying my essential inner self. Fact is, I'd become a bit of a barbarian after having lived alone for so many years. From her, then, I'll learn a few things about manners, how to deal with others, the rules of protocol, what's done and is not done—that basic wisdom in which she is expert and which is part of belonging to ordinary, everyday humanity.

In addition she'll encourage me to make more contact with my mother and the rest of my minimal family, to visit them and phone them from time to time. Lucky for me that she'll do so, as I would have been racked with a paralyzing guilt had I not been in touch with my mom in the years before her untimely death.

But all that still lies in the future.

Expatriation et cetera

[Some Adult Third-Culture Kids] strike their peers . . . as not being able to make up their minds about what they want to do with their lives, where they want to live . . . They have what some call prolonged adolescence.

—RUTH HILL USEEM and ANN BAKER COTTRELL, "Adult Third-Culture Kids," in Carolyn D. Smith, *Strangers at Home*

So, in the summer of '74, having completed my Ph.D., I decline an attractive, full-time, long-term job offer from some gracious folks at the University of Massachusetts's new Harbor Campus. (This despite the fact that there's an academic recession going on; some of my profs and fellow students probably think my decision foolhardy.) And I leave for Europe on a budget flight with Icelandic Airlines.

First I spend time with Audrey in her studio apartment in The Hague, where—with my Ph.D. thesis firmly behind me—I start to read and write on brand-new topics, totally unrelated to my doctorate. During her off hours, Audrey and I meet and hang out on occasion with her various school colleagues (from them we'll actually first hear the term "Third Culture Kids," though it doesn't register as yet); we go for strolls along the orderly, attractive tree-lined streets or in the lively, expansive nineteenth-century beach-resort area of the small but historically rich city; and we feast on the occasional *rysstafel*, the monumental Dutch dish consisting of anywhere from seven to seventeen Indonesian delicacies (one of the more palatable results of Netherlands imperialism in Asia). We take side trips to Amsterdam and to neighboring Belgium, staring at architectural beauties, and marveling at the size and quality of the national art collections. For the first time, I set eyes on the original of Brueghel's *Fall of Icarus* at the Brussels Musées Royaux des Beaux-Arts, a picture made doubly famous in Auden's poem bearing the institution's generic name. Finally, much to Audrey's sadness and mine, I board a silvery, Trans-Europ-Express train for Paris, where after moving into a spacious garret at the Cité Universitaire Internationale, I settle in to read and write on a full-time basis, in preparation for a long-term stay.

It will prove to be an indispensable and fruitful period. From my little room I crank out literary articles and reviews for general periodicals, both in English and in Spanish, and also initiate book-length projects. I write every morning and many an evening, leading the life of a happy scribbler in Paris. During my leisure moments I head for the cafés of *la bohème*, where I meet and mingle with young, free-floating intellectuals from all over Latin America, Europe, and the U.S. And I take in the variegated cultural and street scene—theater, art, politics—at every opportunity. On weekends I make use of successive Eurailpasses to visit Audrey in The Hague, or she comes and stays with me in Paris. We attend dozens of classical concerts together and, during her vacations, travel by train along the length and breadth of the Old World— Spain, Portugal, and Italy; Normandy, Copenhagen, London. At the children's zoo in Denmark we feed the furry goat kids and warm to the sight of a ferocious-looking wild boar mama, who leads her seven boar piglets as they scurry out of the shed. All cubs, all pups can be cute, we remark. Our relationship, formerly U.S.-based, then transatlantic, now burgeons into a trans-European romance.

My long-range plan had been to find work of some kind in Europe and, on the model of many a past American expatriate, to follow my bliss and write as much as possible. At first I depend chiefly on my accumulated savings, with occasional help from Audrey. Enjoying my status as a full-time, freelance reader and scrivener, I keep putting off a job search. By early spring, though, I've got to look seriously into locating employment. Enlisting the help of a Sino-French-American woman friend who lives at the dorm, I draft a letter applying for teaching jobs in Spanish or English, and send it out to dozens of French universities. I also fill in forms at an employment agency for work in tourism, where I might put my language skills to good use.

Unfortunately, 1975 is the year of the worst global recession since the 1930s, with frequent bankruptcies, talk of possible economic collapse, and few openings available—even fewer for an alien living in France. Also, Juan José Barrientos, a Mexican academic whom I know from the Latin Quarter cafés, warns me that, as a gringo, I might have trouble landing a job in a Spanish department in France. "They'd make jokes about your being CIA," he says, with a wry smile.

Meanwhile, Audrey is feeling exhausted from the pressures of her job. For all these reasons we decide to return to the States and settle temporarily in the Boston area, where I might wing it with part-time teaching positions. Ironically, in the last week or so of my Parisian stint, as we prepare for departure, I get calls for two job interviews, one as telephone receptionist at a big hotel, another as English-language instructor at the Université d'Orléans. Over the years I'll sometimes wonder how different a course my life might have taken had I sat for those interviews, and if some French job—however low-level and dead-end—had magically materialized.

Instead, Audrey and I take our return flight in July, find a cramped apartment right in Harvard Square that unforgettably hot summer, and make our wedding plans. I do some casual tutoring in Spanish, inquire about temporary jobs here or there, and accidentally find out about a one-semester vacancy at Williams College, due to a last-minute resignation in their ranks.

I apply. Shortly thereafter I get a call from a gentlemanly Czech named George Pistorius, chair of the romance languages department at Williams, who invites me to come soon for a candidate interview. And so, during a heat wave in early August, still lacking even the slightest notion as to my financial prospects, I drive out in a rented car to the distant northwest corner of the state, the fabled Berkshire mountain range—seat of Williams, founded in the 1790s and indeed the second-oldest college in Massachusetts. Following a whirlwind round of meetings with select Williams administrators and faculty, I once again hit the road, this time for my lightning wedding two days later in Dunkirk, New York, Audrey's home town, where she has been taking care of the preliminaries.

A few days later, postnuptial, we're on our honeymoon, heading west, in yet another rental vehicle, on to our final destination—oh my God! Just as it was with Kanani and me sixteen years ago!—Albuquerque, New Mexico. As I ease the Budget auto into the carport, Mother and Steve come out to greet my newlywed with a warm welcome and hugs. ("Hi, Audrey," says Mom, beaming, "I'm Carmen, and this is Steve!") We set up for a few days' visit; Mom cooks up some stunning Chinese dishes (she has recently been rediscovering her Chinese roots); and Steve takes us to some new and very different kinds of beauties in the state's old ruins and wilderness. We're all spending a relaxing family time there, when Williams calls to inform me that I've been hired. For one semester only. It has been a summer like few others I'll know: flying back; apartment hunting; the wedding; finding a job; cross-country driving—all within weeks . . .

I accept the offer from Williams, but am warned not to entertain any hopes for the future, due to nationwide economic woes and low language enrollment figures at the college. But, in one of life's strange imponderables, over time my "temporary" job will keep being miraculously extended—another month, a semester, and three years followed by a four-year renewal, and eventually tenure.

A decade later, in the wake of Mom's death, I'll come upon the cache of hundreds of letters that will give me adult insight into my father and eventually end any possibility of reconciliation. Apart from Dad's accusatory letter about Valerie, however, the most disturbing discovery comes from a diary my mother had kept when interned at the mental hospital.

In a blue, hardbound notebook with narrow-ruled sheets, she intermingles dry, factual accounts of her daily drug treatments with quiet yet intense reflections on life and on her marriage, the early years particularly. From the opening page of these recollections, I found out that my pop originally did not want my mom to have me. "I couldn't go through with the abortion," she notes flatly.

To this day, I feel awed and discomfited at the astonishing, simple truth of my being on this earth not merely by crass biological happenstance, but by my mother's conscious, firm decision to give birth to me and *be* a mother. In those pages she shows no bitterness toward my father for his pressures to interrupt her pregnancy. Indeed she reproaches herself for not having offered her young husband more "love and assurance than I did," and expresses a powerful self-blame for then shifting her energies toward her newborn baby. Yet she also recalls, "On the birth of the child, he left me to go out on the beach with his friends, or to do barbells to protect and conserve his health. In spite of the fact that I was adjusting to a new environment, a new language, new customs, and the news of Pearl Harbor, I got no solace from Gene" (i.e., my father).

My combined sadness and amazement as I read and reread those lines, nearly a half-century after they were written, remains as potent as when I first set eyes on the journal in 1985. And inevitably I wonder if, while still inside my mother's womb and later as a babe-in-arms, I'd already sensed good reason to distrust my father, wonder if I somehow felt his prenatal rejection of me before I'd even had a life.

Admittedly, Dad was then a twenty-two-year-old boy only just beginning his Haitian business ventures. But in the ensuing years he did precious little to overcome his initial indifference—hostility?—as a father, to work somehow at gaining his two sons' affections. If anything, the most common, vivid memories Kanani and I have of everyday life with our dad are of us being abused verbally. Or barked at gratuitously. Or being addressed by him simply as "Hey."

Later, in response to the less-than-loving attitudes Kanani and I developed toward him, Pop began playing the role of suffering victim. When, in 1984, Steve conveyed to our progenitor the news of Mom's death, suggesting that he seize the moment and make conciliatory overtures to his children, Dad in his reply solemnly declined the offer in a letter concluding, "It was they, after all, who rejected me." Elsewhere in this same missive, my father informs Steve that he often prays to God, "with forgiveness to Carmen for what she did to me."

There was a strange follow-up much later to my father's accusations regarding Mom and Valerie. For years, Mother as well as Steve had urged me to make some sort of contact with him—again, "He *is* your Dad," they'd say. And so, in 1993, having accidentally heard that he'd taken retirement in Florida, I wrote the man a short note; I explained that I was not seeking reconciliation, but that I simply would wish to hear from him as a retiree, a returnee, and a human being. I informed him that I'd since found out about his pressures on my pregnant mom not to give birth to me. And in passing I reminded him that he hadn't been a good father to his children. Nevertheless I was willing to put that past behind me in the interests of a civil exchange.

His reply, two sides in single space, consisted mostly of sermons, and about five lines of personal news. In his third paragraph, though, he expands the accusation:

> . . . Poor Valerie is out of sight, out of mind. I suppose you know that I was not her father. Her biological father was Dr. N. Ravitch, supposedly a friend of the family. *Your mother admitted this.* [Emphasis added.] Dr. Ravitch was a family friend since about 1942 and I even suspect that he may have been the father of Kanani also. I have always loved Kanani as tho' he were my own son but I can discern nothing of me in his physical appearance . . . That does not mean that I have anything against him, except that when you rejected me . . . I continued to write to Kanani, offering to help him continue his studies, but he never wrote me again . . .

Previously he had supposedly merely arrived at that conclusion about Valerie's paternity. Now he asserts that Mother had actually owned up to it. And this time Kanani has been added to the list as a "suspect." It all gets bigger and bigger . . .

And now I've worked at Williams College for nearly three decades, and claimed New England as my home for almost four. This fact amazes me after a youth spent drifting aimlessly among various tropical lands and then wandering from one U.S. college town to another. Paradoxically, having found stability in the oldest and most traditional part of the United States is what has allowed me to work through my identity as an Overseas American. As a teacher of Spanish, I function as a kind of "global nomad," trying to convey to my divers Anglo-American charges the satisfactions of speaking and thinking in a foreign tongue. Living in two languages, after all, is one of the few birthrights I can consciously claim. Meanwhile, as I attempt to transmit to my literature students the joys of savoring Latin America's great authors, I reexperience my own discovery of their work along with that time when I was sorting out my problematical relationship to a vast and contradictory American empire of which I'd always been a marginal citizen.

I know too that, had I not come to terms with my overseas past, my whole life and personhood would have remained sadly truncated as yet another instance of underdevelopment. What sanity and happiness I currently enjoy stems in great measure from my having marshaled that initial overseas self and put it to work within a U.S. setting. Paradoxically, my own writing and teaching about Latin America for U.S. readers and students is what has allowed me the opportunity to feel less foreign, less marginal, and more of a legitimate participant in a small corner of the nation's big stage. I facilitate, I interpret, happily muddling through in my daily tasks as cultural and linguistic middleman. My chosen role . . .

Afterword, without an End:
Overseas American

The high mobility of third-culture families, who usually move every one, two, or four years, seems to have the effect of bringing individual family members closer together.

—RUTH HILL USEEM and RICHARD DOWNIE,
"Third-Culture Kids," in *Today's Education*

In 1978 I'll add my mother's maiden name "Villada" to my byline, and start calling myself "Bell-Villada" in other work-related business as well. The compound surname serves a number of purposes: to claim my complex Hispanic background, to make it clear from the outset that I'm not exactly white-Anglo-Saxon-Protestant, and to differentiate myself from my father. Whenever I set eyes on my original, shorter handle, I'll feel a curious disengagement from it, as if "Gene Bell" belonged to somebody else, some other guy I never much liked.

I nevertheless think it necessary to retain the "Bell" side of my ancestry. I *had* indeed grown up Anglo-American, after a fashion, and I see no point in burying one half of my life history under the moral and political weight of the other, as I'd attempted in vain to do during my early, "immigrant" years. My compound last name is an effort at reconciling two sides of me that had once seemed so far apart.

254

I've also come to realize that there's much of me that's American. A breezy informality. A taste for the direct and colloquial. A discomfort with the pretentious and hifalutin. And a love of the American literary language itself: these are all part of my life, and I look upon them as assets. And then there are the many U.S. authors, artists, and composers I admire. And I love jazz. A solo by Art Tatum, Coltrane, or Milt Jackson, or a skillfully sung old standard by Gershwin or the Duke, can move me as deeply as does a Bach aria or a Mahler finale. I also thrill with fascination at the more extreme, parodic forms of American vulgarianism. There's sheer poetry and real beauty in the hard-boiled novels of Raymond Chandler, in outrageous films like *Repo Man* and *Kentucky Fried Movie,* and in the dazzlingly grotesque cartoon art of R. Crumb.

At the same time, though, I feel repelled by the aggressive know-nothingism and shallow bluster of much of American life, the spiritual void and emptiness. The ideologically based ignorance that is so common within the United States. The myths, superstitions, and simple delusions concerning the role of U.S. power abroad. The libertarian sloganeering wherein any government program automatically equals Communism and Sovietism.

My uneasiness with such bunkum is both personal and political, for hovering implacably over my relationship to the U.S. is the figure of my dad.

My father was the first American I ever knew (the *only* one, really, in my initial fifteen years), an expatriate wheeler-dealer who, for all his overseas experience and trilingualism, never ceased being the midwestern provincial and "typical American" he'd started out to be. Indeed, although he spent his entire professional life all over the Caribbean and eventually married a Cuban, like a good colonialist he never regarded the local peoples and their culture with anything more than contempt.

Whenever I hear right-wing clichés spoken from the lips of Americans, I hear my father's voice. Dad thought of America as the most perfect, absolutely greatest entity on earth. Everything else— French intellectualism, British education, foreign cars ("just a silly fad"), Swedish multilingualism and welfare-statism, Latin warmth, whatever—simply couldn't hold a candle to the universal greatness of America. My rejection of boilerplate, "greatest-country-in-the-world" slogans inevitably includes him too.

Much the same goes for my take on the American rhetoric of "self-reliance." My dad from early on took the entrepreneurial life path and set his sights on accumulating money for its own sake, to the exclusion of almost everything else. Like a hero out of an Ayn Rand novel, he acted on the principle that selfishness is the highest good. Like a trickle-down economist, he justified to Mom his single-minded pursuit of financial gain as beneficial "for you, & for us, & for our future." In this I'm reminded of the comical, bumptious Josiah Bounderby in Dickens's *Hard Times,* the "banker, merchant, manufacturer, and what not" who boasts at length about his bogus rags-to-riches story. My father, like Mr. Bounderby, dwelled obsessively on having "lifted myself out of the gutter," with "nobody to thank . . . but myself." In truth, Mom's savings gave Dad's start-up businesses an initial boost. Her unpaid office labors further kept the enterprise afloat during his pro-longed absences. And he always found a "godfather" to sustain him in his ambitions. He was not alone. My disdain of the American folk cult of the self-reliant entrepreneur—and the worship heaped on such fig-ures for supposedly "creating wealth"— targets my father as well.

A good friend who kindly read an earlier version of this book sees in my dad an embodiment and "grotesque caricature" of American patterns of thought and conduct. Her judgment confirms what I already knew. In my mind, Dad represents—*is*—the U.S.A. For a while, during the '60s, I felt so angered at his American chauvinism, so racked about my own problematical identity within this American nation, that in casual talk with new acquaintances I'd describe Dad as a Scottish immigrant, trying to exorcise that "ugly American" from my past and present. Eventually I'd find that publishing spoofs and satires was a funnier and more fruitful means of refashioning his ideological baggage. That writing realistic fictions was a healthier and more suitable strategy for re-imagining my family background. And that remembering my past for the making of this memoir could serve as a catharsis, a cleansing.

Finally, I also now know enough to grant that, while I inherited Mom's writing side, her cultural bent, and her strong capacities for love, loyalty, and friendship, there is much of my father's character in aspects of my makeup. My musical and then writing compulsions became an activity as single-minded and self-absorbing as his own maniacal quest for monetary wealth. My repudiation of his formulaic flag-waving and religiosity came to be as intemperate and extreme as his fanatical preaching and sermonizing. My occasional brusqueness with and insensitivity to other people bears an uncomfortable resemblance to Dad's everyday dealings with Kanani and me. And his broad failings as a father, along with the enduring negative example they have left in my mind, were what ultimately led me to decide that, in my case, parenting would be too risky, too much of an invitation to follow in his dreaded footsteps. The void I received from him as a young boy, alas, is the void I chose to sustain and continue with as a less-than-complete adult.

One of the many things I've learned from telling my story is how fragile a human psyche is, particularly a young one. The mind and soul of any individual form a delicate balance easily shaken by loss, threats, or just plain neglect. During my youthful years, I now realize, I was incomplete, less than whole, and fairly close to crazy besides. In addition, Kanani and I both lived and still live with a lack of a "tribe" (in his word) that we might genuinely call our own. In the recollections and studies that I've read and reread while working on this memoir, even the happiest of families wistfully report the all-too-recognizable (for me) pangs of TCK growth and development. Our own ongoing dilemmas of adjustment as Overseas Americans, then, would doubtless have existed even had Kanani and I been blessed with the ordinary good fortune of family stability and a supportive dad for whom we might've felt lifelong affection, admiration, and warmth. But as Overseas Americans we're far from typical, not having been raised within any gringo enclaves abroad nor been enrolled at Overseas-American schools until our adolescence.

My brother's and my situation is further complicated by our having lived a family history that, in any setting—even within the U.S. heartland somewhere—would have proved emotionally crippling and possibly destructive. (During his thirties Kanani underwent therapy, yet found himself unable to weep when recalling his personal past. It was the therapist who shed tears.) In this regard, Kanani and I may not be your typical TCKs. In "Third-Culture Kids," Ruth Hill Useem and Richard Downie single out a trend that makes me envious and sad:

> The high mobility of third-culture families, who usually
> move every one, two, or four years, seems to have the effect of
> bringing individual family members closer together. They share
> the common experience of moving into unfamiliar territory and
> offer each other mutual support in the face of change and
> strangeness. Parents are often the only people with whom TCKs
> have a continuing relationship as they move from one location
> to another.
>
> American families overseas spend more time together
> (unless the children are in boarding school) than do their
> stateside counterparts . . .

Such obviously was not the case with us. My brother's and my lot as cultural marginals was instead all the more exaccrbated by our hopelessly makeshift and disjointed—I'll say it: unhappy! miserable! *dysfunctional!*—home life.

So is this a happy ending? Compared to our childhood and adolescence ... well, yes, of course, without a doubt! Kanani and I both started out living in a kind of emotional hellhole cum limbo, yet at least, by some providential series of miracles, we found our way into the new, maze-like purgatory of life in El Norte. Decades of muddling through in another country finally led us, if not to heaven's bliss, then at least to an inner state that feels a great deal better than what we'd known while floating—anchorless, rudderless—overseas. The memory of those first years still casts its dark, fearsome shadow and will not go away, but, with more light from good living, it can be illuminated and, in the process, be shrunk mercifully down in size and strength.

As for us two today, well, better to be more or less sane than pretty nearly crazy; better to be somewhat settled than ever-transient and uprooted; better to have constant and affectionate family ties, however few and scattered, than chronically and intensely sick and delusional ones. Regarding work, in time each of us wandered into some occupational stability (Kanani as art professor, then as a social worker, and I with one of the more desirable jobs on this earth), slowly carving out some modest participatory role on the margins of a land that, though supposedly ours, in certain ways wasn't. We both ended up with loving spouses, and Kanani lavished unconditional love on his son Sebastian Estevan, whom he devoutly cherishes as his flesh and blood, and with whom he now maintains a lively and spirited intellectual relationship.

So there it is, the life I was born into, the only life I've got. I first saw light as an Overseas American, was raised as an Absentee American, grew up as a Third-Culture Kid, became a Global Nomad, and then evolved into an Adult TCK during my years of "reentry" and repatriation. I may be something of a Stranger at Home, but I might as well feel proud to be an Overseas American and all that that entails.

I couldn't have written any of my previous books without my Overseas TCK background, and my being an Adult TCK has enriched my day-to-day life as a foreign-language teacher and as mentor and advisor to my students, and as sharer in things Hispanic with my wife, Audrey.

And finally, growing into and recognizing my existence and role as an Overseas American has afforded me a vital and usable optics, a way of seeing my place here, neither as immigrant nor as resident alien—but as an American, sort of, and (sometimes out) of sorts.